MindWorks

A Practical Guide for
Changing Thoughts, Beliefs, *and*
Emotional Reactions

By

Gary van Warmerdam

Illustrations by Gabriel Manninen

Published by Cairn Publishing
Santa Barbara California

Published in the United States of America

ISBN: 0990584607
ISBN 13: 978-0-9905846-0-5

Cover Design and Artwork by Raess Design www.RaessDesign.com
Author Photo by Alex Erotas

Contents

A Path of Transforming Beliefs and Emotions

As humans we live in two worlds. The first is the external, physical world of family, friends, work, and environment. The second is the internal world of our mind, imagination, thoughts, emotions, and beliefs: an inner world that can feel just as real to us as the first one. This book is about that second world and how to change what happens there.

These two worlds aren't separate—they impact each other all the time. In particular, our internal world invisibly influences how we experience and relate to the external world around us. Our overactive mind, driven by our beliefs, can sabotage our relationships and our attempts at happiness while tempting us to point the finger at everyone else. Our beliefs and thoughts can also convince us that we are somehow lacking, that we don't deserve happiness and success, or that we are essentially failures. The result is a lot of unnecessary, unpleasant emotional reactions and unhappiness.

This internal world draws its power from the beliefs we adopt over the course of our lives. We observe, assess, and interpret our world and ourselves through the filter of our beliefs. Because this process happens constantly and for the most part unconsciously, we have little control over it until we bring these beliefs into our conscious awareness and begin to question their validity.

As children we were naturally happy. As we grew up, our perceptions and experience became conditioned by the values, beliefs, and emotional patterns we absorbed from those around us. We learned to please others and sought approval from them; when we got it, we felt loved and accepted. We also learned to fear their criticism and to feel hurt by it.

Over the years we developed our own thoughts and beliefs about our self-worth and value, and we adopted behavior patterns accordingly. We created our own emotions and emotional reactions based on our own beliefs. If we succeeded or won we felt good about ourselves; if we failed we automatically felt bad about ourselves. We developed a part of our mind to constantly assess ourselves and find ourselves good enough or not good enough throughout the day. Our mind ran automatically with opinions, thinking, and emotional responses whether we wanted it to or not. If we want to live in happiness that is sustainable, we will have to take steps to free ourselves from these automatic thought patterns and emotional reactions.

This book offers clear explanations and several practices to help you change how your mind works. Once developed, you can apply these skills to any situation for the rest of your life. Within these pages you will find and understand in a commonsense way:

- How beliefs are formed.
- Why many of our beliefs are unconscious to us and yet affect our thoughts, emotions, and behaviors.
- Practical exercises to identify and effectively change these beliefs.
- How to focus your attention and perspective in a way that can reduce and eliminate emotional reactions.
- How to inventory and organize your beliefs so that you don't become overwhelmed and confused by your emotional reactions and conflicting thoughts and behaviors.
- How to recover the personal power previously lost to your beliefs and the unnecessary emotions they create.
- Why you feel the emotions you feel and practical tools to make changes in yourself.
- Why many self-help techniques or other attempts at change are often ineffective or make things worse, and how to avoid those pitfalls.

Throughout the book I use real-life examples, drawn from my work with clients, to illustrate how beliefs work and how the processes described here can be applied effectively to bring about real and lasting change. What you will not find is a trite, "just go to a happy place" approach. This is not about projecting happy thoughts and optimistic affirmations as a surface solution to change your emotions. If it was that simple it would have worked already. Instead, I show you how to identify and dismantle those existing beliefs that are triggering painful emotional reactions and interfering with your enjoyment of life.

The final two chapters provide encouragement for the task of change ahead—and the rewards inherent in it. When we eliminate our false and fear-based beliefs, we find another dimension to our internal world. In the state of mind empty of fears and false beliefs, our inner world is peaceful and emotionally beautiful. From this state of mind we perceive the external world as it is and people as they are, without a filter of negative thoughts. Free of the distorting layer of false beliefs, our eyes see clearly and we perceive the beauty that exists everywhere. Most importantly, we are able to perceive the beauty and love within ourselves.

An Invitation

Life is rich with diverse experiences, challenges, and surprises. You cannot bend everything in life, or even in yourself, to match your hopes, goals, and expectations. If you rely on certain criteria being met in order for you to be happy, you will be disappointed and fearful. Your emotions will be dependent on factors outside your control. Outer events, other people, and your own judgments of yourself will determine how much love, acceptance, and happiness you experience. Even in your moments of success, you will feel driven to control external factors and people because of a fear of losing what you have. Your attempts at happiness and enjoyment of life will be unsuccessful and may even be disrespectful or abusive towards others, as well as towards yourself.

However, if you eliminate the false beliefs that make up the negative thoughts, criticisms, fears, and patterns that cause your emotional reactions, then you also eliminate much of your unhappiness. As you learn how you can create your own emotions independently of outside events, you are no longer limited in how much love, acceptance, and respect you can experience. The result is that your love and happiness can expand beyond what you can currently imagine.

What you have in your hands is a guidebook, a manual with step-by-step instructions on how to identify and change the beliefs central to negative thoughts, emotions, and sabotaging behaviors. While great care has been taken to explain what happens in your mind so that you will understand what's behind the emotional reactions you are having, this is not the book's greatest value. The real benefit comes from practicing the exercises provided so that your perspective, thoughts, and emotional patterns will change.

What lies before you is an extraordinary journey to reclaim the inner world of your mind. I wish you happiness on your path, and as your destination. You will find other valuable resources, including videos and audios with a more comprehensive set of exercises and practices helpful for your journey, at www.PathwayToHappiness.com.

Chapter 1

Our Beliefs Affect Our Emotions

If ever there was a person with the potential to become successful and happy, it was Bill. Growing up in Fort Lauderdale with a loving family, he was regarded as "special," "talented," "brilliant," all the adjectives often ascribed to high achievers in our society. And yet, for Bill, living up to this standard became a burden and a source of constant stress. He became afraid of missing the mark, and worked hard to meet the expectations that were placed on him.

Rather than enjoy his college days, Bill felt pressured to make the grades that would give him entrée into medical school, which he wanted very much. Tension headaches plagued him, and he was miserable. He rationalized that this was a temporary and unavoidable unhappiness, the price one paid for exceptional success. He thought, who wouldn't be miserable in this situation?

His acceptance into medical school was a relief, but medical school itself wasn't. The schedule was brutal, and his stress headaches continued. Next came his residency, with its heavy workload and verbal abuse from superiors, which weighed him down further. Still, it was easy to rationalize once again: "All residents are miserable." He convinced himself that he would surely find happiness and peace in the future, just as soon as his training was over.

Although not in the top of his class, Bill was highly regarded by his professors and even his peers, who voted him "most likely to succeed as a premier physician." If only he shared their confidence. Deep down, he knew he was a disappointment waiting to happen.

Several years later, married and with two young children, he accepted a position in a medium-sized medical group. The practice was hectic, but he convinced himself he was trained to deal with the pace. He continued to be admired by his peers, friends, patients, and community. After five years he was voted the head of the cardiology section of this now fifty-four-man group. But as the pedestal grew higher and higher, so did his fear that one day they would all realize that he was not nearly as smart or competent as they believed him to be. He felt like an imposter, a fraud, afraid of being found out.

In spite of all his outward success, the misery had followed him. The tension headaches worsened and he became clinically depressed. He sought help from psychiatrists and psychologists, who told him it was chemical and that he needed to be on medication. To Bill, his chronic unhappiness made no sense—he had no rational reason to be depressed, and he certainly didn't have a Prozac deficiency. He became convinced that it must be the high pressure of his work that led to his depression and misery—so he resigned.

He started a cardiology practice in a small community. It was a nice environment with much less pressure, but for some reason his emotions didn't change. He began to think that his home situation must be causing his pain, and in order to find peace and happiness, he needed to leave his wife and family. He filed for divorce and rented a nice apartment in a trendy part of town, but to his surprise, his gloom followed him. Frustrated with his inability to control his emotions, Bill felt like a failure.

Bill looked for alternative ways to deal with his emotions and stress. He took up yoga and meditation, and read one self-help book after another. He started to see some changes and became hopeful, but the depression lingered. He even started a holistic clinic. Often his clients saw results, but he was disappointed with his own lack of progress and change. Additionally, running and financing the clinic was another source of emotionally stressful chatter in his head. When it became too much to endure, he closed the clinic—and the voices in his head chimed in with more accusations about failure and his worthlessness.

One morning, as Bill looked at himself in the mirror, feeling raw and exhausted, he had a realization. He had left behind all the circumstances he'd believed were causing his deep unhappiness, and yet it was still there.

There was nothing left to point to but himself. Maybe all his years of misery really had more to do with him than with his circumstances. As he looked inward, he discovered that he harbored some deep-seated and pervasive self-judgment and self-hatred. He'd been judging himself constantly for everything, including the emotions he felt, even though the judgments had no basis in reality.

The negative emotions he'd been feeling weren't themselves the problem—they were a symptom caused by something else at work in him. The answer seemed to lie in lessening his own negative thoughts about himself and his judgments about his emotional reactions.

Bill's unhappiness seemed mysterious, both to him and to those who loved and admired him, yet it is typical of many successful people. We think, "They have everything. They *should* be happy." And yet, many outwardly successful people—doctors, business executives, entertainers, or athletes—have achieved their goals, only to end up feeling unfulfilled, depressed, or even suicidal. All of which adds another layer of feeling like a failure because they are unable to be happy in circumstances that they believe should have made them so. What this tells us is that external circumstances aren't the primary source of our emotions.

Ultimately, a person's happiness is determined by factors internal to them, within their own mind. These internal causes include the negative thoughts, opinions, criticisms, self-judgments, and beliefs they hold. Unless a person addresses these factors and develops a healthy belief system, external success will be emotionally empty and the individual will be continually chasing the next goal or wondering, "Is this all there is?"

—ᴡ—

Controlling the external world offers no defense against the unhappiness we create in our mind.

—ᴡ—

The inner world of the mind greatly affects how we feel. Controlling the external world offers no defense against the unhappiness we create in our mind. Like Bill, we can be successful in our field, make lots of money, receive accolades from peers, have a wonderful spouse and family who love us, and still be unhappy. We may then turn to self-help and personal-development programs that suggest we improve our external world by taking control of our life and pursuing the things we are passionate about. But unless we address the internal causes of our unhappiness, we are unlikely to experience the fulfillment and joy we seek.

Changing our beliefs and judgments isn't a simple matter, because we've been accumulating them all our lives. As children, we weren't educated about how our emotions, thoughts, or beliefs operate. We received no training in monitoring how our mind is working, or how to make changes in these things that drive our behaviors. Lacking guidance and training, we still realize our emotional reactions often don't make sense. But when we try to change them—perhaps by willing ourselves to change or by using techniques we've heard about—it doesn't work. So we learn to suppress or reject our emotions throughout our lives, just as Bill did, especially if the emotions don't match what we think we "should" be feeling.

Bill's emotions were actually telling him that he needed to change something. He just didn't know that what needed to change would be found by looking inward at his world of beliefs, instead of at the world outside.

Inner World-Based Emotions

A simple example can illustrate the way our belief system affects our emotions. Bernadette wakes up Saturday morning to discover that the sky is filled with dark clouds and rain is muddying the backyard. She marvels at the watering the earth is receiving, the bright shades of green as the leaves are dusted off, the glistening of the light reflected in each drop. She is so delighted at this show of nature, she might even run outside barefoot and happily get drenched.

Meanwhile, next door, Brigitte wakes up to the same weather and is disheartened. Her mom asks her why she is so down. Brigitte replies that it's because of the rain—it's so depressing.

Here we see a singular event, a rainstorm, resulting in two very different emotional reactions. Both Bernadette and Brigitte would say,

"The weather makes me feel . . .," but Bernadette would conclude with "delighted" while Brigitte would say "sad." What is it about the weather that creates emotions of delight in one person and sadness in another? The answer is nothing—the weather isn't making either of them feel a specific emotion. Weather is as impersonal an event as there can be. Yet both of them will look at the external event, notice how they feel, and unconsciously assume there's a cause-and-effect relationship.

Both believe that the weather is causing their emotions, but neither explains how. Each simply assumes that this external circumstance results in these feelings. But if the cause of the feelings was really the weather, everyone would respond the same way. Rain wouldn't move one person's emotions to happiness and the person next to them into sadness. There must be other factors at work.

Bernadette interprets the experience of rain one way; Brigitte has a different interpretation and even blames the rain for ruining her day. Each girl's emotional experience derives from her interpretation and her beliefs about the rain, and not from the rain itself. The rain is only a trigger for her story and emotional experience.

The emotional event looks more like this:

**Weather
(External World Trigger)**
↓
**Beliefs, Interpretations, Thoughts
(Inner World Reaction)**
↓
Emotions

The Inner World Creates Most of Our Emotions

Let's look at another example. People typically assume that being fired or laid off is enough to cause a person to feel miserable. There is no question that outside events *influence* our emotions, but there is more going on here. Many of those painful feelings are actually created by our own self-criticism and the beliefs we have about being laid off.

Suppose you were laid off from your job. That day and subsequent days might feel like the worst experience of your life. You might believe you're a worthless failure, or you might feel victimized and angrily blame your former boss or company. How you respond to this circumstance is largely determined by what you tell yourself about it—and what you tell yourself originates from your beliefs.

If the event itself was really the source of those emotions, then everyone who gets laid off would have the same emotional experience. But they don't. One person might respond to getting laid off by feeling unworthy, hopeless, and depressed because having a job is integral to their sense of self-worth. Someone else will get angry because they interpret it as unfair. Another individual will be relieved and experience it as freedom because it opens the door to make changes they wanted to make. Yet another person will respond with fear because their mind is focused on issues like feeding their family and health-care worries.

So there is something else in the equation that causes us to feel what we feel and others to feel something different. When we attribute our feelings entirely to external factors, we tend to ignore the beliefs that are at the root of many of our emotions. Our beliefs determine the meaning we give to an event, which in turn influences our emotional experience of the situation.

Imagine that a few years have passed since you were let go. You've found another job or started your own business. Your life is immeasurably better, and now you see the event as propelling you to a new life you hadn't imagined. You may now look back at this event with acceptance and even gratitude. The historical facts of being laid off remain the same, but the interpretation of meaning you give to that time is different. Therefore your emotions are different.

If external circumstances really created our emotions, we would all react the same way to a given circumstance. But we know it doesn't work that way. We go to a movie with our friends, and they love it while we hate it. A person makes a comment that we find funny, while someone else is offended. Was the movie any good? Was the comment funny or offensive? That depends more on the belief system each person uses to interpret their experiences.

Sometimes we get people to agree with our opinions or reactions, making it more difficult to see them as changeable beliefs. We seek out friends or "authorities" to validate our version of the event. The experts may tell us that what we feel is "completely normal," confirming that our thoughts and beliefs are true. They suggest that a person who is laid off would *naturally* feel depressed, unworthy, angry, and so on. Their message confirms that the circumstance makes us feel this way and ignores the role of our beliefs. While it may be true that a majority of people will feel those emotions, that's not because of the event itself. It's because the majority of people have similar beliefs and interpretations, so they create similar emotions. Responding to that situation with anger and depression may be common, but it isn't required, nor is it the only way to respond.

Thomas Edison experienced numerous failures in his attempt to build a working light bulb, but his interpretation was, "I have not failed. I've just found 10,000 ways that won't work." His emotional attitude was clearly independent of external events like success and failure and more dependent on the internal meaning he created.

Many people never get over a painful experience. They are so attached to and controlled by their beliefs about that experience that they hold grudges and resentments until the day they die. For them it still appears that the event caused their emotions, and that it's still causing their emotions decades later. In truth, it is the story in their inner world that hasn't changed.

With awareness and practice, we can become flexible and change our opinions and beliefs at will, even those regarding negative experiences. By changing these beliefs we can change how we feel about things in the past and in the present. We can also learn to adopt perspectives that will help us to avoid emotional reactions to begin with. The result is mastery over our emotions.

Chapter 2

Change: More Than an Intellectual Process

What I've said so far may seem obvious. It's pretty easy to figure out that emotional issues such as anxiety, fear, insecurity, anger, jealousy, depression, and the like are the result of what goes on in our head, and all of these emotional conditions contribute to our unhappiness. Yet *knowing* that what goes on in our head needs to change and *changing* it are two very different things. Labeling the problem is not the same as treating it.

When we first see the problem—that our negative feelings are caused by our thoughts and beliefs—the solution seems simple: just change our negative thoughts and the emotional issues will go away. This quick assessment of the challenge makes for a naïve plan, bolstered by the expectation that change will be easy. We have an idea of how we "should be" different, so we try to shape our thoughts accordingly. But our negative thoughts, emotions, and behaviors don't seem to change. Our habitual ways of thinking are more deeply ingrained and there are more layers to them than we realized. So our surface attempts to change the ones we are aware of are ineffective, and the plan backfires.

Our mind—the same one that is already misinterpreting things—construes this as our own failure to execute and judges us for failing to change our negative thoughts. Our failed attempt then activates our self-critical belief and we end up feeling worse than before we attempted to change. This can be discouraging and demotivating.

If a child tried to fly by jumping out of a tree and flapping his arms, would we scold him for failing to try hard enough or flap his arms well enough? No. The problem was that his expectations were unrealistic. His belief that he could fly that easily was false. Similarly, our failure to reshape our thoughts is actually a failure of naïve expectations.

One lesson learned here is that underestimating the task of changing a negative thought can lead to unnecessary frustration and be detrimental to our success. There is more to this process of changing our negative thoughts than we think. Another lesson is that just exerting personal willpower to change isn't enough. We need some effective tools and techniques to achieve our goals.

Some Negative Thoughts Don't Budge

Let's use the example of Bill again to better understand why some thoughts and emotional patterns don't seem to budge very easily. Realizing the problem must lie within him, he reads a few self-help books and learns about the effects of his thoughts and judgments on his emotions. Intellectually, he *knows* that his emotional reactions and feelings of happiness and fulfillment are not dependent on success, failure, or other external factors. He *knows* that what goes on in his mind will make a lasting impact on his happiness. So why can't he just change his mind and attain the peace and happiness he seeks? Why does he continue to be caught up in work and achievement, worried about what others think of him, or some other emotional dynamic? There are a number of reasons for this.

First, Bill's beliefs have been there for a long time, and for the most part he's unaware of them. He perceives his unhappiness, but his attention remains on the circumstances, not on his beliefs. He doesn't see his inner world and what it is driving him to do. He grew up with these beliefs, which have been reinforced by hundreds, even thousands, of interactions with his parents, teachers, siblings, church leaders, and other authorities. Furthermore, every time he reassures himself that he will be happier when his circumstances change, his beliefs get bolstered. These deeply ingrained beliefs cannot be dislodged simply by introducing an opposing idea.

Second, his beliefs and supporting arguments about achieving happiness through outward success are continually reinforced by the world around him. Self-help experts and people promoting success-formula programs make a strong case for setting and achieving goals, and then working with persistence to achieve them. Carefully selected cases lend credence to their message. Somebody else achieved success and they became happy, so of course it should work for you. Since it fits with his existing beliefs about how to be happy, Bill uses this information to fortify his existing belief structure.

When Bill finally decides to change his beliefs so that he can change his emotions, he is confronted by an inner world of beliefs telling him it is the wrong way to go, it's nonsense, and it won't work. The thoughts stemming from his existing beliefs tell him he must be a success in order to feel better, so he shouldn't bother changing his mind—just get back to work and try harder. This is the struggle within his mind: the new paradigm he is trying to adopt conflicts with the existing structure of beliefs, which pushes back with negative thoughts about this different approach.

As I will point out periodically, reading self-help books is often insufficient to the task of changing the ingrained, self-reinforcing belief patterns of the mind. For simple beliefs, these practices may work. But for larger beliefs, a more comprehensive approach and set of practices are required.

Social Conditioning of Our Emotions

But here is the biggest reason that certain thoughts, beliefs, and emotional patterns are hard to change. Bill was conditioned towards certain modes of behavior and thinking the same way that Pavlov's dogs were conditioned to respond to the sound of a bell. When the sound of the bell was repeatedly followed by the appearance of food, Pavlov's dogs began salivating upon hearing the bell. The pattern was reinforced until it became a natural response of their unconscious nervous system.

While perhaps unintentional, a similar process was at work in Bill's upbringing. As a young child, Bill was rewarded with praise and attention when he did what others wanted. By the time he was forming words, he was starting to mold his behavior and watch his parents' reactions for feedback. Praise and a smile from them reinforced certain actions, developing patterns of behavior and beliefs about what was acceptable. By winning their approval, he formed a positive self-image that resulted in pleasant emotions and feeling happy. Later he strove to earn the praise of teachers and other authority figures, and even of his peers, to ensure that he was successful in their eyes. His mind learned to associate the trigger of accomplishment with good feelings. With time and many repetitions these emotional responses became automatic and happened faster than thinking. Bill also developed a positive image of himself that he identified with. When he was in this positive perspective, he was baffled as to why he sometimes felt miserable or bad about himself.

The same automated conditioning happened with his negative emotions. When Bill failed to meet others' expectations he was reprimanded, punished, rejected, or shamed. Over time and with many repetitions his mind learned to give him the same punishments and rejections whenever he failed at something. With that story, Bill's mind created an image of himself as a failure. At times this image seemed like his identity. His mind would label him as unworthy and produce emotions corresponding to these beliefs. Even when Bill did well and was praised, his mind harbored an opposing belief of himself as a failure. From that belief would arise thoughts like: "If they only knew I'm not as smart or good as they all think." His internal dialog rebuffed compliments and reinforced its existing self-judgment paradigm in these moments.

The result of all this is that Bill has an internal conviction of not being good enough, as well as a set of beliefs that give him a positive self-image. These are two opposing identities within his own mind, each with its own automatic emotions. Bill isn't aware of these beliefs about his identity and so has no idea of how they affect his thoughts and emotions or of the conflict they create. While there are plenty of good feelings, they hardly get noticed. The sharp pain of unpleasant emotions drowns out any good feelings underneath, in the same way stubbing a single toe makes it difficult to notice how healthy and good the rest of our body feels.

Internally Bill's painful emotions are felt more strongly. There is self-judgment that he's a failure, guilt about undeserved praise, fear of failing, and anxiety about being found out as an imposter, not nearly as good as other people believe. Many repetitions have trained him to look at his external circumstances and other people's opinions as the source of his feelings. So Bill works hard to uphold his positive self-image to others by working himself to exhaustion. However, his good feelings become increasingly rare as he gets older and the negative ones drown them out.

If the positive-reinforcement game isn't kept going, Bill might feel bad enough to look inward and see what else is going on. However, occasional small successes might earn him enough approval to keep reinforcing the pattern that accomplishment and other people's opinions determine his happiness. Then, despite his state of misery, he may continue to harbor hope that things will get better. That lingering hope is what enticed Bill to change everything external about his life without looking inward.

Repeated reinforcement strengthens a belief system so much that it takes real work to adopt a behavior or emotional state that contradicts the automated response. When a conditioned response simply ceases to be reinforced, it will naturally extinguish over time. After some time, if food no longer follows, the dogs will no longer salivate at the sound of the bell. However, if the conditioned response is *intermittently* reinforced, it can be sustained indefinitely. For example, if the dogs get food sporadically after hearing the bell, they will still salivate every time they hear it. Similarly, when Bill achieves success, he sometimes feels good momentarily, which reinforces his unconscious association of outer success with good feelings.

The real source of Bill's happiness in those moments of feeling good is his expression of good feeling towards himself in the form of love, approval, self-acceptance, and self-respect. The problem is that he has been conditioned to express these emotions *only* when his mind says he has achieved something worthwhile, something external—when he has "earned" it—and these belief-based conditions are rarely met. Furthermore, when he does begin to feel good, his beliefs of unworthiness immediately rebut the paradigm, tell him he is an imposter, and inject a fear of being found out.

After a lifetime of reinforcing experiences, Bill's mind produces certain emotional responses automatically, and it will take more than an intellectual idea to change this pattern. It will take more than reading several self-help books with great ideas to change the automatically generated emotional responses. Even an experience of not getting food a few times when the bell rings isn't enough to stop Pavlov's dogs from salivating. What is required for emotional change is to retrain the mind's conditioning and automated responses.

Distorted Beliefs Distort Our Understanding of a Process

One of the other challenges in changing beliefs is that beliefs distort how we see things. Beliefs form images in our mind that make things that are false appear to be true, and true things appear false.

In effect, our emotional response doesn't always depend on whether or not something is real. Our emotional response depends on whether we *believe* it is real. Developing awareness that enables us to choose whether to believe the thoughts or images our mind projects is an important part of changing our emotional reactions.

Our mind often uses our emotional responses as evidence that our beliefs are true. When asked by an accusing spouse, "Why do you believe I'm cheating on you?" the accuser replies, "Because it *feels* like you are." This is a case of false beliefs creating real emotion, and the emotion then being used as evidence to support the false beliefs it arose from.

Some approaches attempt to change these emotions by adopting an opposing thought as a replacement. In some cases this may work; however, it can also cause larger problems. Such an approach might leave the original belief in place, by only masking it over. This can make it more difficult to find the deeper core beliefs that drove the original emotions.

These positive-thinking approaches can also fail because of our own self-criticism. Sometimes when we affirm a positive thought, another part of our mind kicks in with criticizing comments like, "You don't really believe that. That's stupid. You are kidding yourself if you think this will have any effect." Often, creating an opposing belief just plain doesn't do the job on a bigger belief. Then the person risks judging themselves as a failure when it was really an inadequate technique they were attempting to apply.

Steps to Internal Happiness: Changing False Beliefs

Changing beliefs is not as easy as we think. Thinking is a surface-level activity, while beliefs are embedded in our mindset and run automatically. It's a simple thing to tell ourselves to stop thinking a negative thought or stop imagining a fearful scenario—it is another thing to do it.

Our mind is complex: it makes a staggering number of associations every minute, particularly in the emotional realm. We are familiar with the mind's ability to think, process information, and relate concepts, but not so familiar with how to change what it does. Changing belief systems and emotional patterns requires more than just telling yourself to think happy thoughts. If it was that simple, it would have worked already for everyone who's tried it.

The following chapters are devoted to understanding your beliefs and learning practical tools for changing and controlling them. Consider this somewhat like learning to drive a car. To control a car you have to have control over the many elements of it: the steering wheel, brake, turn signal, gas pedal, cruise control buttons, and so forth. Our beliefs are similarly made of fundamental elements—perspective, attention, thoughts, and personal power. To control our mind we must discover how to control each element. When you have skillful control over these different elements, you can change the inner world of your beliefs at will, and therefore the emotions that result. This is vastly different than the automated way our mind has been trained that leaves us reacting emotionally to whatever it projects.

The approach I introduce in this material is systematic and thorough. It also includes several practices for you to work with. These practices might seem awkward in the beginning, and you will likely feel some resistance to doing them. The same would happen if you went to a foreign country and started to drive on the opposite side of the road. With practice, they will become easier and you will become more skillful. Reading this material and absorbing it intellectually may be helpful, but it is by doing the practices that you will gain the most benefit from this book. Engaging in regular practice of the exercises will retrain your mind out of the automated conditioning and give you more control of your mind, your emotions, and your life.

Chapter 3

Understanding Beliefs

With one thought our imagination can create an entire world. The following story illustrates the ways we surround ourselves with belief-based thoughts and interpretations. If you can see how another person structures their beliefs and considers them reality, then you have better insight to perceive how your own mind does the same. You can also become aware of how we blend facts with false beliefs. Going forward, we will take a closer look at beliefs that drive negative thoughts and emotions and revolve around self-image. These beliefs are more difficult to see clearly as separate from reality because they are so personal. This example is an easier starting point because it uses beliefs about how the world works.

> *Two guys are sitting together in a bar in the remote Alaskan wilderness. Greg is religious, Al is an atheist, and the two are arguing about the existence of God with that special intensity that comes after about the fourth beer.*
>
> *Al, the atheist, says: "Look, it's not like I don't have actual reasons for not believing in God. It's not like I haven't ever experimented with the whole God and prayer thing. Just last month I got caught away from the camp in that terrible blizzard, and I was totally lost. I couldn't see a thing, and it was fifty below, and so I tried it: I fell to my knees in the snow and cried out, 'Oh, God, if there is a God, I'm lost in this blizzard, and I'm gonna die if you don't help me.'"*
>
> *Greg, the religious guy, looks at Al, feeling puzzled. "Well then you must believe now," he says. "After all, here you are, and alive."*

Al just rolls his eyes. "No, man, all that happened was a couple Eskimos came wandering by and showed me the way back to camp. It was completely random chance."[1]

In this example, Al and Greg look at the same event but somehow draw completely different conclusions. They do agree on one thing. Each is absolutely certain that he is correct in his understanding of reality and that the other has it wrong. I'm not interested in resolving their debate but in something more fundamental: how facts get blended with beliefs so that a person can no longer discern the difference between reality and the inner world of their personal beliefs. What happened in each of their minds to create completely different interpretations? This is where we will find the cause of disagreements.

How can two intelligent people look at the same set of facts and with absolute certainty draw two different conclusions? Quite easily, once you realize that neither is looking purely at the facts. Each is looking at *his own belief system's version* of the facts. If we can understand the dynamic in this example, then we can more easily see how beliefs operate in our own mind, relationships, and emotional reactions. Being able to distinguish between beliefs and facts is an essential step in learning to change our beliefs and, therefore, our experience.

Beliefs Determine Our Interpretation of Events

Greg's belief system is based on the assumption that there is a God whose hand is ever present in people's lives. To him, the facts are clear: Al was out in the blizzard, he prayed for help, God answered the prayer, and the Eskimos found him. Greg's beliefs pair the observed facts with his convictions about God, resulting in the conclusion that Al was found *because* God answered his prayer. The facts are "what" happened, and Greg's beliefs provide an explanation of "why" it happened. In this example, Greg's strongly held beliefs merge the "what" and the "why," creating a cause-and-effect relationship in his mind.

---

1 Adapted from David Foster Wallace, Kenyon College commencement speech, 2005.

Al believes that the events of the day are random, unconnected oc-currences. The appearance of the Eskimos was coincidental, unrelated to his prayer for help. As far as Al is concerned, things happen independently of each other. He sees this not as a belief but as reality. In fact, he would probably claim that, unlike Greg, he has no beliefs—he's just impartially observing the facts. Therefore it's difficult for him to question his belief, because he believes it isn't one! Al believes he is describing "reality." He sees events as random and chaotic because his belief projects this pattern onto events.

Beliefs form interpretations, and
those interpretations support beliefs.

Both Al and Greg have woven their beliefs into the facts of this story. Those beliefs are the basis for how they interpret events. For Greg it is a "known fact" that God intervened. For Al it is a "known fact" that his rescue by Eskimos was a random event. Each man's interpretation supports the beliefs he started with. This is a closed-loop system in which events are used to substantiate beliefs, even if a belief is false. This is one of the early obstacles in changing beliefs. To change a belief you have to step out of the loop.

Both Al and Greg operate within a closed-loop mindset, seeing their own belief-generated interpretation of events as the only true version. Therefore, they are unable to see the possibility that another interpretation might be valid. This kind of closed mindset creates a self-sustaining illusion. I refer to these self-sustaining closed-loop illusions as *belief bubbles*.

Living within a belief bubble, it is very difficult to see alternate possibilities as viable. You may be able to acknowledge there's some logic to support a different version, but it won't appear believable. You can't clearly see past your own bubble, even if the alternate version is indeed factual or "true."

Belief bubbles both distort our perception of reality and cause us to accept our false mental projections *as* reality. We then dismiss factual evidence or other interpretations without fully considering whether they might be true. A stark example of this is the way a woman with anorexia perceives herself. Her illusion is so strong that when she looks in the mirror at her thin body, even if her bones are clearly outlined, she still thinks, "I'm overweight. I should lose a few more pounds." Her perception of reality is distorted by her belief.

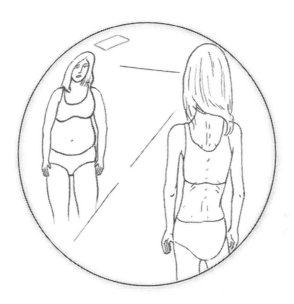

It's very difficult to perceive that our beliefs are merely mental constructs because they seem so real. Beliefs provide a mental model as to how the world works and why things are the way they are. Our beliefs map explanations and interpretations onto the real world. This becomes such an automated process that the line between our belief-system-based understanding of the world and the real world becomes blurred. To change beliefs, we must learn to perceive them as abstract ideas separate from the world.

Now back to our story. Al "knows" that Greg's explanations of God are only conceptual ideas in his friend's head, none of which could be true. It doesn't occur to Al that his own belief bubble may be nothing but conceptual ideas as well. In his view, every explanation he offers to support his case is "factual," and every argument offered by Greg is dismissed as merely "coincidence." This reinforces Al's allegiance to what he already believes.

This conflict between their beliefs has gone on for a long time. The principal reason they cannot come to a resolution is that they inhabit different inner worlds. While each man claims he can "see both sides," he perceives his own story as reality and the other's version as fiction. When he does consider the other person's ideas, he does so from a perspective within his own belief bubble, so he doesn't actually see it the same way the other is seeing.

Adding Emotion to Your Belief Bubble

To complicate matters, we add emotion to our experience and our beliefs, making them seem even more real. We interpret an event based on emotional experience, and that lends validity to our beliefs. Emotions are real sensations, but that doesn't mean what we believe is real. The anorexic woman has real fears of gaining too much weight, but that doesn't make the associated beliefs true.

A loud motorcycle drives by: this is a fact. But two people will experience two different emotional reactions. One person experiences joyful admiration of a work of engineering art. Another person experiences annoyance, frustration, or even anger at the intrusion of this loud, obnoxious machine. The stimulus is identical—the passing motorcycle—but the emotional experiences vary because the individuals live in two different belief bubbles. These emotions, congruent with the beliefs they arise from, appear to validate and intensify the beliefs. Both individuals attribute their emotional experience to the motorcycle, and neither notices how their belief system played a role. Fundamental to changing beliefs is the awareness of the influence your belief bubbles have in creating your emotional *experience* of events.

20

Further emotion is added when we associate our opinion with *being right*. Being right has a conditioned feel-good emotional response going back to early childhood and reinforced through years of school. Anybody else's divergent opinion is interpreted as false or "wrong." It may even be perceived as a threat to our own feel-good experience of being "right." The other person's contradictory beliefs threaten to burst the bubble of emotion in which we feel comfortable. If our bubble were to collapse, we might be ushered into the alternative belief bubble of being "wrong" or looking "stupid," and that would feel unpleasant.

Conditioned emotions leverage our position in a belief bubble of "right" and help us avoid a bubble of "wrong," independent of the facts. When we have emotions like this associated with our belief it seems better to keep our bubble intact, even if it is an illusion. Bursting our belief bubble is an emotional experience we are conditioned to avoid, even if the belief itself is false.

Belief Bubbles Versus Reality

One of the major challenges in changing negative thoughts and beliefs is that alternate interpretations appear false. Once a belief is accepted as true, it forms a bubble around us, conditioning the way we see things. After that, truth and facts that contradict it appear to be fictional and are dismissed. Even scientists can feel defensive when a new theory or research is introduced that challenges previously held paradigms. This is one of the reasons that negative thoughts and beliefs are so resistant to change. We tend to cling to them as truths because that is how we perceive them from within our bubble. It is easy to label such behaviors with words like "denial" and "confirmation bias" but this doesn't change them. It is more valuable to see their inner workings.

When our belief system's inner world/mental model and the real world of physical reality are congruent we can operate pretty well. When our belief system's mental model is incongruent with reality we will have difficulties emotionally and in getting the results we want. When things aren't working in a person's life, or they are having a lot of emotional reactions about the world, it is likely because their beliefs about the world are faulty. If we struggle behaviorally or emotionally in an area, it is likely that our unconscious beliefs are having us operate by a mental model that is incongruent with reality.

Another reason we resist changing beliefs is because we have construed this mental model as reality; it becomes the foundation upon which we operate. When we are not aware of our beliefs as separate from reality, and beliefs start to shift, it appears that reality or how the world works is changing. The anorexic woman is not merely changing how she thinks about herself—she is also displacing the idea of how everyone in the world perceives her, and what is important in the world. Greg is not merely changing his story of how Al got saved—he is changing his understanding of how the universe works. Indirectly, this is experienced as the universe changing. Bill, from the example in Chapter 1, believed he was an imposter, undeserving of success, and would be found out. To change this belief bubble of being undeserving involves more than just a singular thought. It includes his imagined version of how everyone perceives him, measures him, and will treat him in the future.

Changing these singular beliefs also requires a different understanding of how the world works, how people are, and a different version of ourselves that will be interacting with this new reality. As a result, when we begin changing beliefs it seems like the world is being displaced with an alternate world, and that is usually too big of a leap to fathom comfortably in one step.

The internal nature of belief bubbles explains why a supermodel can believe she is ugly even though her picture graces the covers of magazines. Belief bubbles are the reason a wealthy tycoon can still feel he hasn't been successful enough. Belief bubbles can make a person feel unlovable, even though many people love and care about them. They are also the reason we can feel unworthy or inadequate no matter how much we accomplish or how "good" we are.

We don't have to go as far as Alaska to see these belief systems at work. We can see their influence in a friend's self-image or sense of self-worth, in a coworker's opinions of others, and in the emotions a person expresses. Belief bubbles are at work when we casually dismiss a compliment. Perhaps you are told you did a great job, or that you are good-looking, very smart, or skillful. When you notice an impulse to dismiss the compliment, you are witnessing your belief bubble pushing away an idea that doesn't fit with existing beliefs about your self-image.

The story of Greg and Al gives us the following insights:

1. Our belief systems (bubbles) cause us to see our own beliefs as "facts" and "reality."
2. Our belief systems cause us to dismiss other interpretations, or even facts and truth, as invalid because alternate ideas appear false.
3. A belief bubble forms a closed-loop system. We see what we believe is there and confirm to ourselves that it is reality. We reinforce what we already believe because the belief bubble is the basis for interpretation.
4. All of this impedes our ability to see a situation from any point of view other than the one we already hold.

If you have found it difficult to change your beliefs in the past, or even to be aware of what your beliefs were, it may be due to some of these factors. It's important to be aware of these dynamics in your mind so that you can avoid these closed-loop traps. When it comes to changing beliefs, it is unlikely that you will be able to change what you are not aware of.

—⚒—

When the illusions of our beliefs are identified for what they are, they tend to fall apart, along with the fear and unhappiness attached to them.

—⚒—

For Best Results: Focus on Your Own Beliefs

Challenging the beliefs of others rarely benefits us or them. However, there is great value in challenging our own beliefs. When we can shift our perspective out of our belief bubble and scrutinize our assumptions, we have the opportunity to develop clarity and distinguish between truth and our own illusions. Those illusions are usually what cause our unhappiness and emotional reactions. When the illusions of our beliefs are identified for what they are, they tend to fall apart, along with the fear and unhappiness attached to them.

One of the interesting things about a bubble of false beliefs is that we are very quick to see when someone else is operating from their inner world of beliefs and very slow to perceive when we are doing the same thing. Like Al and Greg, we go about our lives with opinions and thoughts arising from our beliefs and we assume they are true. Then we defend our interpretations and try to change other people's beliefs when they don't fit with our own.

What happens when we try to change another person's beliefs? For starters, our ideas and proposals appear false to them from within their belief bubble. Second, they may get upset or annoyed, feeling their beliefs are being attacked and invalidated. If their beliefs are tightly held and charged with emotion, the person might feel the challenge to their beliefs is a personal attack. Third, they defend their beliefs by attacking back. In defending their beliefs they reinforce their commitment to them as being valid and factual. The result is that their belief bubble becomes a thicker fog around them.

The overall result of challenging another person's beliefs is often that the beliefs become more deeply entrenched. For some people, this means spending a massive amount of personal energy challenging other people, creating frustration, aggravation, and disappointment, while changing nothing. We might experience a similar internal resistance, aggravation, and ensuing reinforcement if we attempt to change our own beliefs in the same confrontational way.

Without much awareness, we assume that the thoughts running through our head are true, and therefore we rarely examine them skeptically. We also assume that if someone disagrees with us, their beliefs are false. With those assumptions as a starting point, we are skeptical of other people's beliefs but not of our own. In this manner, our belief system automatically directs our attention to reinforce our existing belief bubbles. We push away interpretations that would open our mind to other perspectives, ideas, and thoughts. This is one of the self-preservation strategies of the belief system. It directs our attention to be skeptical of the beliefs and behaviors of others and distracts us from directing our attention inward with any skepticism. We see this happen in the example of Bill whenever he was complimented or praised. His beliefs would immediately throw out thoughts of rebuttal such as, "If they only knew I'm not nearly as good as they think."

A word of caution: As with all techniques and tools, there is a near-enemy downside of looking at issues using this new paradigm. Some people will use this information to point out the belief bubbles of another party and justify labeling them as false. In the process, they are using the tools presented here to reinforce and defend their own closed mind. If you plan to use what you learn in this book to change someone else's beliefs while holding on to your own, you should know it will probably backfire. The best use of this material is for you to change your own beliefs.

The Real Work: Changing Thoughts and Beliefs So You Can Change How You Feel

You probably had some emotional motivation when you selected this book. It might be an issue with anger, insecurity, jealousy, fear of what others think of you, fear of the future, or any of a thousand different negative thoughts and emotions. You may have noticed that you want to change not only your emotional state but also the many negative thoughts and images that your mind projects. This is the real work that we will address in the coming pages.

To do this, we'll first dissect belief bubbles and belief systems into their fundamental elements, detailing how they form and how they work. The imagination is an extraordinary tool, and we have spent years using it to create our own worlds of beliefs and then forgetting that those self-created bubbles still surround us. The following chapters will give you a systematic approach to understand what goes on in your mind, how your emotions get generated from your beliefs, and, most importantly, how to change them. In order to do that, it is important that you understand the different elements that make up your beliefs. We'll begin with attention and awareness.

Chapter 4

Attention

A critical but often overlooked factor in forming and maintaining beliefs—and therefore in determining the quality of our lives—is how we use our attention.

Attention is the process of focusing on some features of the environment to the exclusion of our vast field of perception. A simple example of this is when we are in a crowded room and we concentrate on what one person is saying and ignore everyone else. How we direct our attention is a fundamental component in creating our experience and our beliefs. By gaining control of our attention we can eliminate or change beliefs that are no longer useful and are perhaps even harmful.

How Attention Works

Out of a myriad of stimuli, we only consciously focus on a small number of them at any given moment. Most of the time we filter out the majority of our perceptions. By narrowing our focus, it becomes possible to read a book on a train while filtering out the noise around us, or to complete a project at work while ignoring a pain somewhere in our body.

While we always perceive the world in many modalities, such as light, sound, touch, smell, and emotions, it is our attention that determines the dominant experience of each moment. Other factors, feelings, and sensations are ignored and, for the moment, are left outside the realm of our conscious awareness and experience. What you are experiencing in this very moment is a product of your attention. You are using your attention to focus on these words and on your mind's ideas about them, and excluding a million other experiences. Your experience in every moment of your life is created through the action of your attention.

Selective attention is essential to function successfully in the world. It protects us from becoming overwhelmed by every bit of data our senses can perceive. When we are driving, we automatically key on important factors like the traffic lights and other vehicles. We avoid becoming absorbed with the color of other cars, clouds in the sky, the pebbles of asphalt that make up the road, or doing our hair and makeup.

We also use selective attention to structure the inner world of our mind. Sometimes this means ignoring or suppressing certain thoughts and feelings. Those thoughts and feelings don't cease to exist—we merely stop noticing them without conscious attention.

The Role of Attention in Forming Beliefs

Because our attention largely determines what we *perceive*, it also plays a huge role in determining what we *believe* about the world and about ourselves. From the limited range of input that our attention allows into our awareness, we draw conclusions and construct beliefs about what is and isn't true. By creating a system of beliefs in the form of simple rules, we create a mental model of the world that automates future meaning and behavior. Our mental model maps onto the world explanations of how things work and interact. These automatic interpretations are essential so we don't become overwhelmed trying to make sense of every stimulus every time. However, when these mental-model beliefs are applied falsely, they usually cause unpleasant emotional responses.

Five-year-old Sam wanted a cookie. He climbed onto a chair to reach the cookie jar and was happily munching when his mother walked in. He wondered what she would do. She frowned. Sam interpreted this to mean that his mother disapproved of him and that he had done something "bad." Past experience had taught Sam to give his mother's reactions priority over anything else he might pay attention to: his hunger, the delicious cookie, and the fun of climbing on the chair all receded into the background once his mother appeared.

Sam's attention became fixed externally on his mother's expression and internally on the meaning that he derived from it—that he had done something wrong and was therefore a bad boy. Sam accepted this "bad boy who has done something wrong" mental-model idea of himself as true. With this act of agreement a belief bubble was imprinted on his mind. It happened without any conscious consideration of other interpretations or choices.

Beliefs form when we put our attention on a certain interpretation of an event and agree that it's true. In five-year-old Sam's case, the interpretation appeared true because his mom was standing right there with a disapproving look on her face. However, many distortions and exaggerations accompanied that belief, including a guilty-feeling "bad boy" identity that he carried into the future and projected into many situations. We will look more closely at the identity portion of the belief later.

Years later, when a girlfriend looked at Sam a certain way, he would feel guilty, as if he had done something wrong, even though he couldn't figure out what. He would wonder, "What did I do?" and scramble to answer a question that had no basis in present-day reality. This was his imprinted belief at work, using its mental model for explanation, and reinforcing itself by directing his attention even years later.

Eventually, as Sam developed skill in noticing his emotions, he discovered there were many triggers that could activate his "bad boy" belief and generate feelings of guilt and shame. For many years, Sam didn't notice these feelings much, since he had learned to ignore them and to "pay attention" to other people, or to try to answer the faulty question his belief system reacted with, as to what he had done wrong.

The Development of Attention Habits

As a child, you gave adults your attention, and they gave you their instructions along with their opinions, emotions, ideas, values, and beliefs. You largely accepted these without question, and they became yours as well. It became a habit to pay attention to other people and for them to tell you what to do, how to be, and how to feel. You didn't yet have the awareness and discernment to decide what to believe or not to believe. If your parents told you that a person named Santa Claus would come from the North Pole to bring presents, you believed them. If they said what you got was based on whether you were good or bad that year, you believed them. You didn't have enough wisdom to discern between facts, fiction, and opinions.

Nor did you have the awareness to question other people's opinions of *you*. Whether people said you were beautiful, ugly, a good person, a bad person, good at math or bad at math, you largely accepted it as true. You also lacked the awareness to question your own interpretations and conclusions.

Unaware that you were accepting all those ideas at a young age, you could not have known the consequences. You had no awareness of what you were doing with your attention or that you were forming beliefs. There was no way to know that these mental models would be used for future interpretations, even if they didn't exactly apply. The end result is that you did not consciously choose most of what you believe or who you got it from.

The Habit of Looking to Others

As you grew older, paying attention to external authorities as a guide for what to do and how to feel became an ingrained habit. This habit is a part of what needs to change if we are to live in a state of self-acceptance instead of fearing what others think of us or hoping to gain approval from others.

When five-year-old Sam climbed onto the chair, the cookie was the focus of his attention. When his mother looked at him, his attention shifted to her. Sam was now set up to react to whatever she did. It didn't matter what else was going on in the room or in his mind. Sam was focused on his mother because of years of conditioning. It was as automated as the response of Pavlov's dogs.

Gradually, Sam became trapped in the belief bubble of always feeling like he has done something wrong. As an adult, he continually tries to compensate by seeking to gain approval from women in order to feel better. When this behavior pattern is played out with a woman who is unhappy and critical, it amplifies Sam's chronic guilt and can drive him to physical and emotional exhaustion.

Sometimes adults are so used to looking to others for guidance that they feel lost and uncomfortable if they don't have someone else telling them what to do. When we start a new job, we want to know who the boss is so that we can follow the right instructions. In the military, people follow the orders of the sergeant, who follows someone else's orders, who follows someone else's orders. In the larger picture, the actions of large groups of people are controlled because of the habit of having other people direct their attention. A few fashion designers decide what is "in style" and what is out of style. Millions of people pay attention and respond accordingly.

Magazine covers at the grocery store are a small example of how popular media tries to hook your attention and direct you towards how your body should look, how your home should be decorated, and what cigars you should smoke. But it's not just advertisers that make monumental efforts to get your attention and keep it. Politicians often evoke fear to get people's attention and agreement.

We automatically pay attention to external authority figures or groups of people for approval, guidance, and instruction, even if they are just following someone else or are going the wrong way. Since everyone around us is putting their attention on other people to tell them what to think, and has been for so long, we don't easily notice the option of using our attention in a different way or forming beliefs and actions independent of groups.

Nor is the world busily trying to get you to have control over your own attention and make your own choices. Rather it is the complete opposite. The world can keep your attention so busy that you won't have time to direct it yourself, unless you commit to it.

Conditioning by Rules

One way that other people can control our attention and behavior over time is by giving us rules to follow. Eventually, the authority figures no longer need to be present to control our attention and behavior because we have internalized their rules and made them our own.

Following rules can be productive and useful. A peaceful society depends in large part on the willingness of its members to follow its laws and rules. But it becomes a personal problem when, as adults, we still rely on the fear-based reactions or other emotionally charged responses we learned when we were young. Many a workaholic puts in numerous hours, consciously or unconsciously driven by their wish to be recognized, or by their fear of what others would think of them if they left the office before their colleagues did.

The rules we learned as children often become powerful beliefs that we live by, powerful enough to elicit emotions years later whenever they're activated. These rules can often be recognized by the words *should, shouldn't, supposed to, not supposed to,* and *have to* in our thoughts. If we act in a way that opposes the rules of our belief system, we can often feel guilty or uncomfortable, even if the belief we are challenging is false. Our mental model projects that we have broken a rule, that we will get caught, and we are made to feel bad for it.

At the same time, some part of us dislikes the rules and harbors a desire to be free of these conditions and restrictions. An instinct from an authentic side of our being makes us want to rebel. We tried to rebel as a toddler and as a teenager, but the pressure of rules was usually too big. They were not our rules, but we were made to adopt them in the household and community we lived in until we internalized them. As adults wanting to change our beliefs, we have a chance to rebel against these rules in our head, without judging the people we got them from or externally challenging our community. Unfortunately, too often the rebel instinct goes off track and focuses attention on other people instead of the false beliefs we have internalized.

A Growing Problem

The mind is not a static thing. It continues to extrapolate and expand from the original belief. Sam took a simple belief, "I did a bad thing," and grew an associated belief of "That makes me a bad person." Again, we see that the look from his mom may have been about the action, but Sam's mind builds an associated belief about his identity. Later chapters will explore these false beliefs about our identity and how it affects our perception.

Later that day Sam thought, "If I hadn't gone for that cookie that I wanted, I wouldn't have gotten into trouble." So his mind developed a general rule to follow as a preventative measure: "I shouldn't try to get what I want—ever." To accomplish this, it became easier just to suppress feelings of inspiration, desire, passion, or interest about things. Each of these rules, or beliefs, formed part of a belief system, created another false identity in his personality, and affected his future behavior.

Years later, many people marveled at how capable Sam was and how much potential he had. And everyone, including Sam, was completely baffled because he could not find anything he was motivated by and he seemed just plain lazy. Sam's self-reflective process as a five-year-old might be admirable, but because of some misinterpretations and exaggerations, he lived many years of his life with limiting beliefs and not really accomplishing much.

Sam's attention, under the control of his beliefs, only allowed him to perceive aspects of himself and of life that confirmed his belief bubbles. Awareness of his authentic nature and interests was obscured, along with any aspects of the world that might inspire him. It's an oversimplification to judge that Sam has a self-esteem problem or is lazy. At its root, Sam has a perception problem. Sam's beliefs continually direct his attention to the same false self-image presented by his belief bubble.

Beliefs Control Your Attention

If a person looks at you and smiles, you can have a number of different interpretations depending on your belief system. If you have a belief that you are good-looking, you are likely to have a congruent thought: "They are smiling at me because they think I'm attractive." If your belief system includes a belief that you are ugly or unattractive, then a congruent thought might be, "They are smiling because they are laughing at me for the way I look." The stimulus of someone smiling is the same, but the belief bubble generates different interpretations to reinforce the original belief. In either case the belief system captures the attention with a thought, to produce an affirming interpretation and emotion.

Because of this reinforcing cycle, it is critical to become aware of your thoughts and begin to be skeptical of them if you wish to change them. Your thoughts don't tell you why that person smiled; instead, your thoughts give clues about the beliefs in your mind.

In Sam's case, his thoughts as an adult are being directed by his beliefs. Although those beliefs originated in childhood, they have been added to and perpetuated in his mind to the point that they are now his own beliefs, affecting how he interprets things and thereby supporting his belief bubbles.

Sam sometimes had thoughts of being an entrepreneur and starting a business. When he saw an opportunity he liked he would feel that inspiration and desire. However, shortly thereafter his rule-based beliefs about getting caught, reprimanded, and feeling guilty for breaking his rule and going after what he wanted would affect him unconsciously. In order to avoid this unpleasant imagined outcome his mind would then find reasons that the business would be a bad idea, and he would abandon it. Sam's belief system projected a mental model of the future outcome and directed his attention towards avoiding the projected pain. Months or years later Sam would reflect back on what he didn't do and wonder why he hadn't pursued that business. Another belief bubble ingrained over time, acting as a mental model to interpret this behavior, would automatically send him the thought that he was just lazy.

Sam was stuck in the narrative of the stories his belief system wove in his mind. By believing the thoughts arising from his beliefs, Sam reinforced them. With the self-image belief that he was lazy, Sam became less motivated to look for things to be inspired about. This is how a person's beliefs control their attention and lead them to repeating behavior patterns in life.

I Didn't See That Coming

Just as our attention automatically focuses on certain details, our mind automatically classifies much of what we can perceive as irrelevant and ignores it.

In new relationships (especially romantic ones), we sometimes ignore annoying or disturbing traits in the other person because they contradict the idealized image we prefer to have of them. David met a woman named Dawn and was immediately attracted to her. He pursued her, and eventually they married. After some time had passed, David became aware of aspects of Dawn's personality that surprised him. Her emotional reactions to his absences while on business seemed excessive. The numerous phone calls when he was gone were no longer about caring; they were about control. She was obsessive about knowing where he was and who he was with. As David paid closer attention to Dawn's emotional cycles, he noticed a great deal of fear, insecurity, and jealous behavior.

Likewise, Dawn began to realize some things about David that hadn't seemed important prior to their marriage. In the beginning, she had enjoyed his lavish attention and gifts. Caught up in the excitement of his pursuit and courtship, she never paid attention to his financial situation. Now she realized that, in spite of making good money, he was deeply in debt. By her standards, his spending habits were out of control. She worried about his lack of concern and his failure to plan for the future.

You might say David and Dawn "overlooked" these important issues at the beginning of the relationship. "Overlooking" something points to an issue of perception, which at its root is an attention issue. Distracted by the exhilaration of their courtship, Dawn and David unknowingly focused on the most pleasing personality traits of the other, ignoring everything else. In doing so, they completely missed important attitudes and behaviors that would impact their relationship down the road.

Looking back, people usually realize that all the signs of a problem were there right from the beginning. Even if they had a fleeting thought about an issue, it was easy for their belief system's mental model to dismiss it as "unimportant" or "not really a problem."

Dawn and David each had a belief bubble version of their partner and a projection of how the relationship would play out in the future.

Because their attention was focused on these idealized versions of each other, they overlooked signs pointing to real behaviors in their partner. Concerns mentioned by friends or family bounced off their existing belief bubbles. When a flag was raised in their perception, their beliefs redirected their attention to a dismissive explanation so that their belief bubble could remain unchallenged.

That this happened is not surprising. Like everyone else, Dawn and David were used to having their attention controlled by other people, outside activities, and, most of all, by the stories and beliefs in their mind. Since much of their attention was automatically directed by their conditioned mind and existing belief bubble, they couldn't perceive potential problems with their partner. The decisions they made about the relationship were based on what they "knew" about each other, which was limited to their belief bubble version. What they didn't "know"—the things their attention ignored—became the source of problems.

If you can't control what you focus your attention on, then you can't control what you perceive and what you miss. Without a clear perception of what is going on, it's impossible to make a good decision. Good decisions are based on awareness of the difference between the mind's projected belief and reality. Although we weren't trained to make this distinction consciously, we can learn to do it by gaining control of our attention.

—⁂—

Good decisions are based on awareness of the difference between the mind's projected belief and reality.

—⁂—

Discipline Versus Habit

To what extent can we control our attention? It depends. Completely absorbed in a novel or engaged in a project, we might find it easy to focus for hours without distraction. But we have all experienced the opposite— for example, being unable to focus at work, or enduring a sleepless night, with many beliefs and emotions active, and unwanted thoughts raging through our minds, leaving us feeling futile and exhausted. Why is it that we can focus so well at some times but not others?

The fact is, the quality of our attention varies. Being able to focus our attention on a novel or on work doesn't necessarily translate to other situations. Our lack of control over our attention can become apparent when we first attempt something new like studying another language, playing a musical instrument, or meditating. If focusing on our breath is something we have no practice in, we might be easily distracted by thoughts or by anything else in the room. We might interpret this to mean that we are undisciplined or incapable of meditating. Our attention then focuses on this thought of being lousy at it. From there it goes to the next tangential thought. These uncontrolled thoughts—which aren't true, by the way—are then controlling our attention.

Developing focused control of your attention comes from repetition. When you first learned to read or do schoolwork, your attention span was measured in minutes. As you practiced reading over the years, you increased your ability to direct your attention. You developed your mind's ability to picture all the imagery conveyed in the story and construct related meaning as you read. Similarly, your ability to focus your attention at work developed over time as you learned to immerse yourself in all the elements that make up a complex project. Only after years of practice did it become a habit that is "easy" to do for hours. The same development and practice must be applied to focus your attention when learning something new, like meditation, a language, or how to play a musical instrument. It's not a matter of poor discipline or lack of ability, but rather that your mind needs to be retrained.

From one point of view, the ability to stay focused can be a powerful skill, but if taken to an extreme it becomes obsessive and unhealthy. For example, if you are at home having dinner with the family and your mind is still busy at work or absorbed in the novel, the automated thoughts from your beliefs are controlling your attention out of habit. This is an indication that you don't have control over your attention because you don't have the flexibility to shift your focus to other things.

What can look like an ability to focus your attention on an activity like reading or work might actually be a conditioned habit, albeit a positive one. It does not mean that you have control over your attention and can focus it in another way with the same acuity or length of time. Sometimes it just means your beliefs conditionally and habitually focus your attention. For the workaholic, it is not necessarily a matter of having such disciplined attention that they can work straight through things. It might just be that their belief system is so conditioned that it doesn't allow them to contemplate or focus on much else.

At some point in the process of self-awareness, individuals learn that they do not have control over their attention to the degree that they want to, particularly when it comes to certain emotions, reactions, negative thoughts, or behaviors. While a person might have great skill directing their attention in other matters, or be able to maintain a calm mind during a practice such as meditation, it may not translate to control over emotional issues, negative thoughts, and the like elsewhere. Using your attention the way you want is like developing a set of muscles. Focusing your attention on reading uses one muscle, but to focus it on writing a computer program, understanding your emotions, or meditating involves separate muscles to be strengthened through their own specific exercises.

—∽—

The first step of the solution is simply an awareness of what is going on.

—∽—

The First Step: Awareness

By the time we become adults, the people who gave us their beliefs no longer control our attention. Rather, it is our beliefs themselves that control our attention, make interpretations for us, and, through these interpretations, further reinforce the beliefs. This is the trap of a belief bubble: it is difficult to see something other than what's in the bubble, namely what we believe. Our attention is controlled by the beliefs we created in the past and are no longer aware of.

38

Over the years, as our internalized set of rules grows, layers of beliefs reinforce one another and discount alternative thoughts, giving an impression of reality. When someone proposes a different idea it bounces off our belief bubble before we have a chance to consider it thoroughly. Living in a belief bubble, it can be difficult to imagine how life could be different, or even how we might think differently about things.

Before we can become free, we first need to be aware that we are trapped. The first step of the solution is simply an awareness of what is going on. We must become aware of what we are doing with our attention so that we can gain more control over it. With this awareness we can begin to choose what beliefs we will create today. When we are aware and can control our attention, we can also use it to stop reinforcing, and even break free from, old beliefs that run our emotions and behaviors. Our attention was fundamental in building the structure of our beliefs, and it is through the use of our attention that beliefs will be dissolved.

Although gaining control over your attention and changing beliefs may seem hard, not having control over your attention is harder. Being at the mercy of an emotional reaction with no control over it is a much more difficult and emotionally painful way to live. Letting those false beliefs run stories in your head and determine your behaviors is exhausting. If you want to be free from emotional reactions and negative thinking and live your own life, you must gain control over your attention, choose what you will believe or not believe, and that in turn will lead to different emotional experiences. Without some control over your attention—which is the most basic mechanism of your mind—you will have little chance for control over other parts of your life.

Gaining Control of Your Attention

Since our belief bubbles make it difficult to imagine other possibilities, sometimes the most practical and effective approach is simply to become aware of what blinds our perception. We begin this process by using our attention to observe our beliefs in operation. The more we are aware of our mind's habitual patterns, the better we will be able to see past them.

If you sit still and watch your mind, you'll realize that it is very busy, generating one thought after another, often even contradicting itself.

Every thought, when accepted as true or valid, can generate its own little emotion. We have thousands of thoughts each day. If we let our attention follow them and automatically accept them as true, we create many beliefs that are false and continue to reinforce existing false belief bubbles. We also experience many small emotional reactions that are unnecessary. By the end of the day we can be exhausted from the emotional dramas that took place in our head.

As mentioned earlier, the skill and discipline that you gradually develop over your attention in meditation won't automatically apply to other areas, such as thoughts about your relationship issues or fears about money. Unquestioned beliefs remain, generate thoughts and images, and demand or seduce your attention away once again.

As adults, what principally directs our attention is our own false and fear-based beliefs and rules. Therefore, the fastest way to gain control over our attention is to identify these beliefs and dismantle them. When we break the beliefs, they no longer tug at our attention, and it is much easier to put our attention where we choose.

Focusing attention on your beliefs can modify and even dissolve them. In the same way that sunlight burns away the fog and clears the sky, your awareness and attention can dissipate the fog of beliefs. It is critical that when you look at a belief, you do so as an observer and apply a bit of skepticism, rather than simply accepting it as true, as you have in the past. It is also not just a matter of mentally rejecting the belief or embracing an opposing one. In later chapters I provide some practical exercises and techniques you can implement to dismantle your beliefs.

The process I outline in this book is about getting control over your attention by dismantling beliefs. The apparent catch-22 here is: How do we use our attention to dismantle our beliefs when our beliefs already have so much control over our attention?

We have to assume that you do have some ability to control your attention, even just a little bit. The truth is, the beliefs in your mind don't control your attention *all* of the time. Right now, you are using your attention to read these pages, absorb these ideas, and connect them with other things you believe. In the beginning, you will have a small amount of control over your attention and maintain it for short intervals of time. This means that breaking down your fear-based beliefs will start out slowly. You will probably also be most effective at changing smaller beliefs. However, as you dissolve each belief, you will have more control over your attention and be able to apply that control to breaking other beliefs.

Each time you break a false belief, you will recover the personal power that was holding it together. You will then have more personal power with which to control your attention and identify and change other beliefs. As you continue this process you will notice an acceleration in the gaining of personal power and in the speed with which you can identify and change your limiting beliefs.

Focus on the Positive: The Self-Help Trap

There is a common misconception in the self-help community that because what we put our attention on grows, we should avoid focusing on "negative thoughts" and focus only on the positive. Optimism and a positive focus can be helpful, but if we refuse to face our negative beliefs or acknowledge the fact of their influence, we leave in power a belief system that is distorting our view of reality. The common name for this behavior is denial.

For change to happen, we must focus our attention on our false beliefs. By doing so, we will not generate "more of it," but rather a clarity that comes from exposing the false assumptions at their core and seeing what is true. To deny what the belief system is doing and focus on "the positive" is to ignore significant factors affecting us.

If you were to go to the doctor with a broken arm, would you want him to say, "Well, just look at the good one—why don't you focus on that?" No, you wouldn't. If your car had a flat tire, would it help to focus on the three other tires that were fine? Of course not, it sounds ridiculous. Yet this sort of advice, to focus only on your positive points, is often given to people who are struggling with insecurity, low self-esteem, anger, jealousy, and other belief-based issues.

To fix a car and make it run better, the mechanic must identify and focus on what's wrong with the car. His work is made more effective and enjoyable if he does so with a pleasant and optimistic attitude. He can even celebrate the moments when he discovers the core cause of a problem.

In the same way, if you have unnecessary emotional suffering, you must put your attention on the false beliefs that are the root cause in order to change them. This is not the same as being negative. By focusing your attention on fear-based and false beliefs, you are merely addressing what isn't working in your emotional life at the level of cause so it can be changed. Then, as these false beliefs are cleared away, it is much easier to focus on things you enjoy.

Chapter 5

Perspective

The perspective from which we view our world has a great impact in creating our experience. It works hand in hand with our attention. Attention determines *what* you focus on, while perspective is the *position* from which you view things. Let's consider two examples to illustrate how strongly the element of perspective affects our emotions.

Perspective and Experience

Perhaps you experienced an embarrassing incident sometime during your teenage years. Recalling the incident in the days that followed, you felt the same emotions of shame, humiliation, and embarrassment. However, as years passed, you probably seemed to "outgrow" that youthful embarrassment. More precisely, your *perspective* of the event changed. Remembering the event now might make you laugh out loud. Rather than hiding it, you might even share the story with other people and laugh together at what happened.

The facts of the event haven't changed. However, *your interpretation* of the event and what it means has changed, because your perspective is different. When your perspective changes, the thought, interpretation, belief, meaning, and, most importantly, the emotion associated with the incident also change.

Your original embarrassment may have stemmed from the belief that all your teenage peers were judging you. This belief was created from a perspective where the emotions were principally insecurity and fear. From that myopic perception you assumed that what happened on that one day as a teenager would affect you for the rest of your life.

As you grew older, you acquired more experiences that you used to define yourself. You became more confident and no longer viewed yourself and the world through the myopic perception of one event associated with rejection. Years later, you don't have that teenage myopia that magnifies the impact of small things on your "whole life." Just as a building appears smaller when viewed from 10,000 feet away, the past event, which was huge when you were inside it, doesn't hold as much significance from today's viewpoint.

Often we attribute this emotional change to age and maturity, but merely growing older is not what alters beliefs and emotions about an event. One person might laugh at an embarrassing event that happened thirty years ago, while another might still feel horrified and embarrassed thirty years later. Time is not the essential factor in changing emotions. More time only allows for other real factors to change. Shifting perspective is what changes your interpretation, meaning, and emotions related to a past event.

If you have difficulty letting go of the events of the past, then perhaps you can consider another approach. First consider that events of the past don't change. What happened happened—the facts of history are not going to alter. However, the story you tell, the way you tell it, and the interpretations you make—and therefore the emotions you feel—about the past are all based in a perspective and are changeable. Being aware of your own perspective will begin the process of changing the way you interpret past and present-day events.

—⁓—

Perspective is the steering wheel of your belief system. Get hold of it and your thoughts and beliefs will move more easily.

—⁓—

Perspective, Beliefs, and Emotions

Suppose your partner has some traits that you like or find admirable. Perhaps this person is somewhat aloof and immune to what others think.

You might interpret this to mean that they have a strong sense of themselves and can think and act independently, and you admire that quality. But later you look at those same traits and they annoy you. That same aloofness now looks like indifference and a lack of caring. Your partner didn't change, their personality didn't change, but you changed your opinion or interpretation about that characteristic.

However, it wasn't simply a matter of altering your opinion. What changed is the perspective from which you view your partner. You might think of this as the eyes through which you are looking at them. You went from looking at this trait through the eyes of respect to viewing it through the eyes of annoyance.

Yes, your interpretations and beliefs about your partner changed, because beliefs and perspectives are closely intertwined. Perspective is the viewpoint from inside a belief bubble that allows the projected belief to appear real. Although the two are closely linked, it is important to understand the distinction between them, just like a mechanic needs to know about the different parts of a car and how they interact. Once you change the perspective that relates to that belief, the belief no longer appears the same or impacts you in the same way emotionally.

Often the easiest way to change a belief is to change the perspective part of it first. You can push on a moving car in a lot of different ways and you won't change where it's going, but put just a little force on the steering wheel and you begin moving in a different direction. Perspective is the steering wheel of your belief system. Get hold of it and your thoughts and beliefs will move more easily.

Your perspective is the vantage point from which you view experiences. It precedes any interpretations, thoughts, beliefs, and decisions. Your perspective affects not just *what* you perceive but *how* you perceive it, and therefore your experience of the world. Awareness of your perspective is essential to changing beliefs, because you can't consciously control or change something you are not aware of.

We can use our eyes as a physical metaphor for perspective. When we look at a building, we are putting our attention on it. Our eye is our tool of physical perception. If we stand in a different place, the building appears very different.

45

We would have a very different experience of the building if we were inside, versus outside. From the ground level outside, it appears mammoth and immovable. From inside a room, it appears much smaller, but tends to surround and enclose us. From an aircraft at altitude, the building becomes small and insignificant. As our perspective of the building changes, so do its significance and our relationship with it. In each scenario our attention is still on the building, but each change in perspective gives us a different experience of the building.

In no case do we actually see where our eye is located. We can only notice what the eye perceives, and then infer where the eye is located and how the head is tilted. Likewise, when it comes to events or relationships in your life, you can't directly perceive what your perspective is, but you can infer it based on context and other information you have. It is like figuring out the location of a camera just from seeing the photograph it took.

Discovering the structures of the beliefs in our mind is much like discovering the structure of a building. We can view a room from within a building and have no idea how big the building is, where it is located, or what floor we are on. Similarly, when we are within a belief bubble we are unable to tell how big it is, what other false beliefs support it, whether it is true, or whether it is helping us be happy or making us miserable. Someone may go about their day believing they're in danger of losing their job. Miserable and nervous all day long, they might defend that belief as being helpful because it makes them work harder. However, they might not notice how their anxiety about possibly losing their job makes them inefficient and difficult for others to work with. When that belief bubble and its associated behavior are viewed from an outside perspective, it reveals things the person didn't see from within it.

The stories you tell yourself and what you believe about your experiences are all based on a perspective, even if it isn't obvious at the time. That perspective resides within a belief bubble. Having flexibility in perspective, or point of view, is fundamental to changing the thoughts you believe. I'm taking some extra time here to explain perspective so that when I introduce methods for moving your perspective outside your belief bubble interpretations you will understand why they work and the importance of doing those practices.

46

When you learn to change your perspective of an event, not only do your thoughts and beliefs change, but so do your emotions. The facts won't change, but the interpretations you make, and therefore the emotions you feel, will change. Your beliefs will seem smaller, less valid, and changeable. In the beginning, perspective might seem so obvious or abstract that you will feel like glossing over the topic. However, when it comes to identifying and changing beliefs that affect our emotions, the importance of perspective cannot be overstated.

Perspective Determines Experience

Suppose you're preparing to give a presentation. If you're feeling confident you will probably focus on all the things that are likely to go well in the presentation. Even when you imagine what might go poorly, you will consider what you can do about it so it will all turn out well; you will reorient your inner story towards a positive conclusion because that is congruent with a confident person's perspective. Conversely, if you are feeling insecure, your mind will focus on all the good and bad things that might happen but will anticipate a negative outcome. Prior to the presentation, this negative scenario will play out in the inner world of your imagination. Not only will your attention focus on negative things, but you will experience yourself from the perspective of an insecure person before you ever step onto the podium. From a confident perspective and the insecure perspective you will consider the same problems, but the perspective you adopt will result in different attitudes about the problems, different feelings, and different imagined outcomes.

In the example of the insecure presenter the solution isn't simply to change the negative thoughts to positive ones. The confident presenter also considers negative thoughts but doesn't experience them as problems. When they arise, you know that you can deal with what shows up and get to a good outcome. So the negative thoughts about potential problems during the presentation aren't the issue. The perspective you view them from is what changes the experience of them. Instead of wasting your time wrestling with the negative thoughts, if you make a change in perspective you will change how you feel about any scenario.

More About the Self-Help Trap

As mentioned in Chapter 4, my approach to dissolving beliefs differs from most self-help and personal development doctrine, which suggests focusing your attention on positive things. But where you focus your attention is only part of the process. Equally important is the perspective you adopt when you focus your attention. If you focus on the positive image of giving a good presentation but are in the perspective of an insecure state of mind, you aren't going to feel good. If you focus your attention on what you want to create but are in the perspective of a depressed and hopeless person, you aren't going to believe your own positive self-talk. You are more likely to feel like a fraud pretending things will work out, which adds a layer of self-judgment to what you're already dealing with.

Paradoxically, you could put your attention fully on the failings of your past, which sounds very negative, but if you do it from a perspective of curiosity with the intention of learning and growing from them, it can be a valuable and positive experience. Putting your attention on fears you have, while coming from a perspective of curiosity and skepticism about the beliefs behind them, can be a revealing growth experience. Putting your attention on how you project a self-image to others while you step back from it a bit and laugh about it can be liberating.

Often we learn a great deal more from our failings than from our successes. In cases where we have hurt others' feelings, we can become aware of our behavior patterns, beliefs, and fears, and grow from them. If we become introspective and reflect on our fear-based beliefs, we can bring them into our conscious awareness and break the pattern of unconscious sabotage that happens when they remain hidden.

The prerequisite to reflecting on these past experiences and growing from them is to perceive them from a neutral observer perspective, with an attitude towards learning and growing. Deviation from this perspective will usually bring our mind into judgmental interpretations that result in beating ourselves up emotionally for so-called mistakes, and this isn't helpful. The perspective we start with and maintain in the process determines the outcome. There is a great deal we can learn and grow from by focusing on the "negative," provided we do it from a positive or neutral perspective.

If we follow the mantra of always focusing on the positive we will miss opportunities to learn and grow. However, we can focus on something that is a problem, or painful, from a not only neutral perspective but a perspective of love, respect, compassion, and acceptance. This perspective is not only possible but essential in order to facilitate real and lasting change.

Chapter 6

Personality and Characters

When we change our perspective, everything looks different. At some level, many of us already know this. When we are troubled emotionally, we are often advised to "change your point of view," or "look at it differently." After we've heard this a few times we might even tell ourselves the same thing.

But being aware of our perspective is difficult because it is a very abstract component of the inner world of our mind. Just like the photo metaphor, where the camera is one thing that you can't see in the picture, we can't point to our perspective and say, "There it is." It takes some practice to develop awareness of this aspect of the mind. I will introduce some exercises later to help you do this.

A more practical way to think of perspective is in terms of attitude, mood, and mindset. We all have experience understanding attitude and mood. How many times have people asked, perhaps about a parent or boss, "What mood is she in?" If you know what her mood is or what kind of attitude she has, you can predict how she might respond to you. If she's in a good mood, she will more likely respond positively, even to bad news. If she's in a bad mood, she may respond poorly even if the news is good.

A person's mood or attitude tells you about their perspective and how they are likely to view and therefore react to things. We seek this information about someone because we know their mindset is as much a factor in their reaction as the information they're receiving. When we ask the boss's secretary, "What kind of mood is she in today?" we want to know about the perspective part of her belief system that is dominant and active in her personality at that moment. The secretary might reply that the boss is a bear, rushed, or "Just closed a sale so she's a 'pushover.'" From just a few words we gain a lot of awareness about the perspective of the person we will be dealing with.

Heading forward we will call these different aspects *characters*. A character is a facet of someone's personality and more clearly identifies the perspective component of their belief system.

The Characters of a Story

I was in my twenties and home visiting my parents. My dad's back was in bad shape, so my mom made an appointment for him with a chiropractor. My dad was a farmer, a strong bear of a man with an amazing tolerance for pain. If he was going to the doctor it was pretty bad. We lived in the country twenty minutes outside of town and I was to drive him.

We left our house and my dad sat next to me in the passenger seat. I drove over the railroad tracks at the intersection and I could see him wincing in pain as we went over the bumps. It didn't feel good to me, watching him like that.

It was a two-lane country road most of the way into town. Traffic was busy enough that there weren't many opportunities to pass. I normally drove that road about 65 miles per hour when I could and hated drivers who slowed things down.

I hadn't gotten up to 60 when our car went over a small bump in the country road. My dad, in a hushed, breathy voice of pain, said, "Please slow down." I hadn't realized he was that sensitive to the movement of the car. My mood changed as I realized this wasn't going to be a casual drive to town. I paid closer attention to the road and kept a cautious eye on how he was doing as I drove. We hit another bump in the road and he winced again. I slowed some more. With each bump I slowed down even more. In a short time I was driving just over 40 miles per hour. Soon there were four cars and then six lined up close behind me.

I'd always hated driving behind slow drivers. Like any normal twenty-year-old, I had a penchant for speed. When I was behind a slow driver I swore about how stupid they were to drive so slowly. Trapped behind them, I felt they must have some personal agenda against me. Whether it was my impatient mindset or their stupidity, either way I was quick to get frustrated by a driver going only the speed limit.

As I drove with my dad in the car, I felt I could hear the voices in the other drivers' heads screaming with the same attitude I'd had so many times: "You stupid freaking idiot! What the hell is the matter with you? Speed up, you moron!" I could imagine them yelling at me in their heads or possibly even out loud. I was now the stupid freaking idiot that I had so often yelled at.

I kept glancing at my dad. He occasionally moved a little, trying to find a less painful position but afraid of aggravating his pain in the process. His slow movements, tightness of breath, and tension in his body conveyed his fear that another shooting pain would come. Even if the drivers behind me screamed for me to speed up, I wouldn't do that to my dad. Unfortunately, pulling over to let them pass would only add more bumps getting on and off the road, and I wouldn't do that to him either.

Stuck at the head of this slow-moving line of cars, I reflected on all those times I'd felt frustrated and angry at being trapped behind slow drivers. I had called them idiots, morons, and other choice words. Now I realized how ignorant I'd been. I'd assumed there was no valid reason for them to drive slow. I'd assumed I knew so much more than they did about how fast they should drive. I'd assumed I was so much smarter, with my sense for faster being better, and I'd assumed they were so stupid. The truth was that I'd never known what was going on with any of those drivers in front of me. In reality I was the ignorant one, and I was doubly ignorant for thinking I knew better than them. Maybe they had a good reason for their slowness. Maybe they were driving slowly out of love and caring for someone.

Just as I hadn't known what was really going on at those times, the drivers behind me right now didn't know about my dad being in so much pain next to me. If they were upset, frustrated, and maybe even angry, it was mostly because of what they were imagining in their own mind that didn't have anything to do with reality. They didn't know I was just trying to help my dad, or that if they were to find themselves in a similar situation they'd be driving slow too.

Since then, whenever I'm behind a slow driver, I never believe a complaining thought in my head. The thoughts might come up, but I know the false assumptions behind them and how they don't apply to reality. I'm aware that I don't know what's going on in the car ahead of me. I simply decide that the driver is doing the best that they can.

Multiple Perspectives in a Story

When we think a thought, have opinions, or react emotionally, what we say usually takes the form of a story. A story is always told from a particular perspective. When you read or listen to a story, your imagination can adopt the perspective of the storyteller or of characters in the story. We'll use the story above so you can see how different thoughts come from different perspectives.

I told the story in the first person, as myself, but let's step outside the story and examine it in the third person, as "Gary's experience." If we dissect the story we can see several different perspectives within Gary's experience. For starters, there are five different versions of Gary alone, and two other characters adopted via imagination about other people's experience:

1. Impatient Gary, who gets angry and frustrated at slow drivers.
2. Idiot Gary, who feels he is the stupid slow driver this time.
3. Kind Gary, who is helping his dad by driving him to the doctor.
4. Reflective Gary, who is processing and having realizations.
5. Aware Gary at the end, who is at peace with slow drivers.
6. Dad in the passenger seat, in pain.
7. Drivers behind Gary, feeling frustrated and angry.

Then there's an eighth perspective, the observer stance that we are using right now to dissect the story's characters.

As you read the story you move into the perspective of the different characters and imagine the experience from their points of view. You can imagine going through the experience and realizations of change that Gary is undergoing. You might jump into the dad's perspective of being in pain, or the perspective of a driver behind a slow car.

As a reader or listener, you create your own version of the story in your mind. Using your imagination, you build a virtual experience, complete with people, cars, scenery, conversations, and an internal dialog of thoughts and emotions. As the story goes along, you travel in and out of the perspectives of each of the characters and imagine experiencing what each of them feels emotionally and even physically. When the storytelling is over you step out of the story and look at it as something you created in your imagination. When Gary goes back and reads his own story, he can adopt the perspective of the observer as well.

As a listener, you can also take in the story from an observer perspective, sitting outside others' experiences, never engaging in any character's perspective. You experience the story as an observer instead of building it in your imagination as if it were happening to you. This might happen when you are editing a written story. You know all the different parts of the story, but your perspective isn't within those bubbles of experience. However, if the story is emotionally engaging or dramatic, it might draw you into various perspectives of the characters and you'll lose the neutrality of the observer perspective.

Go back and read the story again, this time paying attention to how Gary shifts from one character to another, even though it is all told by one person. By reading with the intent to observe the character shifts, you might also notice that you have adopted more of an observer perspective the second time through.

A Skeptic Steps Out of the Story

Now we can take this approach one step further and create a ninth perspective, that of a skeptic. The skeptic originates from the neutral observer perspective and then begins to scrutinize the assumptions and structure of the story. A skeptic might start by wondering whether this is a true story or one that was made up.

The skeptic might also notice that although Gary claimed a more enlightened perspective at the end of the story—admitting that he hadn't known what was going on in the cars in front of him—he nevertheless assumed that he knew what was in the minds of the people behind him. He assumed the drivers behind him were having the same kinds of reactions as Impatient Gary. He didn't imagine that any of them would have more maturity and awareness than an impatient twenty-something. He assumed he was the only person in that line of cars with this understanding. This is another limited assumption about people he doesn't know.

After writing his story, Gary can go back and read it from a more neutral observer perspective. From a skeptic perspective we can see that this Aware Gary still has a limiting belief paradigm with a somewhat spiritually arrogant perspective. Gary has moved past one set of limiting beliefs and is calmer, but he is still limited by other assumptions that he's not aware of. By actively scrutinizing the assumptions of each character, he adopts the perspective of the skeptic. The skeptic can view the story and see the false assumption of the Aware Gary belief bubble.

The experience of each character perspective within the story is limited to its belief bubble. Idiot Gary can't see things that Reflective Gary does, nor do Aware Gary and Impatient Gary see slow drivers the same way. The observer and skeptic, however, are not in the story. They look at the story and the beliefs from outside all the different belief bubbles. Being outside, they can see how the different parts fit together or are separated, and more easily question the assumptions. The observer and skeptic are able to see how each of the characters is limited in how they view and experience things. In our earlier analogy, this is like viewing a building from outside. Each character is in a room or a floor of the building and is having a full experience, but only by being outside the building can you see how the rooms and stories fit together.

—◊◊◊—

The use of characters will help identify and isolate the specific beliefs that cause emotional reactions.

—◊◊◊—

Characters, Interpretations, and Meanings

Every story, opinion, and thought is based in a point of view and has its own belief bubble. Impatient Gary is within a belief bubble where all slow drivers are idiots. There are no other interpretations available to this character. Idiot Gary feels like he is stupid for driving slow. There is no other interpretation available for this character. Kind Gary perceives driving slow as a compassionate act. With that perspective, and that belief bubble, he is not going to look at it any other way. Each character has the same raw data but creates its own interpretation, meaning, and emotion because of its perspective within its belief bubble.

We probably have been aware of different people having different points of view. When it comes to belief systems, a single person can also have multiple points of view. These perspectives can change moment to moment or coexist in the same moment. Reflective Gary was considering the perspectives of Impatient Gary, Idiot Gary, and Kind Gary by being outside all of them. In effect, Reflective Gary was holding four viewpoints at once. While reading this story, you might find yourself adopting the perspective of Gary, his dad, and the drivers behind him, all at the same time. Simultaneously holding multiple viewpoints is not new; however, being *aware* that this is what we are doing, or how often we do it, might be.

We can't use the description "Gary's perspective" with much precision because, as we've seen, there are several different versions of it, depending on the moment and how we slice it. Towards the end, Gary is the observer of his experience, and later, when studying the story, a skeptic who perceives the various belief bubbles of different characters.

Identifying these various perspectives as characters—Gary the Impatient, Gary the Kind Son, Gary the Idiot, Gary the Reflective, Aware Gary, Gary the Observer, Gary the Skeptic, Gary imagining the other drivers, and Gary imagining his dad—helps us clarify attitude and state of mind in each moment of Gary's experience. This use of characters in dissecting thoughts and beliefs becomes very useful when we want to eliminate certain emotional reactions from our life. Although many of our thoughts and beliefs are just fine and don't need dissolving, the use of characters will help identify and isolate the specific beliefs that cause emotional reactions.

As we go forward in understanding and changing belief systems, I will rarely use the terms *point of view* and *perspective*. Instead, I will explain this element of our belief system in the more practical forms of *characters* and *archetypes*, which are easier to identify and more telling. Perspectives that generate emotional drama in our lives and relationships correspond well to characters. However, for expressions like kindness, compassion, humility, and love, the use of characters doesn't map as well, because these expressions are more genuine and not based in a false belief construct or limited perspective of a character identity. This generally isn't a problem because there isn't much need to dissect and get rid of expressions of love, compassion, and respect.

—〽—

Simultaneously holding multiple viewpoints is not new; however, being aware that this is what we are doing, or how often we do it, might be.

—〽—

Using Characters to Change Beliefs

As discussed earlier, when a belief is false it creates a belief bubble. The perspective of a character can be found within its corresponding belief bubble, and identifying it is essential in changing a belief. In Gary's story, his beliefs and therefore his emotional reactions towards slow drivers changed as a result of a change in his perspective. If we can understand how this worked in Gary's case, we can apply this same approach to our own beliefs.

Having a good reason to drive 40 miles per hour and hold up traffic forced Gary to adopt a Kind Gary perspective of what goes on in the mind of a slow driver. This conflicted with Impatient Gary's belief that slow drivers are morons. Kind Gary had the experience that slow drivers are compassionate and caring people with good reasons for driving slow. As Reflective Gary observed these contradictory ideas, he was forced to step outside the bubbles of Idiot Gary, Impatient Gary, and even Kind Gary. Reflective Gary put his attention on the beliefs of Impatient Gary and the experience of Kind Gary and examined them side by side.

In doing so, he also discovered a hidden belief. While it might appear that Impatient Gary's belief was simply "slow drivers are idiots," this was more the surface-level thought or conclusion. It was based on the assumption that "that driver has no good reason for driving slow, so they must be doing it because they are an idiot." When these hidden assumptions are identified and seen as false, the surface-level belief can fall apart quickly.

From the perspective of Reflective Gary, the belief bubble of Impatient Gary appeared false and unfounded. Impatient Gary's beliefs about slow drivers being idiots and having no reason to drive slowly didn't map onto the reality that Kind Gary was experiencing. With that shift in perspective, not only did the beliefs of Impatient Gary dissolve, but all the opinions, judgments, and emotional reactions that arose from them dissolved as well.

Fundamental to awareness and growth is the ability to expand and change perspective and look at things from multiple points of view. Gary's shift in perspective happened by accident. He hadn't intended to change his beliefs that day. He stumbled into the mechanism of a different perspective and combined it with self-reflection, and it was effective.

Often such shifts are explained away as an epiphany, as if it were some kind of accidental magic, but there is a mechanism or process in the mind that allows these shifts to occur. While Gary's unplanned experience in driving his dad to town forced him to adopt another perspective, we don't have to leave our changes to chance. We can consciously utilize the technique of changing perspective to intentionally change negative thoughts, beliefs, and emotional reactions.

Another element that helped change the beliefs of Impatient Gary was the use of attention. When Reflective Gary was considering beliefs about driving slow, he put his attention on the beliefs themselves. This specific use of attention, from a skeptic's perspective, on the beliefs of Impatient Gary and Kind Gary allowed him to see the inconsistencies. Although his experience of driving slowly as a kind and compassionate gesture helped to invalidate his previous stories, it was by putting his attention on certain beliefs and perspectives that the permanent change came about. Without paying attention to those impatient beliefs, Gary would likely have had the same thoughts again the next time he found himself behind a slow driver, even though he'd had an experience that contradicted them.

Perspective Is Key to Change

This technique of combining perspective, attention, and skepticism can be intentionally applied to effectively change other beliefs, which in turn alters thoughts and emotional experience.

In this story, it wasn't just Gary's beliefs that changed. He also shed the perspective of the impatient character and subsequently the negative thoughts and emotions that arose from that character. You will discover that, for an emotional change to happen, changing character perspectives is of fundamental importance. Too often people want to change how they feel or think about something, but they don't realize that the steering wheel to those thoughts and emotions is their perspective, nor are they aware how to use it.

Notice that this process of changing beliefs and emotional reactions about slow drivers occurred in the absence of any intent to do so. Gary's beliefs changed without him *trying* to change them. His emotional reactions stopped permanently without *trying* to stop them. It didn't take willful, disciplined effort to change his beliefs and thoughts or to hold back his emotions. The effort applied was to the steering wheel of his belief system. He first shifted his perspective, and then focused his attention on how his beliefs looked from this new perspective. From a skeptical, reflective perspective, outside existing belief bubbles, the underlying assumptions were seen as false, and the bubble fell apart rather quickly from there.

Our perspectives are interwoven in our beliefs. Programs or techniques that attempt to change the conceptual belief or thought without changing the perspective can often fail. If they do work it is because the perspective changed without there being any awareness of it. If you have used a technique that seemed to work, but later the belief and emotional reaction came back, it may be because you have re-adopted a character's perspective. Techniques to change beliefs will be more effective when you consciously include the element of perspective in the process and don't leave it to chance.

How Not to Change Perspective: Unhelpful Reminders

Sometimes people try to facilitate change by reminding themselves, or others, that they should change their perspective. The problem is that it's usually said in a way that has a judgmental impact and produces a feeling of failure or rejection.

It's like giving someone the advice, "You should do that differently." As a byproduct you're implying that they shouldn't be doing it the way they are. Whether intended or not, this can be experienced as a criticism because it has all the elements of a judgmental thought. A similar, self-rejecting experience can happen when we remind ourselves to change our perspective. "I should just change my perspective about this" is interpreted as "I have the wrong perspective," or even as "I am wrong." It can be felt as a reprimand or self-rejection, or it can reinforce a failure belief, depending on the character perspective. When this occurs, well-intentioned advice and reminders are not helping—they are hurting because they are being voiced and interpreted through the Judge and Victim character perspectives. What is needed is an actual shift in perspective, not reminders to do it or reprimands for not doing it.

Chapter 7

Adopting an Observer Perspective

Two types of stories we commonly tell ourselves that produce unnecessary emotional drama are those of an imagined future and those that we remember from our past. In telling these stories, or thinking in this way, we adopt the identity of the person who would be experiencing them—either an imagined future version of ourselves or a remembered past version. In stepping into that false identity, we take on its perspective, seeing the story through its eyes, experiencing the interpretations it makes as if they were the only factual ones. The perspective and its accompanying emotions often trick our senses by giving these stories a feeling of being real.

Emotionally dramatic scenarios of the future often create fear in the present moment. We begin to worry, become fearful, have anxiety, and can even create panic attacks about something that hasn't happened and likely won't. In imagining the future scenario we then feel the real emotions of fear and nervous system responses as if the event were actually happening. Similarly, memory allows us to re-create past events in our imagination, along with their accompanying emotional responses as if the imagined event was real and happening again in present time. The emotions we experience are real, even if they are responses to imagined scenarios in our mind.

During these imagined scenarios our perspective shifts into false characters. In a future scenario we assume the perspective of a fictitious future self. When we replay a past event, we assume the character of a past self with its particular attitude and interpretation. Both of these are characters separate from the present-moment perspective and our genuine identity. Reminding ourselves to live in the present moment is usually only a temporary fix before our imagination wanders into scenarios of past and future again.

A more comprehensive and therefore effective way of changing these types of emotional drama is to identify these future and past selves as characters. To do this you have to make yourself aware of the distinctive time shift taking place in your mind. Using that awareness as leverage for separation, let's explore a method for changing these emotional cycles by separating ourselves from past- and future-distorting character perspectives.

Perspective on the Future

Let's use as an example someone who has the thought, "I am afraid that I am going to lose my job, I won't be able to pay my mortgage, and I will end up on the street pushing a shopping cart." The thought is not only about an imagined future. It also has an implied character identity. The word *I* in that future scenario refers not to who we are now but to an imagined future character who is pessimistic and fearful. Emotions of fear become amplified and exaggerated when we adopt this character's perspective and assume its identity. The use of the term *I* tricks our mind and emotions into the belief bubble of this future doomsday character and the imagined experience seems more real than it is.

The first step to making the scenario less believable and reducing the emotional component is to separate from that false identity and place our perspective outside that future character's belief bubble. This is commonly known as adopting an observer perspective. In the English language, we don't have a simple term for speaking of a future version of ourselves, the way we can express the future tense of a verb. Nor do we have words that would clarify that this future character was made up in our imagination. The statement "I am afraid that I won't be able to pay my mortgage" is certainly referring to a future event, which would mean an imagined version of ourselves. However, just by thinking those words, our perspective slips into the belief bubble of this character. To change these thoughts, beliefs, and emotional reactions of the future, we have to change our use of language in a way that makes our perspective shift out of these false identities.

One simple way to do this is to journal and drop the use of words like *I* and *me*, since the imagined future self isn't really you. Instead, you refer to that self as *he* or *she*, or by name, in third person. After some time writing this way you can substitute the specific character you see and drop the general he/she. As you write about events this way you develop an observer perspective of your thoughts and false character identities. If you have difficulty identifying your characters at first, writing in third person will help you so you soon can.

After rewriting the scenario above and adding some detail, it might look something like this when you journal about it:

Bob watched his imagination generate a scenario about the future. In it, Future Fearful Bob said he was afraid he was going to lose his job. Future Bob's scene carried forward with not being able to pay his mortgage. In a few seconds Future Bob warped time and covered six months and imagined he was on the street pushing a shopping cart. Future Bob then warped time again, freezing the shopping cart scene at a standstill, so it seemed like he would be there for the rest of his life.

I've taken the original sentence and clarified that it is Future Fearful Bob throughout. Other first-person references are converted to *him, his,* or *he* as well. Writing this way trains us to have the clarity that what the mind is projecting is not actually happening to us in this moment. I've also detailed the time-warp things the mind does so we are more aware that what is taking place is only happening in a belief bubble. Making note of these differences between imagined version and reality helps us be mindful and skeptical of what the projected character thinks or feels. By including these details, or "holes" in the story, the imagined scenario becomes less believable.

It is easy to tell when someone else is caught up in a story in their head, creating unnecessary emotional drama, because we are outside their perspective watching what they are doing. This technique of writing employs that same kind of shift in perspective so we can be an observer and skeptical with our own emotional thoughts.

Revisiting the Past

A similar dynamic happens when we remember past events and experience emotions coming up again. What gives the appearance of reality to these memories is that we replay them from the perspective of the person we were in the past. When this happens we are no longer just remembering something—we are re-experiencing it emotionally as the person we were *then*, from the perspective we lived in at that time. This perspective of the experience exaggerates the emotion we create and feel. This might be enjoyable if we are reminiscing about happy times. However, if we have a painful or unhappy memory, and we replay it over and over again, we re-create the emotion repeatedly, and this can be exhausting.

Revisiting past events can produce emotions of judgmental criticism, regret, anger, sadness, guilt, and shame. These emotions often arise from the interpretations made about that event by our characters. One result is that we become less connected to the present moment. Shifting our mind into an observer perspective will allow us to think about the past, or observe past memories, without getting caught in many of the interpretations and the emotions they produce.

The same language problem we experience in speaking about the future happens when we speak of the past. In talking or thinking about the past we also use words like *I, me, myself,* which actually belong only to the person who is experiencing things in present time, not to the person we used to be. Because of this character shift, our mind can tend to imagine past events in a way that we relive them, or re-experience them, and respond emotionally as if they are happening again. The solution here is the same: We have to retrain our mind to view past events as an observer instead of from the character of a past self. Writing in third person is an effective way to train your mind to make this shift to an observer perspective.

Examples for Shifting Perspective

The return to our old perspective is one reason we can still have emotional reactions to something that happened years ago, that we wish we had gotten over. Our perspective returns us to the identity of that past person and that past event in an exaggerated emotional way. As we remember a past event, we are no longer our current self, present in this moment. We are in a belief bubble complete with a past identity and memory, and we lose our present-moment awareness and perspective that would temper those emotional responses.

Again, an easy way to start changing emotional reactions to your thoughts is to write about yourself and your experiences in the third person. Let's look at how Sam, from Chapter 4, might use this exercise to shift his perspective. Here's how Sam could write in the third person about that incident with the cookie jar:

> Sam recalled that day when Happy Little Sam was sitting on the countertop enjoying the cookie. He was proud of himself for going after what he wanted and figuring out how to get it. Positioning the chair and climbing up on onto the counter was a challenge, but worth it.
>
> Happy Little Sam was caught off guard by Mom standing in the doorway looking at him. Happy Little Sam didn't know what to make of the look on her face because it didn't make any sense to Happy Little Sam. He was always happy. To rescue him from the confusion, Bad Little Sam jumped in with an idea. Bad Little Sam proposed that he'd done something wrong. Bad Little Sam quickly went to guilt, as he was the one who always took the blame for everything. Bad Little Sam watched Mom's face to see if she responded and if his guilty response was what she wanted. When Mom's face changed, Bad Little Sam used it as confirmation that yes, indeed, he had done something wrong. Bad Little Sam took this to mean that he was now the "good" guy for making sense of Mom's reaction and acting accordingly, and "Happy Little Sam" was bad for getting them in trouble.

When Sam writes about his past in this manner, he is retraining his mind to *not* adopt the bad-boy character that produces guilt as an automated response. He can also more easily see what is going on in his belief bubbles and decide whether he wants to continue to believe these characters and their other thoughts.

If you have found it difficult to let go of emotional reactions or feelings about something from your past, it is probably because you are still perceiving them from the same past character perspective.

People who still have emotional issues about past events usually think about and imagine their memories from a first-person perspective. People who no longer have an emotional charge about things of their past see the memory from outside, as if they were watching a movie of someone they used to be. Writing from a different perspective will help make this emotional shift.

—⚏—

If you have found it difficult to let go of emotional reactions or feelings about something from your past, it is probably because you are still perceiving them from the same past character perspective.

—⚏—

Practice: A Different Way to Journal

Suppose I'm anticipating an unpleasant conversation that I need to have with my friend John. I might write about it this way:

Gary felt nervous about bringing up to John the matter of changing travel plans. Gary imagined how John would respond with anger at the proposal; his mind also flashed to similar scenarios from the past. Gary could feel the fear of his imagined self in the story, and also felt the fear in his body as he sat and wrote about it. Gary watched his mind scramble for ways to modify this imagined scenario. One part of his mind looked for just the right words to say, at the right time, in the right place, that would not trigger John's anger. Another part of his mind tried to come up with alternate work schedule adjustments so he could avoid the conversation entirely.

This simplified example doesn't identify characters. However, as Gary writes about what is going on in his mind and emotions, he is getting more awareness as to how different parts of his mind have different agendas. This will help him to identify the various characters at work in his belief system creating conflicts and stress. Some people will have difficulty seeing their various characters in the beginning. In that case, write using terms like *he/she* and *his/her* to practice being in the observer perspective. With time the different characters will become more apparent.

After spending some time writing as an observer, you will begin to find it easier to shift out of some of your habitual negative attitudes or old mindsets. With more practice, you will begin to be able to shift perspective during emotional moments when you typically would have reacted in a way that you'd later regret. The shift in perspective is critical for refraining from repeating past patterns and for seeing other choices.

Understand that you are *training* your mind so it will eventually do this automatically. Spending time writing in a third-person perspective is making the neural pathways in your mind operate differently. These new neural pathways are not created by wishing, or by reading about the idea. They will develop because you practice making your mind adopt a different perspective. Since you can write for ten, twenty, or thirty minutes or more, your mind gets lots of practice holding a different perspective. Gradually, that perspective becomes easier and easier to maintain in other parts of your day. Sometimes you will notice an immediate emotional shift when you are writing about certain things.

If it helps, consider that you are adopting the perspective of a journalist or anthropologist performing a study of the person you used to be, even if it was just yesterday. Include observations of your emotions, thoughts, feelings in the body, actions, and behavior. Remember that an anthropologist is only there to document the facts of what happened, and not to give an editorial on what should have happened or what needs to be done about it. Those types of thoughts often lead to another layer of emotional opinions like judgmental criticism and regret. In those narratives we are no longer observing. The Judge is comparing the observation to a fictional version we wished would have happened.

In the beginning, write about events and experiences that involved only mild emotions. This will make it easier to be a neutral observer. Stronger emotional events tend to pull us back into our old belief bubble and past or future perspective. Avoid the bigger emotional experiences or topics until you have developed your skill as an observer by writing about smaller events first.

The goal in the beginning is not to dissolve emotions or change the entire belief. At this point we are working on changing the perspective part of the belief only. You are learning the critical skill of shifting to a neutral observer perspective and *holding it* while you observe your emotional reactions. Developing this skill of choosing your perspective will make changing the remaining parts of the belief bubble much easier.

It may feel odd at first to write about yourself in third person, as if you were writing about someone else, a person you're observing in a detached way. It is certainly different, but if you are suffering from emotional reactions, "different" is what you need. After a while you will consider it odd to identify yourself as the person you were in the past, or as a fictional future self.

Once you have spent some time writing in the third person, it won't seem strange anymore. Eventually the observer perspective will seem more normal, and the *I* and *me* in your stories will seem more like just what they are: drama-making characters in your mind instead of you.

Dealing with Resistance

A common objection I hear regarding this exercise is the fear that memories of the past will be lost or dissolved. What you are detaching from is the old perspective from which you viewed them, not the whole memory. By shifting perspective you are detaching from the interpretations, meaning, and beliefs you created from those past experiences. You will still be able to remember events of the past, just not with the same emotions. With your new perspective the *interpretations and beliefs* about the event change.

For example, thinking back to the slow driver story in Chapter 6, I can still remember times when I got impatient and upset at slow drivers. However, I no longer believe any of my past interpretations or opinions about those experiences. I am no longer that impatient person. I see that as a past version of self, or as an emotional role I played in those moments.

If you feel resistant to this practice, there is likely a character that has a negative attitude about this exercise. To address this, write from a third-person perspective about your resistance. Write what you feel in your body, emotions, and thoughts about doing the exercise. Your writing might look something like this:

Samantha sat at her desk, staring at the paper. She knew what the assignment was, and some part of her mind knew it would help. At the same time she could sense another part of her mind resisting. The two sides were pulling at each other, creating a tension in Samantha's body. The tension stretched down Samantha's arm, pulling at her hand as she wrote. Samantha found it necessary to will herself to keep writing in order to override this resistant impulse from another part of her mind.

The struggle extended into her head in the form of various arguments. One part of her mind wanted to write something that happened yesterday and keep it simple to start. Another impulse thought wanted to write about the big emotional stuff that happened last week. Some other part of her argued against that, fearing she wasn't ready to take on that big event. Because she didn't know the "right" thing to be writing about, another part of her concluded she would get it wrong; that part felt fearful about getting it wrong and therefore didn't want to do the assignment. As Samantha sat there she began to observe these four different agendas in her mind in conflict with each other.

In the beginning, your writing might not have this much detail. That's fine. As you spend time looking inward at these different thoughts, emotions, and stories you will tend to see more detail, interpretations, and emotions at play. The more detail you are aware of, the more likely you will be the observer of it and the less likely you will fall into the drama of it.

The Need to Shift Perspective

I developed the idea of writing in the third person out of necessity. A client named Janice wanted to get rid of sabotaging beliefs and emotions that were causing drama with her current boyfriend. We were identifying patterns in her relationships with men and the character roles she would play out. While backtracking through her ex-husband issues, her mind took a jump to when she was eight years old. She discovered that she was repeating a pattern with her ex-husband that she had as a little girl with her dad. This was a great realization, as it was foundational to her sabotaging relationships with men. However, I noticed her emotions had shifted and they were heavy. She said she wanted to tell me the story of what happened. I told her no.

Janice was dismayed at my refusal to listen to her story. She was used to sharing a very honest and open communication with me. But my concern was that if Janice told me the story, the emotion would be strong enough to pull her into her past perspective and reinforce the interpretations she created when she was eight years old. I knew that it was an emotional memory, and that use of the words *I* and *me* might thrust her back into the viewpoint of the frightened eight-year-old girl of her memory. I didn't want her to revisit the memory from that perspective.

She needed to revisit those past beliefs so that she could see clearly what they were, but she had to do it as a neutral observer so the beliefs would not be reinforced. So I told her instead to write the story in the third-person perspective. She went home and did the writing. The next time we talked, her beliefs and the emotions associated with them had dissolved. It didn't require anything dramatic and she didn't have to tell anyone the story. She just needed to be present with the emotions and put her attention on the interpretations and beliefs she had made as an eight-year-old girl from a present-day adult's viewpoint that would allow her to see them as false.

It isn't always necessary to retell a past story from a third-person perspective in order to detach from it. Not everyone's mind works the same. Some people talk about themselves in the past using *I* and *me* without shifting back into the memory bubble of an old identity. But in places we do get emotionally triggered, we can speed up the detachment process by consciously shifting perspective through writing in the third-person perspective.

Take time to journal in this third-person perspective and use this tool to help shift your point of view. Whether you do it three minutes at a time, five minutes a day, twenty, or more, the time invested in retraining your mind to gain flexibility of perspective will yield rewards going forward.

Chapter 8

Character Perspectives in Belief Bubbles

Jane wanted to get rid of some insecure and jealous thoughts that were causing her to be angry and controlling over the smallest of things in her relationship with Steve. The first step was to become aware of the different belief systems her mind was subjecting her to.

Jane is a partner in a law firm and is confident and capable in her career as a litigator. She has been in a relationship with Steve for a couple years, and she says that when they are together it is the best. They've talked about getting married, but Jane is a little tentative after her previous marriage. It ended badly, with her husband being abusive to her and eventually cheating on her. He had beaten her down verbally and emotionally until she felt powerless. She doesn't want to repeat the same kind of mistake.

Because of that painful experience, she is worried about getting hurt again, and she has become suspicious of Steve's activities. She checks his phone to see what text messages he has gotten. When he takes a phone call from his ex-wife and talks for a few minutes, Jane quizzes him on what they talked about. She worries that Steve has a wandering eye, and imagines him going back to his ex-wife or getting together with someone at work, so she looks for inconsistencies in his story. Steve sometimes feels like he is under deposition.

Yet Steve's perspective is entirely different. Jane is the only girl for him. She is a wonderful woman who makes him happy. But as much as Steve professes his love and commitment for her, on some days Jane doesn't fully believe him—his words can't penetrate or dissolve her existing fear-based belief bubble. On other days they melt her heart.

Jane then shares another telling piece. The other day, when she knew Steve was working and wouldn't be home until late, Jane sensed that her mind was going to take her down a fearful story road of Steve betraying her. Instead of letting her mind wander that way, she went to the gym, knowing it would make her feel better. A tough workout drained off the tension from work, got her endorphins fired up, and took her mind off Steve.

After the workout she was noticing how good she felt. Her body felt alive and strong, her energy was up, and she felt empowered, attractive and confident about her looks. She reflected on her day at the law firm. Things were going well. She was a solid partner bringing in money and getting things done. In this empowered state, when her mind flashed on the idea of Steve cheating on her that she last visited two hours before, her response was, "I hope he does. Then I'll know he wants to be with someone else and I can move on. It will be a relief to be free of this situation."

At first glance it might appear that Jane has gotten rid of her negative thoughts, but that's not actually what happened. Jane had a positive thought about herself and what would happen if Steve cheated. She is still having a negative thought about Steve cheating, but this time she feels differently about it. She's considering the scenario from an empowered state of mind, that of a confident character instead of an insecure one.

Our Character Perspective Determines Our Experience

How can Jane feel like a victim one moment, frightened of being hurt by her partner cheating on her, and then a short while later feel completely confident that she would be fine if that happened? Two different character perspectives about the same event produce two very different responses of thought and emotion. In one belief paradigm, Jane has an image of herself as a victim who will be rejected, hurt, and alone. From Victim Jane's perspective, her negative thoughts appear true and she projects a future of being hurt, alone, and unlovable. The idea that she is attractive, capable, or desirable to Steve is a foreign thought and quickly dismissed.

After the workout, another part of Jane's belief system is active. Now she is strong, capable, and attractive and knows that many men would want to be with her. We will call this confident character Strong Jane.

Strong Jane perceives that she can handle anything life throws at her. Strong Jane's perspective is in a different belief bubble of how the world appears. Her victim image of herself doesn't exist here.

There is a third perspective as well. Jane initially characterized the couple as "madly in love, meant to be together." We can call this the viewpoint of Romantic Jane. Romantic Jane sees Steve as the perfect man for her. He will always be faithful and there for her.

From the perspective of Jane the Romantic, Steve seems to be the man of her dreams. From the perspective of Jane the Victim, Steve appears to be someone who will cheat on her. From the perspective of Strong Jane, Steve still appears to be a guy who will cheat on her, but she interprets that possibility as being a relief and knows Steve is someone she is better off without. Steve didn't actually change from one moment to the next, but Jane has different imaginary versions of him. Each belief bubble has its own version of Steve and of the future. The world we perceive, how we see other people, and interpretations we make change depending on the character we adopt.

Jane's perspectives of Romantic Jane, Strong Jane, and Victim Jane are generated by different sets of beliefs about her identity. When her Strong Jane beliefs are active, she has a positive self-image and positive beliefs. When her Victim Jane beliefs are active, she has a negative self-image. When Romantic Jane is active, her feelings are positive as well and the world looks different. Jane recognizes that she has these contradictory beliefs about herself, but she is unaware that her perspective is shifting between different characters. As a result, she feels confused and can't figure out who she is.

Jane has different, contradictory versions of Steve as well, depending on which of her belief bubbles is active. When she looks at these contradictory images side by side, she feels confused. She doesn't know "who" Steve really is and whether she can trust him. This problem stems from the fact that Jane's images of Steve are only projections. No wonder she has difficulty committing to their relationship! She'd be committing to at least three versions of herself and multiple versions of Steve.

—⚊—

The world we perceive, how we see other people,
and interpretations we make change depending
on the character we adopt.

—⚊—

Defining the Problem

Unaccustomed to viewing her emotions as a function of character perspectives and belief bubbles, Jane thinks solving her relationship problem of insecurity and jealousy is a matter of getting rid of some negative thoughts. She wants to adopt the beliefs of Romantic Jane, as they are the most appealing, and be done with it. This is somewhat like putting a Band-Aid over an infected wound that needs to be cleaned.

Most often, Jane views the situation as the Victim, who always imagines that *I* will get hurt. This pattern derives from previous relationship experiences, as in the Pavlov's dog scenario. Even if she were to somehow erase her negative thoughts, the Victim character would generate new ones about something else. The Victim expects to get hurt, assumes failure and impending doom, so it will continue to generate new negative thoughts—if not about Steve, then in other areas of her life.

Jane's Victim character perspective is held in place by other beliefs related to self-image and self-esteem. These might include, "Bad things happen to me," "I will get hurt if I fall in love," "I am powerless over my emotions," "My emotions depend on him, because he makes me happy," "Men will leave me," "I am not worthy or lovable," and so on. These negative self-image beliefs form the false Victim identity. From this identity Jane creates interpretations and thoughts that she doesn't make when she is in her Romantic Jane or Strong Jane characters.

Jane isn't aware of how her mind shifts from one character-based belief bubble to another, so she ends up being confused by what "she" thinks. The Victim Jane, Strong Jane, and Romantic Jane create and sustain three sides of the argument in her head and she is bounced between them. Because each perspective appears true within its own bubble, she believes each thought as it arises. Then when she shifts perspectives, the thought she just had from a previous character now appears false. This causes a lot of conflicting thoughts with each one appearing true and then false at different times.

Thoughts arise from beliefs, and the active set of beliefs originates from a particular character perspective. People who attempt to change their negative thoughts without addressing the character structure of the beliefs they arise from are only pursuing symptoms and are not addressing causes.

Practice: Inventory Your System of Beliefs

Illustrations of belief bubbles and pictures of characters can be helpful in representing what is going on in our imagination. Another way to present an inventory of beliefs is with text in a table. Both are suitable mind maps to see the various belief systems going on in our head. The following chart is a mind map for Jane's conflicting thoughts, beliefs, and resulting emotions with regards to Steve. Make your own inventory charts for the thoughts, beliefs, and emotions you want to address. Begin by using the format below.

Character	Thought/Belief/Behavior	Emotion
Jane the Romantic	Steve and I are perfect for each other. Implied Belief: Steve is a great guy.	Love, gratitude. Feels secure in how she feels about him.
The Victim	He will cheat on me. I will be hurt. Implied Belief: He can't be trusted.	Fear. Powerlessness over emotions. Dependent on Steve for being happy.
The Controller	I have to know what he's doing. I have to know where he is. Behavior: checks his phone and emails. By checking on him I will avoid pain.	Fear. Fear of being hurt by him. Suspicious. False sense of power/ protection.

Strong Jane:	I don't care if he cheats on me. I'll land on my feet. It will be his loss.	Relief.
		Confidence.
	I won't be hurt by him.	Worthy, strong.
	(Denial of what emotions she is likely to feel based on other perspectives.)	Empowered.
		Repressing/Ignoring emotions from other beliefs when in this bubble.
	Implied Belief: Steve is an Average Guy and I can do better than that.	

We'll use this format for inventorying and mapping belief systems in future chapters. In your own inventory or mapping process be sure to include a minimum of the elements that make up a belief from the columns in this list.

A Unique System of Characters

Each person has unique experiences of life and has developed their own interpretations, perspectives, and belief bubbles. As a result, each person has their own set of character perspectives, although there are often some we share. Each person also has their own collection of conceptual ideas that they have formed into beliefs. Because each person's belief system is unique, you can't just read a book and suddenly be aware of what your beliefs are. You have to look inward and discover them yourself.

It is also difficult for another person to tell you what your beliefs are and what perspectives you hold. For starters, that person isn't inside your mind and doesn't have all the information that you have access to. An experienced guide can help, primarily by asking questions that guide your attention to critical factors affecting your emotions. However, when another person is offering opinions or conclusions about what you believe, they run the risk of projecting their beliefs onto you.

Even if someone else could clearly explain what your beliefs are, it would be of little use. Simply knowing what beliefs you have, and even knowing that they are false, is not enough to change them. You will also have to change your perspective. It is more important to change your point of view than to know what you believe.

For instance, Jane might look at the chart above and understand that she has a Victim character and a belief that she is emotionally dependent on Steve, but simply knowing these things doesn't change the belief. The automatic Pavlov's-dog-type emotional responses are still there. If she looks at this situation from a judgmental perspective, a Judge character might think she is stupid for believing this. Her Victim character might feel trapped by this belief and feel powerless. The result is Judge and Victim criticisms adding layers of opinions and emotions to the original problem.

In order to avoid doing harm in this process, a person must first shift their perspective to that of a neutral observer. If they don't, they will likely fall into debilitating and painful Judge and Victim opinions that cloud what they discover. Also see Chapter 13 on acceptance to avoid some of these traps in your thinking.

A book or another person can't tell you what your beliefs are because that book or person doesn't have an inventory of your personal beliefs. To discover your beliefs, you must engage in a self-reflective process of awareness and mindfulness from an observer perspective. Once you've identified these elements of your belief system, you can then begin to question them.

—⟋⟍⟋—

***It is more important to change your point
of view than to know what you believe.***

—⟋⟍⟋—

Practice: Identify the Characters of Your Personality

Here are the steps to using the characters tool in changing your beliefs:

1. Begin observing the various aspects of your personality. Make a list of the different moods, emotions, and attitudes that you have during the day.

2. Identify the different aspects of your personality in terms of characters. Give each character a name. Naming them will help you recognize that they are not your essential, authentic self. Characters that express in a kind, loving, and respectful way are generally more closely aligned with your authentic self. Characters that generate emotional reactions and drama are usually indications of false self-images of the ego. Give names to both the authentic and the drama characters. Don't assume you know which ones are on your authentic side. We feel better in some characters, but that doesn't mean they are genuine.

3. Use character names that have some comical or entertainment value. This will help make what they say less believable, which can make it easier for you to shift perspective and remain an observer of those aspects of your personality.

4. Look for these different characters in both the way you think and the way you interact externally in the world. Some of our internal characters will show up in how we think about things, the opinions we have, and the interpretations we make. Other characters will be more noticeable as behaviors. For instance, we might have judgmental or angry thoughts about someone but be too polite to say them aloud, giving no external clues to this inner part of our personality. In this case, the quiet and shy behavior is part of one character and different from the judgmental or angry thoughts from another internal character.

Below are some examples of characters that people have identified and named as a result of their inventories. These should help give you ideas to get started on your own list and improve your skills as an observer.

Freddie the Forecaster: Freddie is always talking about the future in dramatic ways. He is absolutely sure he knows what is going to happen, what people are going to do, and he speaks with absolute confidence that things will turn out for the worst. Freddie never looks back to check if any of his doomsday predictions came true. He just goes on making more.

Arnold the Enforcer: Arnold is the character with the Terminator solution to everything. He comes out when there is anger to be expressed. His solution to every problem involves punching someone in the nose. If a driver cuts me off, Arnold wants to punch them in the nose. If the boss doesn't give credit and recognition for an idea I had, Arnold wants to punch him in the nose. From Arnold's perspective all problems can be solved this way. Arnold believes the world would be a better place if he ran it his way and everyone obeyed him.

Abandoned Abner: Abner is the sad little boy whose mother just dropped him off at the orphanage. He shows up either standing on the porch watching his mom drive off, or standing on that same porch and looking wistfully at the horizon, hoping to see her car. He doesn't think he's unlovable, so he's surprised that nobody loves him; yet when evidence is presented that he *is* loved by someone, Abner is slow to believe it. He's suspicious that they might leave at any moment.

Bad Boy Boyd: Bad Boy Boyd, or BBB, only shows up when one of the other characters haven't had their expectations met— especially when they feel stood up. BBB can't find anything to do with himself. He doesn't want to watch TV or play on the computer. He doesn't want to call a friend or take the dog to the park. He doesn't *want* to sit around and mope, but let's face it—what else is there to do? His life is boring and it is other people's fault. There are many things that could be done but BBB finds reasons not to do anything, and then blames other people for his boredom.

Happy Gilmore: Happy puts on a happy face for people. When people ask how he is, he always says, "Fine," even if he is feeling awful. Happy believes it is his job to cheer other people up and so he shouldn't burden them with how he is really feeling. Happy cheers himself up by telling himself he is making other people feel better. He is somewhat of a fraud and knows it, but it's a good fraud. He is often a mask that Abner and Arnold hide behind.

Gladys the Gossip: Gladys always wants to know what is going on with other people. She trades in the currency of gossip. The more dramatic the information she has on someone, the more valuable is the conversation. If she can get the scoop of what is going on, she feels her own worth increase because she possesses the more valuable information. This is how Gladys connects with people and feels loved and appreciated by them.

Patty the Pleaser: Patty is always doing things for other people. She has a great love for volunteering and serving people. Sometimes she sees someone struggling and she jumps in to help, without even thinking. At other times she doesn't even need to see someone with a need—she just jumps in and goes to work. At an extreme Patty can work herself to exhaustion for others and not take very good care of herself. Patty also seems to want something in return for her giving. She wants some recognition and praise. She wants to make sure people like her. Parallel to this need is a fear that she won't be liked unless she does these things. She's afraid people wouldn't like her if she were simply herself.

Use these examples as hints of what to look for to create your own list of characters and a profile on each of them. Write out their characteristics. Make note of what emotions, attitudes, and moods they exhibit. What types of things do they say or do? Your list of characters will be unique to you.

Remember that the purpose of using this tool of identifying the different aspects of your personality in terms of characters is to help you shift your perspective outside their limited belief bubble paradigms. By shifting your perspective outside your belief bubbles, you will find it much easier to disbelieve a thought or impulse and therefore avoid an emotional reaction or negative behavior. Defining these characters will also help you clarify beliefs you have acquired and perpetuated regarding your identity.

Resistance to the Process

Questions and reactions that often come up are, "If I'm not any of these characters, then who am I?" or "If I dissolve all these characters, I won't have a personality—I won't exist." It might be an interesting exercise to note the emotion or attitude behind these concerns. Is there a fear of not existing? Is there a state of confusion behind "Who am I then?" What parts of the mind are asking these questions? More specifically, what *characters* are expressing emotions through these thoughts? The practice of identifying characters can be used directly on the resistance that comes up.

The goal with this practice is not necessarily to find your authentic or real self. Rather the practice is to identify what self-images and ego-based identities falsely claim to be you and detach from them. These characters expressing from your belief system in your mind use *I* and *me* in their thoughts. Detaching from these false ego identities will make it easier for you to discover the authentic and genuine that is underneath these belief-based character masks.

Your characters might feel like they won't exist once they are exposed. This may cause the characters to be uncomfortable emotionally, and this is okay for the process. What is authentic and genuine will not be lost simply by developing self-awareness of these false identity beliefs.

A Word About Ego

I've used the word *ego* a couple times in this chapter and will use it again later in the book. So what is this thing called the ego? While many definitions have been offered by many people, it can remain an abstract concept; the words are empty of meaning if you don't have anything concrete to relate them to.

Perhaps a better word than ego is *self-importance*. The mind's exaggerated sense of the individual's importance, where everything is about "me" and how things affect "me," is a central cause of many emotional reactions and unhappiness. Ego or self-importance can manifest in two opposite ways. The first is in considering ourselves to be more important or better than someone else. Taken to an extreme, it means we believe we are better than *anyone* else. We believe that we have the right answer, that our worthier opinions should be noticed and valued by others, and that we should be respected and honored. Certain archetype characters support this version of self-importance.

The second way self-importance manifests is in the beliefs that make us seem *less* worthy or significant than others. At the extreme is the belief that we are the worst person in the world. Believing that we are less than others may not seem like it involves being important, but it does. The thoughts, stories, and beliefs all revolve around us, our pathetic identity, and the negative impact we have on others. People don't like us because of *us*, and what others do is a direct result of how terrible or incompetent we are. We are at the center of self-blame and judgment. We are the cause of everyone else's problems and behaviors. Being less than others means dismissing ourself, or believing others are dismissing us more than they dismiss anyone else. Again, there are archetype characters that thrive in these negative stories.

The ego is built on false beliefs that we have acquired and sustain, including beliefs about our identity that support our drama-making characters. The ego or self-importance structure also includes the beliefs and belief bubbles of these archetype characters. The thoughts that arise from our internal characters are all arising from the ego part of the mind. The sum total of our false beliefs, including false beliefs about our identity, create multiple layers of belief bubbles that act like a field of fog between us and the world.

The ego is difficult to identify because it hides behind words like *I* and *me*, making it extremely difficult to perceive because we are standing in its focal point, looking through its eyes at the world. As we saw in

Jane's example, it can also shape-shift from one moment to the next, adopting the hurt voice of a Victim, the angry stance of a Judge, the privileged attitude of a Princess, and so on. (We will explore these archetype characters further in Chapter 9.) It is difficult to get a good look at the ego as it changes masks so quickly. At the same time it draws our attention away from its masks and towards the subjects of its stories and opinions. The result is that we are less likely to direct our attention inward and notice the source of these expressions without committed conscious effort.

We also often overlook the ego's role in causing our emotions because we pretend to be all right. When others ask how we are, we usually say, "Fine" because that's what's socially acceptable. We may experience emotional reactions but if, later in the day, either through conscious effort or just by getting involved in something else, our emotional state has changed and we no longer feel bad, we don't go back and look at which character's false beliefs caused the earlier reaction. We feel okay now so we imagine we'll be fine from now on. Even if we've had the same reaction multiple times, as long as we come back to a place of feeling okay, we ignore the repeating pattern once it's over, until it comes up again. So we never investigate or challenge the false self-importance that creates our emotional experience.

When it comes to finding and changing our belief systems, the concept of *ego* is too broad. You will have better luck looking for specific qualities of the archetype characters and the negative thoughts and emotions they express. As you practice being the observer and investigating, you will see each of their masks more clearly and become familiar with their different dances of drama. You will get less distracted by looking at what the ego points your attention to and notice these layers of beliefs generating drama instead.

Chapter 9

Archetypes of Emotional Drama

After you write in third person for a while (practice from Chapter 8) your self-awareness begins to change. You develop the ability to observe with more clarity and detachment the thoughts in your head and your emotional reactions. As you practice you also begin to observe larger patterns.

Observing larger patterns is helpful because it allows you to speed up the process of change. If you have an issue of anger at work, you might also see anger expressed at traffic, or at your relationship partner. A feeling of fear about what others think of you might be part of a larger pattern of fears, including financial and relationship concerns. The same kinds of emotions indicate the same characters of our belief system at work in different areas of our life.

In observing these emotional reactions we find a standard group of six characters common to emotional dramas. They not only show up in our thoughts and behaviors but are common in our culture and even in our storytelling. When you identify these characters in your belief system and remove your perspective from their belief bubble, you will be making large changes to the patterns in your life.

What Is an Archetype?

Archetypes are simple images that quickly communicate a great deal about a character and a belief system. The Victim is an archetype character. A person in the Victim state feels powerless, without choices, and experiences their circumstance as being unfair to them. Feeling defeated and walking away is one possible response of the Victim, but so is becoming defensive and going on the attack. Being aware of certain archetype characters won't tell you what is going to happen, but it can reveal a lot about the different beliefs operating behind the behavior or emotional reaction.

The use of archetypes isn't original; however, the approach I'll describe here is probably different from most. Typically archetypes are used as a way to understand ourselves, or to explain or define our personality. Using such a system we tend to identify with those archetype characters, reinforcing the paradigm that we *are* that character. Instead, I use archetypes to identify characters that were developed through conditioning as part of our limiting beliefs. In this approach we look at these characters as constructs of conditioned beliefs so that we can detach from them.

As we proceed with this exploration, remember that these archetype characters don't describe *you*. They describe a conditioned part of how your beliefs operate, often automatically. I propose that you look at your archetype characters as constructs of your belief system, separate from you. For example, if you identify with your archetypes you might say, "I am a judgmental person." This kind of statement reinforces the perspective within the belief bubble. Instead, we are working to be the observer and say, "There is a part of my belief system that voices a lot of judgmental thoughts." Practicing the exercises described in this book will help you become more comfortable saying and thinking the latter, and facilitate changing the judgmental activity of your mind.

Behavior and emotions largely have a basis in integrity and are natural. However, any emotional behavior can become inauthentic and even destructive when exaggerated by our belief system. Anger is a natural response to a threatening situation and comes from our emotional integrity for self-protection; however, we can also become angry at people we love or at ourselves for minor instances. Caring for another human being is a natural expression of love from our emotional integrity; however, we can take the behavior of looking after others too far and become exhausted and resentful. In each case where an archetype character could be creating emotional drama from our belief system, we might also find a motivation from our genuine self. The key to emotionally balanced and centered living is to eliminate the character belief-based emotions that exaggerate our feelings and behaviors and leave intact our natural, genuine expressions.

The Archetype Characters of Drama: Definitions

To identify the drama-making characters of our belief system we will typically work with a specific group of archetypes going forward. The six common archetypes that create most of our emotional drama are Judge, Victim, Pleaser, Fixer, Princess, and Villain. Because they are such big players we will take some time to get to know them better.

The Judge: The Judge is the critical voice in our head, whether we think or speak it. Occasionally it praises, but mostly it points out what's wrong with us, with our body, other people, and the world. The Judge speaks with the authority of an expert, feeling that it is right about everything and knows what is best. It often seems to have our best interest in mind, yet it doesn't seem to hold our emotional well-being and happiness as a priority. It is more focused on being "right" and following an acquired set of "should" rules. It places a higher priority on following these rules than on being kind, respectful, or happy. When we break one of these many rules we have acquired it can be very condemning of us or of others.

The Judge, which generates emotional reactions through criticism and rejection, is not to be confused with our ability to make clear and helpful assessments of benefits, drawbacks, and consequences for different actions. Making good assessments and decisions is wise and supports our genuine integrity.

The Victim: While the Judge lays out the verbal abuse or adds an emotional edge to an assessment, the Victim character receives it. This is particularly true when it comes to self-judgments. The Victim is willing to accept the Judge's criticisms because it believes that it deserves them. It also interprets what others say in a way that causes it to feel rejected and unworthy. The Victim embodies our unworthiness, our powerlessness, and all that we believe is "wrong" with us, and takes the blame for all our mistakes. It is usually at the center of our fears of being blamed, getting things wrong, being rejected, failing, or being judged. In spite of being able to generate powerful emotional experiences, the Victim feels powerless.

The Victim character should not be confused with actual experiences where we were or are victimized, either physically or emotionally. There are real-life experiences where we are mistreated and our fears and emotional hurt are natural and have integrity. However, the Victim archetype lives in the story and perspective of the belief bubble long after the actual abuse has taken place.

The Pleaser: The Pleaser often comes out as a reaction to the Victim's sense of unworthiness or belief about not being loved or liked. The Victim's underlying feeling is that "people will reject me." To compensate for this state of mind, the Pleaser engages in behaviors to try to "get people to like me." The compensating strategies of the Pleaser can lead to trying harder or worrying about what people think. The Pleaser works hard to do things for others, make a good impression, and get favorable attention. The Pleaser operates under the assumption that love, respect, and acceptance have to be earned; they are conditional upon what one does for someone else. The Victim's starting point is that it lacks these things, so the Pleaser goes looking for them from other people. As much as the Pleaser might get recognition, acceptance, and love from others, the Victim still feels those same emotions of unworthiness and fear, so the Pleaser has to go right back to work.

Of course, these same behaviors of caring for people and being generous can also be done from the stance of integrity rather than as the Pleaser. When we extend love, kindness, and service to others in our actions from our authentic nature it feels good and is without the need for approval or acceptance. From the outside the actions may look the same. The difference between acting as the Pleaser and being genuine is the emotion that motivates the behavior. Sometimes we may even find in our actions both a genuine desire to give and a Pleaser hoping to get something back.

The Fixer: The Fixer is the answer man who follows up on what the Judge finds wrong. Another name for the Fixer is the Hero. However, it is a false Hero because it comes out in response to the false beliefs of the Judge. If the Judge says there is something wrong with the world, the Fixer will go fix it. The nature of the Fixer is to try and get attention, credit, recognition, and the reward of praise. The Fixer/Hero wants to show people how smart, capable, and skilled it is. The Fixer is similar to the Pleaser in that it is doing things to earn love and recognition, but its starting point is a positive self-image, in contrast to the Victim's (and Pleaser's) negative self-image. The Fixer often assumes that it is right and has a better answer or idea than other people and therefore should be respected and appreciated. The Fixer is often quick to give advice and make suggestions, and prides itself on being smart. In this regard it is making expressions for the benefit of its own self-image and not necessarily helping others in a way that is effective.

Again, we can be helpful to others and lift them up, but without the need or desire for recognition or respect; in that case, it's not the Fixer at work but our authentic self.

The Princess: The Princess is defined by an attitude of entitlement. She lives in a bubble world where she believes she deserves or is entitled to things. The Princess may not cause emotional drama herself. She often operates silently in the realm of expectations. The emotional reaction comes from the Victim or Judge characters when something or someone doesn't meet the Princess's expectations.

The integrity part of our being has a natural inclination to make sure our physical and emotional needs are met. This helps us focus on pursuing what we want and enjoying our life. However, the attitude of the Princess character is that people and the world are *supposed to* behave to her benefit, the way she wants it. A Princess might feel entitled to a parking place just because "I saw it first." (*Note:* Although we tend to refer to the Princess with female pronouns, these archetypes are all gender-neutral.)

The Villain: The Villain, which can also be called the Rebel, Perpetrator, Avenger, or Saboteur, tends to operate with an attitude of anger, resentment, disgust, or vengeance. It may also be backed by the Judge's righteousness, which provides a moral justification for the Villain's emotion and behavior. Sometimes the Villain is just angry and wants to punch someone. But it can also have a well-articulated argument or use edgy, put-down humor that can make people feel small, disrespected, or stupid.

These emotions and behaviors can occur with integrity and legitimately act in our defense when we are truly mistreated, putting up boundaries with people who are unkind to us. Because of this the Villain can mask itself as our Defender. The problem is that the Victim falsely interprets many situations as mistreatment, invoking the Villain with anger even when there isn't any mistreatment at all. The result is that we overreact, and the Villain becomes the destroyer of our relationships.

Practice: Use Archetypes to Identify False Beliefs

Take some of your third person writings and replace the pronouns of he/she or characters with archetypes where you see they fit.

Note: This example of observing your beliefs will make more sense if you've spent some time doing the earlier exercise of writing in third person.

Suppose you were doing something and it failed to turn out like you planned or hoped. One of the thoughts and feelings you might have is "I'm a stupid idiot."

When you take a step back and write this dialog in third person it becomes: "The voice in his head says, 'I am a stupid idiot,'" or "He thinks that he is stupid." A second step back might be, "The voice in his head said, 'You are a stupid idiot.'" By writing it this way we are attempting to step back further outside the belief bubble into an observer perspective.

Using archetypes, we can identify the different voices in our head as having their own perspectives and belief bubbles. In this example, the first voice we've noticed is that of the Judge, so we'll rewrite the sentence: "The Judge said, 'You are a stupid idiot.'" The "you" to whom the Judge is speaking refers to the Victim character, so converting it all to third person the line becomes: "The Judge said the Victim character is a stupid idiot."

Next we notice that the Victim heard the Judge and automatically, silently agreed with what it heard. The Judge sent the message of rejection and the Victim received and accepted that message. The result was that the Victim generated emotions of shame or unworthiness for being a "stupid idiot."

When we write the story this way, we are the observer witnessing these two characters of our mind having their own conversation with each other.

The *application* of this exercise will shift your feelings more than the intellectual analysis of it. Please note: Simply writing things down this way doesn't guarantee that your point of view will change, but it does gives your mind a better chance for change. Seeing the situation written on a piece of paper puts you at arm's distance from the belief bubble rather than inside of it, which is where you stay when you merely "think" about these things. This tool of writing about things differently is an attempt to shift your perspective into that of a neutral observer.

How long it takes to get this result will vary. It's kind of like those Magic Eye pictures that have a 3-D picture hidden within the dots. Sometimes you see it right away, and sometimes you have to work to get your perception to change. Each person's flexibility with their perspective is different, so don't bother measuring your results against someone else's.

Further Examination

Why should we look at what goes on in the mind this way? When we consider that we have developed different characters, which think within their own bubbles, we have a more accurate model with which to understand what is going on in our head.

This act of separating ourselves from these thoughts also allows us to scrutinize them and be more skeptical of these beliefs. When we look at the statement "I'm stupid" a bit closer, a number of assumptions become more apparent. Noticing these embedded assumptions hidden in the statement makes the idea that we are stupid less believable.

The statement "I'm stupid" is being made with an attitude of authority and a sense of being "right." A smart, authoritative person would make this statement. This is the attitude and personality of the Judge, who is certain that it knows better than anyone else. The Judge in our mind acts as if it is always right, never wrong, so don't even question it. From the Judge's perspective, the fact is clear.

However, the Judge couldn't possibly be calling *itself* "stupid," because its nature is to be smart and have all the right answers all the time. The Judge is talking about another image of ourselves, the Victim. The Victim immediately accepts whatever negative, rejecting comment the Judge makes, because negative comments make perfect sense to this character. They are entirely congruent with its self-image. It willingly accepts that "stupid" is an accurate assessment and doesn't fight against it.

From the Judge's belief bubble, the idea that it "knows better" is completely congruent. Yet the Victim's belief in its stupidity is congruent within its paradigm. So here we have two opposite assumptions, or hidden beliefs—we "know better" and we are "stupid." These contradicting paradigms can't both be true. When we see this contradiction our awareness instinctively moves us further away from the Judge and Victim bubbles. This skepticism is not possible from within the Judge or Victim belief bubbles.

Separating out these disparate archetypes lets us see how illogical the comment is and begin to question it effectively. If we were actually stupid, we wouldn't know what would have been "better," the way the Judge does. If our inner Judge does "know" better, how can we believe that we're stupid? With this awareness we now have a wedge of skepticism with which to doubt what previously felt true.

Use of the Inventory

When you start breaking down emotional reactions into archetype character roles, you shift your perspective outside these bubbles. From outside the bubble of these archetypes you can see hidden beliefs and assumptions that you didn't notice before. Observing these contradictory details makes your beliefs immediately less believable.

Paul was walking to the subway and a man rushing past bumped into him. Paul's unspoken reaction was, "You jerk! That was rude." He refrained from saying anything, but he felt both offended and angry. This triggered some internal dialog about how the guy should have behaved and what Paul might have done to set him straight. Later, when Paul reflected on his reaction and looked closer, details of different characters revealed themselves stemming from just a couple thoughts. The following chart lists their appearances in chronological order.

Archetype/ Event	Story/Belief/Behavior	Emotion/Attitude
Princess	Subway travelers should behave properly at all times. No one is ever allowed to hurry. Everyone has to be completely vigilant of everyone around them so no one ever bumps into another. (These beliefs existed before the day of the incident.)	Sense of entitlement. I am entitled to an ideal world of perfection and politeness in a crowded subway station. How "I" should be treated.
Event	Stranger bumps into Paul.	
Genuine physical and emotional instinct	Physical discomfort and a small natural emotional response when startled. By itself it would dissolve quickly once the man moves on.	Small amount of surprise. A natural amount of emotional response.
Victim 1	Stories of possibly being hurt pop up in the mind (so quickly he didn't see them until he reflected on it later).	Fear.
Victim 2	The rules of my Princess have been violated by this stranger. That guy is at fault for making me feel this way (blame).	Offended. Blame at the physical discomfort, and fear.

Judge	That person broke the rules of my Princess. He should apologize, not be in such a hurry, pay more attention to where he's going, etc. He is a bad person. The Judge uses the beliefs of the Princess as a standard to judge others.	Righteous indignation. Authoritative, empowered, justified.
Villain	I should go beat him up. I should yell at him and scold him so he doesn't do it again. I'll fix this situation by punishing that guy verbally and emotionally until he behaves. This is the Villain hiding under the mask of Defender.	Anger, frustration. Righteousness in alignment with the Judge.
Fixer/Hero	I should tell him to pay attention to where he is going. I should . . . (imagines all the corrective roles that he would play to make the person's behavior right). Attempting to restore order and make people on the subway operate according to the expectations of the Princess.	Seeing himself in a good light in his imagination. Feelings of being a problem solver and good self-worth.
Full cycle	Paul feels better emotionally after playing up his Fixer personality in his imagination. This helps to put his emotions back to normal after the fear, anger, and offended feelings he created with the Victim and Judge reactions.	

At first glance, Paul's offended reaction had just one layer. But as he worked through this inventory over a couple days, he realized that it was a chain reaction, from one character to another. By itself, getting bumped produced only a minimal reaction, but it was the trigger for the belief system to create the rest of his emotions.

When Paul saw this belief system written out as a systematic inventory, his perspective shifted. It shifted because he became the *observer* of his characters and stepped outside their belief bubble perspectives. He didn't have to try not to believe his thoughts—they simply became less believable as a function of his new perspective, and his emotions lessened in the process. Paul was able to take responsibility for the reaction of his own belief system. He could see how his characters worked to create many of his emotions. Once he did that, it became difficult to believe the story of "blaming the other guy" for how he felt. The agenda of the Fixer and Villain to change another person then seemed contrived as well. Once he detached from one belief in the chain, the others in the sequence started to fall apart.

In doing the detailed inventory, the last piece that Paul got clarity on was his Princess expectation. He only saw it and wrote it into the top of his inventory after he'd written out everything else. When he realized that his expectation required people to be aware, polite, and considerate at all times, he recognized that it was ridiculous. Sometimes people are just preoccupied with what they are doing, stressed, in a hurry, or have an emergency, despite what his Princess expects. The well-behaved world only appeared possible from the unconscious Princess perspective.

—⁕—

When you take an inventory of the different characters' stories and emotions, your perspective naturally shifts to the observer as a byproduct of looking for these characters.

—⁕—

96

Archetypes Are Part of a Larger Pattern

Paul's story was about a small emotional reaction to an incidental bump. However, these patterns of archetype characters and their hidden beliefs make up Paul's bigger emotional reactions as well. If he is unable to stay ahead of these characters in small interactions, then he hasn't much chance of staying ahead of his interpretations in larger emotional reactions. By reflecting on the small instances, Paul is more aware of the automatic patterns of his mind. Developing his skills of awareness and skepticism in small situations gives him a better chance to apply them to the larger situations of his life.

Some people look for a trick or some bit of knowledge that will provide a quick way to change their emotional reactions. They get hung up looking for a quick fix. This is often their Fixer thinking it can solve emotional reactions easily just because it is smart and has solved other problems. Years of conditioning in other situations, like the classroom, have taught them that having the right answers brings them success. However, when the problem is a fixated point of view, the character looking for an "answer" is part of the problem.

Changing an emotionally driven behavior isn't done with information. It's more akin to a skill we develop, like dancing, public speaking, playing a musical instrument, or hitting a tennis ball. We learn to hit a tennis ball by starting with how to hold a racquet and where to plant our feet. We then practice hitting slow ones lobbed at us. Next we move up to faster balls to our backhand. Over time we develop the hand-eye coordination and can hit the ball while on the run. In the same way, by starting with smaller challenges of observing reactions on paper at arm's length, we can learn to handle our attention, perspective, and interpretations when people are throwing fast ones at us. The key to success is taking time to build the skills.

By studying and classifying the characters of your personality, you are turning your attention to your belief system in a way that builds awareness. Most importantly, by reflecting on your behaviors, attitudes, and emotions in a structured way, you are adopting and developing *the perspective of the witness observer.* You don't have to try to make this happen. When you take an inventory of the different characters' stories and emotions, your perspective naturally shifts to the observer as a byproduct of looking for these characters. As an added benefit, the more time you spend in the witness observer state, the less time you will spend reinforcing the perspective, interpretations, and emotions of the Judge, Victim, and other archetype characters.

Having a system to do a "belief inventory" will give you a way to organize what you observe. Most likely, the first time you try it, you won't be able to do this inventory with the level of detail and understanding of the archetypes demonstrated in Paul's example. It's a skill you'll develop with practice. Even being able to observe archetype characters might be difficult in the beginning, as we are inclined to mistakenly identify all these aspects of our beliefs as "me." That's why I have people begin with the exercises of writing in third person and making a list, profiling their characters. These are some of the smaller exercises helpful in the skill-building process.

In the beginning, you will typically see the layers of beliefs and emotional reactions *after* they happen. It is always easier to discern these characters and their stories/beliefs as an observer an hour or a day later. While you're in the midst of an emotional reaction, you are conditioned to assume the identity of one or more of those characters and can't see the beliefs. From the perspective of a character, your inner belief world appears to be "reality." For Paul, it appeared from the Victim bubble that the person who bumped him was solely responsible for making him afraid and angry. After doing the belief inventory, Paul realized that he was making himself angry with the beliefs he had about that person. So even if you're caught up in a character's reactive emotions at first, later that day or the next day you may be able to start writing out the events of your emotional reactions from a more detached point of view. With some practice, you'll get skilled at maintaining the observer perspective, and you'll be able to see these characters tugging at your emotions in real time. That is the opportunity for making a different choice.

Hurry Up and Change

In the beginning, you may find there is a voice in your head telling you to hurry up and change. This can be the Hero/Fixer. You might also find one that tells you that these characters are a painful part of your life and they should get the hell out. Perhaps this is a Judge archetype. You might find a voice that says, "I hate them and I hate what they are doing and how they make me feel." The emotion of hate is a clue to a Villain, while the "me" that hates the way it feels is likely a Victim voice. Yes, these voices in our head can and do complain loudly about each other. As a matter of fact, nobody will complain more loudly about the process of cleaning up the voices in your head than the voices of the archetypes in your head!

At times, they will tell you that you aren't doing enough. This is a Judge and Victim conversation of rejection. In the next breath they might complain that this approach isn't working and you should just quit. This is a Victim and Saboteur comment. Later they will say that you have these reactions under control and you don't have to try that hard anymore. This is the voice of the overconfident Hero claiming victory. When you notice this happening, include in your list of characters the different ones that complain about your belief system and the process of change. No matter how good their intentions seem to be, they are not helping you create a quiet and peaceful mind.

Warning!

One of the risks in applying archetype character labels to aspects of our personality is that the Judge will use it to chime in with negative criticism: "You *shouldn't be* such a Victim, you shouldn't be such a Princess, or you should be more of a . . ." This can happen with any tool you use to heighten awareness and change beliefs. The characters themselves can take hold of that tool and use it against you emotionally, resulting in a lot of hurtful self-criticism based on what you discover. If you observe something like this happening in your process, pay close attention to the sections on acceptance (see Chapter 13), and go back to the exercises for being the neutral observer. Write out what these new voices are saying from a third-person perspective until you can identify them as separate characters.

Chapter 10

How Archetype Characters Develop

A common reaction to discovering the presence of these archetype characters in our mind and personality is to judge and feel victimized by them for the ways they influence our life and our emotional reactions. It may seem at times that there is nothing good about them. At other times we feel like they protect us from getting hurt emotionally, and we get nervous when we don't follow their rules. These interpretations are themselves the Judge and Victim archetypes at work. To dissolve these reactive thoughts and the influence of these archetype characters, it will help to know how they developed in the first place.

Note: In this book I use the words *judge* and *judgmental* to describe expressions of criticism, rejection, or condemnation. They might be subtle or harsh, but the common denominator is an unpleasant quality of emotion. This is distinctly different from an *assessment,* or discernment, which is made with a detached clarity and equanimity. In order to better our lives, we need to make assessments of what works for us. An example is, "I'm much happier when I am not around that person." This becomes a judgment when the emotional attitude shifts to an unpleasant or accusatory expression such as, "They are a bad person." These examples aren't perfectly clear because it is left to the reader to include the correct tone and emotion with each, but hopefully you get the idea of a difference. This book is not concerned with changing assessments, because they don't cause emotional drama. It's the judgments that we are addressing, because they pack the emotional charge that causes unhappiness in ourselves and our relationships.

The Judge: The Critical Voice in Your Head

For many adults, the mind has developed an aspect that incessantly describes, compares, judges, and criticizes. I call this part of the mind the Judge. It's a pretty active character in the mind of a person who is unhappy or prone to emotional reactions. Without awareness, we don't notice how busy the Judge is and how much it dominates our internal dialog.

Sometimes we don't consider our judgmental thoughts to be negative; we think they are just opinions. However, given that our perspective is within the belief bubble of the Judge, our opinions appear to be true, so we believe them as if they were fact. Our belief system habitually defends and justifies our criticisms so they appear rational and we appear smart. We comfort ourselves in the ego cloak of being smart as we express emotionally unpleasant criticisms.

Often, from this critical perspective, only other people and the rest of the world have problems. We feel fine about ourselves. If we're unhappy and upset, it's the world's fault, or someone else's fault. As soon as the other person or group changes, we'll feel better. This fits with the Victim paradigm assumption that the external world is responsible for our emotions. However, in stressful situations, the voice in our head can become critical of us, and even berate us, and the Judge no longer looks like a smart friend. For some people, this is the Judge's default stance: it looks outward at the world and concludes that everything and everyone else is just fine, then looks inward at us and continually tells us how we don't measure up. The theme of its comments is always that we are not good enough.

Most people have this kind of judgmental chatter in their mind to varying degrees. Some people identify with this perspective and feel it is who they are, while others realize that the Judge has taken on a life of its own and become a tyrant. It has a list of how we should be different and how we are such a failure for not meeting the criteria on its "should" list. When it finishes rattling off its list of our failings it starts over again. The resulting feelings are those of unworthiness, insecurity, failure, and shame. We haven't acted in all the ways that it approves. For some, the Judge provides a constant chatter of criticisms about us that can be emotionally debilitating, generating hopelessness and depression when we believe what it says.

Understanding how the Judge developed can lessen our emotional reaction to it and can help towards dissolving it.

Origin of the Judge

When seeking to eliminate self-judgments and chatter in the mind, it helps to recognize that *the Judge doesn't mean you harm*. It may be the source of self-criticism and unkind comments, but that was not its original intent. Paradoxically, we developed this critical part of our mind to help us feel emotionally safe and happy. *The Judge's intention is to help us gain pleasant rewards and avoid unpleasant consequences.* The problem is that since its well-intentioned start, the Judge part of our mind has grown into something else.

The inner voice of self-judgment develops in a young mind with the merging of memory and logic. Before memory and logic developed, we stayed in the present moment where there is only the desire and action to express ourselves. We acted innocently, on impulse and inspiration. If we wanted to go outside and play, but Mom had told us to pick up our toys, we would just run out and play. We didn't remember what Mom told us, and we had no logical reasoning to give it importance.

As memory and logic developed, we could recall Mom scolding us on a prior occasion for not cleaning up our toys. We began to remember things in our past and relate them to our present-moment actions, and then imagine what would come next. Our conditioned memory was working just fine to make these connections, even if our thoughts were not completely conscious.

Our memory would link the emotionally unpleasant scolding to not having picked up our toys. Eventually, as we ran outside to play one time and noticed our toys on the floor, a little voice in our head would remind us, "I should pick those up." This was our Judge voice, an echo from memory with a helpful reminder telling us how to avoid the emotional pain of future punishment. The voice in our head was a good friend looking after our happiness.

Sometimes, after we'd been punished by a parent, this voice would act as an advisor, saying things like, "I should have picked up my toys."

The Judge was instructing us in how to avoid unhappy punishments in the future. If we got yelled at for playing in the street, the Judge would remind us of this unpleasant fact the next time we considered playing in the street. The Judge stored the memories of what had happened and filed away rules to follow so we wouldn't get in trouble. Over the years it added many rules and echoed them back to us: "I should look nice," "I should get good grades," "I should be smart," "I shouldn't be a loser," "I shouldn't get the answer wrong," "I shouldn't leave my desk such a mess," and so on. We learned to listen to the Judge in order to avoid breaking Mom and Dad's rules so we wouldn't get punished. Later we added rules from teachers, clergy, siblings, and friends. As teenagers, our Judge developed complex rules based on our peers' reactions about what was "cool" and "not cool."

The Judge didn't know the future but echoed rules from the past to warn us about what would cause us pain. It used these rules, based on past experiences, to project assumptions about future punishments and tell us what we'd better not do.

The Judge also told us what to do in order to get rewarded with attention, acceptance, and love: "I should clean up my room, eat my vegetables, be quiet, sit still, stay in line, get good grades, win, make lots of money." The Judge echoed all the emotional rewards and punishments stored in memory: Do these things and people will like you, accept you, respect you, and love you. Follow these rules and you will be happy. If you don't do these things you will be punished, rejected, and feel hurt.

As we grew up, we experienced positive emotions whenever our inner Judge approved of how well we did or how we looked. Many people who are very unhappy or depressed are failing to meet so many of their internal rules that hardly any good feelings are generated anymore. Even when they hear some positive comments, their inner Judge drowns them out with many more negative ones about the ways they are failing.

As a young child, we might have seen adults as very unpredictable. Some adults may have had different sets of expectations and rules for us to follow, or reacted differently to the same things. This could cause some confusion, so we began to trust the little Judge in our head more than anyone else. Even our parents, who loved us, couldn't be completely trusted because they would punish us if we did something wrong, and sometimes even if we didn't. Maybe we were wrongly blamed and punished for what our brother did, and concluded that we couldn't trust Mom or Dad.

With its growing number of rules, our inner Judge became the guide to emotional safety. (*Note:* Instead of the word *rules* here we could also use *beliefs, agreements,* or *assumptions*. However, given that we are talking about the Judge, the term *rules* fits better, as the Judge often uses beliefs as if they are rules of law.) Over time, we invested a lot of faith in the Judge and made it our trusted advisor who told us what to do, what not to do, what we should be, and what we should not be. The Judge part of our mind became a very strong voice with great authority and power, and we trusted it to help us make the right choices.

While some people hear the voice of their parents when their Judge speaks, most people grow up recording their rules into memory with their own internal voice. Later, when the Judge repeats them back to us, it sounds like us speaking and thinking because it is our own voice from memory. Sometimes we mistake our trust in the Judge as an indication that we trust ourselves. We look at the world from the perspective within the Judge's belief bubble and assume it is our own. From its perspective, everything the Judge says appears true. Because the Judge speaks with such authority and often in their own voice, some people mistakenly label it their "higher self."

For all its rules and certainty, the Judge is not without some contradictions and confusion. Maybe we told the truth, and that got us in trouble. We would then make a rule that we shouldn't tell the truth, but that would conflict with another belief that we *should* tell the truth. The Judge seems very logical and methodical, particularly when we're younger. Yet as we get older and have more experiences that add more rules, it contradicts itself without trying to reconcile the conflict. It just tries to get us to follow all of its rules, even if they oppose each other.

If we continue to live our life by following all the rules stored in our memory, we run into problems. As children, we internalized the rules of the adults in our lives. As we get older, we find that people don't punish and reward us in the same way they did when we were children, yet we continue to try to live by all the contradictory rules we collected. By the time we are adults, we live by a set of old rules from long ago, even when no one is punishing or rewarding us anymore. The Judge continues to hold us accountable to these standards, with its own internal punishments, even if the rules from when we were eight years old no longer apply.

An example of these lingering rules is George. Nearing seventy years old, George had done quite well for himself and hadn't needed to work in years. He still did some real estate business part-time, but he had decided that he really was retired and that it was okay to enjoy his time in whatever ways he chose. The problem was, when he would get on the computer, play a game of bridge, or spend time playing the piano, the Judge in his head would say, "You should be doing something productive." His father's voice from George's teenage years still echoed in his head. One of the problems with these rules stored in our belief bubble is that the Judge hasn't noticed that we've grown up. For George, that Judge still sees him as a teenager character even though he is retired.

—⚏—

Many people who are very unhappy or depressed are failing to meet so many of their internal rules that hardly any good feelings are generated anymore.

—⚏—

Faulty Logic and Illusions

Problems also arise because rules in the mind can be based on faulty assumptions. Mom might be upset at something else in her life but snap at us when we ask for something we want. We incorrectly assume that we got punished for asking, when it may have been for some unrelated issue Mom had going on that day at work. So the Judge makes the rule, "I shouldn't ask for what I want," and we store that belief in memory. It then gets reinforced with selective evidence, and as an adult we hesitate to ask for what we want, even when it would be appropriate. The Judge says we are being selfish when we consider what we want and what will be good for us.

Even if Mom is kind and not feeling stressed, she may have the good sense not to give us the pony or dog that we ask for. Our sense of disappointment is painful and strengthens the agreement: "I shouldn't ask for what I want because it will just lead to pain." In these ways, our mind can create faulty protocols for us to follow, which, once we accept them as beliefs or agreements, can remain in our unconscious memory, continuing to affect our decisions and behaviors decades later.

If we question these beliefs or rules, the characters of the belief system defend them with statements like, "I don't ask for what I want so I don't get hurt or disappointed." At first glance this might appear as a true statement of how we protect ourselves. However, on closer scrutiny we see that the hurt doesn't come from asking. It is the Victim character bubble that creates disappointment and hurt as a reaction to not receiving what is asked for. Not asking is just a compensating strategy to avoid our Victim responses. From a paradigm of mutual respect we can ask for what we want. And from that same paradigm of mutual respect it is possible to be told no and not have an emotional reaction.

As children, there was no other part of our mind monitoring the Judge for exaggerations, misinterpretations, fear-based beliefs, and lies. We trusted its rules and agreed to them with no consideration of how they might limit our happiness and choices. We weren't aware that we were collecting these rules or how strong they would become later in our life. We were simply doing the best we could to interpret our experiences and navigate the world of adults around us.

Even as adults, our inner Judge makes rules that are based not in truth but in reaction to our limited experience. If we suffer a broken heart, the Judge will make rules so we don't get hurt again. It will declare, "Love hurts. Love will only end in heartbreak. All men are _____," or "Women are just _____." The Judge might swear off a whole gender as a solution for feeling emotionally hurt. This belief-based rule doesn't go away once the emotion of heartache fades. The Judge brings it back and reminds us of it whenever we begin to feel love again. Later in life we feel afraid to express our love because the Judge and Victim say it will lead to heartbreak and pain.

The Judge is prescribing rules to follow so we don't get hurt, but it is also not allowing us to express love and be loved by another person.

Sometimes we are not conscious of any thoughts or internal dialog of words associated to these rules. We might just feel uneasy or anxious around someone as they express their love to us or as we begin to feel love for them. Outside of our awareness, a character might then begin to sabotage the relationship in order to avoid those uneasy feelings.

Most of us receive no guidance or instruction in being aware and changing our thoughts, beliefs, and emotions. We don't realize that these rules we've created can be stored in memory and echoed back to us for decades. We learn to follow these rules in a trusting way, unaware of the consequences. We invest faith in the voice of the Judge and treat it as a trusted advisor that we do not question. In Chapter 11 we'll explore how to divest our faith from the Judge's authority and rules and dissolve its influence over us.

The Judge Transitions from Helper to Critic

Over the years, the voice of the Judge becomes harsher. Perhaps a second heartbreak brings a stern criticism such as, "I knew better and I didn't listen to myself; I am such an idiot." We accept the painful criticism because within that belief paradigm we assume that following the Judge's rules means we won't get hurt anymore. In other scenarios, following the harsh instructions of the Judge will make us push harder to succeed. Either way, its rules appear to point out the path to emotional safety and happiness.

Eventually the Judge has criticisms not only about us, but about traffic, drivers, work, government, our bodies, strangers, and people we love. It believes that everyone else should follow these rules as well. The Judge cloaks itself in superiority. It is always dictating opinions about how things could be better. The Judge is still interested in our success and happiness, but it is completely wedded to the rules programmed into our memory. Its dominant agenda is to get us to follow all the rules we've acquired since we were children. We lose awareness of the original intent of these rules—our happiness—and so the end goal is lost. All that is left is a dogmatic and perhaps fanatical program of the Judge demanding that we follow its rules.

We've believed in the Judge for so long that it's taken on a life of its own. Its self-judgments and chatter run constantly, like a radio station we can't turn off. No longer a helpful, trusted advisor, it is now a loud cynic and critic making harsh rejections of ourselves and others.

We assume that appeasing this tyrannical voice will quiet it. We spend our energy trying to obey its rules, even when so many of the beliefs are based in fear, out of date, or stem from misinterpretations. We are so busy trying to appease the Judge that we hardly notice how many of its rules contradict each other. "I should go after that promotion" conflicts with "I don't think I could do that job." "I should ask her out" conflicts with fear of judgmental self-rejection if she says no. Then we have the added self-judgment of "I shouldn't be afraid" or "I should be happier with my life."

Amidst this mental chaos we forget that the programming of all the rules was designed to prevent pain and bring us happiness. Yet emotions like love and happiness can hardly be felt while our attention is devoted to rules about what we should and shouldn't do.

Freeing Ourselves from the Judge

For some people, a life crisis comes after they've followed all the rules and haven't ended up happy the way their beliefs claimed they would. An example of this is Bill, the doctor we met in Chapter 1. At every stage of his life, his belief system assured him he would be happy once he accomplished the *next* thing. He went from college to medical school to large practice to small practice to divorce, following the rules of the Judge projecting a future outcome. When you realize how many of the rules were really about fears of avoiding pain, or were carrots to get praise from others as an emotional reward, it's not surprising they didn't lead to happiness.

For some, this kind of crisis provides an opportunity to examine the rules and the beliefs behind them. For others, even midlife crises and disillusionment may not be enough to challenge the false rules in their head. Instead, they might just make more rules and opt for new toys, a new promotion, or a new relationship and leave all the old rules intact. Perhaps their Judge makes new rules about achievement and success and tells them that if they achieve that *higher* level of success, they will then be happy. Once again they try to obey all the Judge's rules, to the point of exhaustion, and allow it to remain the unquestioned tyrant in their head.

An early step to freedom from the tyranny of the Judge is to become aware of a couple simple truths. The first is that *the judgmental voice in your head is not you.* This shift in perspective can be difficult to maintain because we have aligned with the Judge's perspective for a long time. We assume that the thoughts it's promoting are *our* thoughts and that its criticisms and opinions are the only way to see things. We can begin to break this identification with the Judge when we realize that we can't turn off the judgmental thoughts. If the voice of the Judge was really *your* voice, you would be able to consciously direct it at any and every moment. To help make the point clear, do an experiment. Make an agreement with yourself that you won't be critical of anyone, including yourself, for a week. See how long you are able to do it. Finding out you can't control the Judge is a clue that the Judge is not the reality of you.

The second truth to accept is that *the Judge doesn't know how to be happy.* It only knows the rules (beliefs) it's stored in memory from the past about how other people will react towards us and how we should behave. The Judge doesn't know how to express love or joy, or even how to laugh. The critical Judge doesn't know what to do in order for you to accept yourself. The Judge knows and practices self-rejection under the assumption that this is how we get "better." In the Judge's bubble world there is no emotion of self-acceptance or self-love. There are only rules to follow that will allow us to get acceptance from someone else. The Judge's only notion of self-approval comes from following all its rules, even if those rules are outdated.

As much as the Judge appears to be an all-knowing authority figure, it actually only knows patterns from a socialized and conditioned experience of the past. It bases everything on past interpretations, and projects all future experiences to be the same. It adamantly pretends to know the future. It doesn't know the happiness, joy, and freedom that we knew instinctively as children, and is therefore disconnected from a very real and natural part of us. The Judge doesn't know how to enjoy and be present in the moment because it is only concerned with what others will think of us in that moment. This shows how far the inner critic of the

Judge has wandered from its original trusted advisor position that tried to keep us emotionally safe: to the point that, as adults, we need to do something to make ourselves emotionally safe from the Judge.

We can free ourselves from the faulty rules of the Judge by first adopting a different perspective. From a new observer perspective we can begin choosing not to believe its rules anymore—and there are many. We stop succumbing to the Judge's tyranny when we stop taking what it says as gospel. This is simple, but not necessarily easy. It requires awareness to shift perspective and see the Judge from outside its belief bubble, and from outside the Victim bubble as well. Practicing the exercises presented earlier, such as third-person writing and ascribing characters to thoughts and emotional reactions, will help.

Resistance to Changing the Judge

Just the thought of challenging the Judge can bring up fears. Since we have entrusted our emotional well-being to following all its rules, we seem to risk being hurt and unsafe if we deviate from them. At least it appears this way from the Victim archetype perspective, which we'll explore later in this chapter. Despite the fact that it takes so much abuse from the Judge, the Victim is a character of dependency, and looks to the strong personality of the Judge and its rules for guidance.

As mentioned earlier, the Judge doesn't offer real happiness or emotional safety, although the Victim believes that it does. There is no emotional safety from a voice in your head that berates and criticizes. Sometimes the reward for following the rules is acceptance, respect, or praise from the people around us, but looking to others for these things sets up a dependency that reinforces the Victim paradigm, and any happiness achieved that way is fleeting. Our Hero and Pleaser begin each day trying to get acceptance again and again from others, which can be exhausting. The truth is that we experience the greatest happiness when we allow ourselves to express love, and very little when we're trying to appease the Judge.

The Judge we developed in our mind over the years was a very useful guide to navigate the big and perhaps chaotic world of growing up. Its system of rules was a helpful guide to our young minds. It truly was a trusted advisor and served us well for many years. However, the rules about life, love, relationship, money, and happiness that we learned when we were six, sixteen, and twenty-six usually have a lot of distortions and misinterpretations that interfere with our happiness today. If all those rules stored in our memory were really the way to happiness, they would have worked out by now.

We will more easily let go of the Judge perspective when we no longer buy into the illusion of emotional safety and conditioned happiness that it purportedly offers. We will challenge the Judge in our head when the suffering we experience under its harsh rules is greater than the Victim character's fear of being without it, or when we simply become aware that what the Judge is doing isn't working for us emotionally. We will defy the Judge's faulty logic when we are aware enough to realize that its rules are based in fear of what others think, or conditioned responses from when we were a child, and not what will help us be happy today. The desire to be happy is the force that will propel us to take the steps that will lead to freedom from the Judge in our head.

—⁓—

The truth is that we experience the greatest happiness when we allow ourselves to express love, and very little when we're trying to appease the Judge.

—⁓—

Maintaining Balance

Everything the Judge has to say should be scrutinized for inaccuracy and distortions. Yet, behind its rules and berating voice, there may be some wisdom in the form of discernment and assessment. The challenge is to discern between its accurate perceptions of what will help us be happy and its outdated set of stored rules and fears that will lead to unhappiness.

It will take a bit of awareness to extract the useful assessments and dismantle the dogmatic rules and fears. What will evolve from this process is a wise sense of discernment and assessment, but without the berating, criticizing, and rejecting attitude that is so emotionally harsh.

The Judge has accumulated great wisdom and understanding that can be utilized. However, the dogmatic, inflexible, and emotionally reactive aspects of the Judge no longer serve its original intent: our emotional well-being.

—∿—

What will evolve from this process is a wise sense of discernment and assessment, but without the berating, criticizing, and rejecting attitude that is so emotionally harsh.

—∿—

The Judge: Summary

The most useful thing to take away from this discussion is that the Judge originated in our mind as a helpful reminder of how to gain love, acceptance, and approval from others. It also developed many rules to follow in order to avoid rejection, punishment, and the unhappiness that accompanies them. At best, the Judge can guide us to a conditioned emotional response of happiness using the rules it learned from past experiences with other people. At worst, it mandates an outdated program of rules that applied to a much younger version of us and that sabotage our present quest for happiness. In either case, the Judge never intended for us to be miserable. It is, however, a part of that outdated program that needs to be rewritten if we are to be happy.

How We Learned to Play the Role of Victim

Just as the Judge's intention is to help us gain rewards and avoid pain, the Victim archetype in our mind is also concerned for our well-being. Its intent was to get us what we wanted and to keep us safe by reducing or avoiding punishment or mistreatment, whether inflicted by others or by our own internal Judge.

Watch children in a grocery store. When they find a candy bar or toy they want, they escalate through a myriad of behaviors to get it. Perhaps they first ask sweetly (Princess). If that doesn't work, they resort to negotiation: they promise to be so good (Hero), if Mom will just buy this thing for them. If Mom fails to respond, they will switch to sadness, disappointment (Victim), and then to a full-out tantrum (Villain). Maybe the child then tries guilt by telling the parent, "You're mean. I don't like you. I hate you."

At this point the child is behaving as if his parents have actually mistreated him. In his imaginary world, the child feels abused (Victim) by them for not being allowed to have the candy bar.

The parents' emotional reaction to the child's behavior may be sufficient to cause them to give in to what the child wants. Notice that it is their own emotional response to the child that determines whether they buy the candy bar or not. If this is happening in a public place, the child's influence on the parents' emotions might be stronger, triggering their fears of what others might think of them as a parent. They may give him the candy bar in order to eliminate that trigger.

At first glance, it might seem like the problem is solved: the tears and screams have stopped, the child is enjoying the candy, and everyone feels better. However, if this Victim dynamic is successful, the child's mind forms a memory and will try this tactic again the next time he desires something. The child is learning that adopting the Victim identity and expressing Victim emotions will get him what he wants. From the child's perspective, playing the role of a Victim is a way to control these much bigger adults and get what he wants.

This is not an intellectual, rational kind of learning. It's not at all consciously manipulative. Children develop automatic patterns by taking actions and observing reactions in others. We all learned this even before we began to talk. Although later in life there is a social stigma associated with acting like a victim, we learned these behaviors because of their many advantages. As we grow older, there aren't as many benefits to playing the role of the Victim, but the pattern doesn't completely go away. We resort to it automatically at times, particularly when we are stressed, afraid, or emotionally hurt.

Besides triggering guilt in others in order to achieve a goal, the Victim also feels and expresses guilt, shame, and weakness in order to minimize punishment and abuse. Imagine being in school and goofing around or talking in class. The teacher wants us to be quiet, and if her first attempts to get our attention don't work, her voice goes up in volume, her tone changes, and she begins to get angry. At a certain point, it is not enough to just walk back to our seat and be quiet. If we still have a lighthearted demeanor, the angry teacher might continue with a scolding or reprimand, telling us to "Wipe that smile off your face." This is our clue that we need to change our emotional state in order to pacify her.

The message is that we have done something wrong, we are bad, and we must accept this admonishment so we don't do it again. The teacher will continue to escalate punishment until we acknowledge our error and express remorse. The teacher knows we got the message when we lower our head, have a sad look, express guilt, and slink back to our seat. When we adopt this Victim expression of being a bad person, the punishment and reprimands are more likely to stop.

By simple, often unconscious action and reaction, we learn to avoid further anger and deescalate punishment from others by assuming the identity of the Victim. We attempt to slow or stop people's reprimands and judgments towards us by adopting the Victim role. In this case the Victim's story is, "I've done something wrong. I'm a bad person who is unworthy. I feel guilt, sadness, shame, and embarrassment for what I have done." This story conveys the beliefs, character, and emotion of the Victim archetype. We might not have any thoughts or words in our head to this effect, but we embody this feeling and identity mentally, emotionally, and physically with our posture and facial expressions as well. The sooner we behave this way, the sooner the criticism and punishment might stop.

In childhood these responses were automatic and genuine. In later years, we unconsciously and automatically express them to influence the behavior of other people. An example of this is how some people insert the phrase "I'm sorry" into their conversations. Their unconscious beliefs have projected that other people will feel offended by them and will be critical of them. Their frequent apologies are meant as a defense against these imagined judgments, hoping to lessen the faultfinding and criticism people direct towards them.

Notice that I said we *influence* other people's behavior, not that we *control* it. People respond to the Victim's emotional reactions according to their own belief systems. The idea that the Victim controls another person's behavior is false. In the candy bar scenario, the parents' Judge

114

and Victim reactions of guilt, shame, and fear of what others might think of them determine their behavior. The child can only influence them by acting as a trigger to their archetype characters and belief system. If those archetypes aren't strong in the parent, the child's acting out may have no effect.

The developing belief system of the child doesn't take into account Mom's belief system. The child simply adjusts his actions to Mom's reaction, unaware that the facets of Mom's belief system are affecting her emotions. Thus, the child develops a false understanding of the world, one in which he assumes he can change other people's behavior by his actions.

Seeing the Victim Tree in the Collective Forest of Society

As children, we learned to do so much with our imagination. In one moment, we believed we were a cowboy; in the next, we were Superman! We played with action figures or dolls and imagined serving tea as a princess where everything we could see was our kingdom. We adopted the whole personality, voice inflection, emotion, and state of mind of each character. We were masters of imagination, building a virtual world in our mind, and then playing roles.

We did the same thing when we played the Victim character. We really believed we were being mistreated if we didn't get a cookie or something didn't go our way. We could even create feelings of emotional pain because we didn't get what we wanted. By creating these powerful experiences in our imagination, we firmly established our Victim perspective with its own belief bubble understanding of the world, and adopted this persona in response to certain triggers.

I am not saying that some of us didn't also experience actual abuse and mistreatment from our parents or other authority figures when we were children. There are many experiences of real abuse that create genuine responses of emotion. In fact, in households where there was real abuse, we assumed Victim paradigms even in calm moments because we remembered past fearful scenarios and imagined future ones. However, even in the best of homes, under the best of circumstances, in the absence of any actual mistreatment, we are still going to create some kind of Victim character within our belief system.

Victim roles are not limited to the realm of children or to beliefs in our minds; they are also perpetuated and reinforced within our society. Because so many people are conditioned with a Victim archetype in their belief system, it looks normal to most of us. Mind you, "normal" does not mean emotionally healthy. "Normal" means that it is a common archetype and socially accepted behavior. The fact that it's so widely accepted makes it more difficult to identify our own Victim beliefs as a conditioned layer or something that could usefully be changed.

When a public official or sports figure has committed an indiscretion in his marriage, the media cries out for an apology, despite this being a personal issue for his family. The public and media will continue the criticism until the person confesses his wrongdoing in some way and makes a public statement of apology. It is expected that he will have a public press conference and act contrite. Much like the teacher in the classroom, the media will comment on whether the person has demonstrated the appropriate amount of remorse, sorrow, and guilt over the offense. If he has, criticism will cease and everyone will move on to the next story. If the person was considered not to be remorseful enough, then the criticism from other people's Judge characters will continue. In this manner, we have a public example of how using the Victim role can change the media's stance and public opinion as well as their emotions.

Although the Victim is generally associated with powerlessness, people in positions of significant power often adopt it for their own benefit. A leader of a political group will stand at a podium and explain how they have been offended. They will point to what someone in an opposing group said and describe how they were hurt by that person or group's actions or words. They will request an apology and ask that the offending group revise their actions, statements, or position on an issue. At a fundamental emotional level this is similar to a child feeling offended when the parent doesn't give him what he wants, and acting out with accusations that the parent isn't a good parent. The only difference is that the politician playing the Victim role is speaking in the intelligent language of an adult, so they don't look blatantly childish in their reaction. The emotions and roles are the same, but articulate words mask the childish Victim dynamic.

How much of this is gamesmanship to court public opinion and how much is heartfelt can't be known. But seeing people portray Victim characters to influence others perpetuates our personal paradigms of the Victim perspective, providing an external confirmation of our own Victim thought processes and beliefs as being "normal." If nothing else, it reminds us how appealing it is to play the role of a Victim so we can get what the Victim wants. Separating ourselves from the Victim archetype is all the more difficult when people around us make it appear normal and justified. However commonplace Victim behavior is in society, it comes with an emotional price of unhappiness. We may get what the Victim character wants, but that doesn't mean we get what we genuinely want or express what will make us happy.

The Victim and the Inner Judge

Unfortunately, the Victim's automatic acceptance of a reprimand in order to reduce punishment doesn't work with our own inner Judge. The Victim accepts the Judge's criticism in the hope that it will let up once there is an adequate demonstration of guilt and shame. However, our Judge character continues to dole out its criticisms, unable to see that the Victim has already been punished and is remorseful. It punishes and criticizes over and over again, as if the Victim didn't hear it the fifteenth time. The Victim doesn't push back because in its belief bubble it still deserves punishment, or believes that if it takes enough, the abuse will eventually lessen. It doesn't. Trapped in their paradigm, the characters do the same things over and over while we genuinely hope for a different emotional outcome.

The Self-Help Enemy: "Don't Be a Victim"

A common mantra in the personal development world is "Don't be a victim." This suggestion is actually more often hurtful than helpful, accomplishing the opposite of what we intend. When we tell someone, "Don't be a victim," the words carry implied messages that cause the advice to backfire.

When we say to someone, "Don't be stupid," we are also saying, "I think you are being stupid"—at least that's how the receiver is likely to hear it. In the same way, telling someone "Don't be a victim" implies,

"You are being a victim, and you are wrong to do so." In all likelihood this is going to be interpreted as criticism. It's likely to perpetuate a Victim experience of rejection and reinforce that identity.

Perhaps the intended communication is more accurately, "The essence of what you are is beautiful. You are not a victim so there is no need to behave like one." However, this isn't what is said, heard, or reinforced.

When we tell ourselves, "Don't be a victim," the command is typically coming from our Judge perspective, carrying implied meanings, whether intentionally or not. Some of the implied meanings of this well-intended advice are:

1. You are a victim.
2. I judge you and reject you for being a victim.
3. You should be something other than what you are.
4. That other thing is what would be acceptable, and you are not that.
5. You are not acceptable the way you are.
6. I don't accept you or respect you.

Although we're trying to encourage ourselves or someone else "not to be a victim," through these implied meanings we are actually reinforcing all the beliefs, identity, and negative self-image of the Victim. This is how the road to emotional hell gets paved with good intentions.

At a more subtle level of triggers, notice the language used to start the sentence. "*Don't be . . .*" is the beginning of the kind of admonishment that dates back to our childhood. Those two words can trigger a shift into the Victim character perspective and emotion before the rest of the sentence has been spoken.

So what should we say, then, to someone who is acting like a victim, or even to ourselves? At this point it's more important to know what not to say. It may not be completely clear how to put out the Victim's emotional fire, but at least we can refrain from throwing gasoline on it. That in itself will help a great deal. Also consider that since most of the meaning in communication is conveyed through tone, attitude, and emotion, perhaps the words are not that important. Perhaps it is more important to put yourself in a kind and respectful emotional state before saying anything. Compassion, acceptance, respect, and love can be conveyed through silent gestures as well as through words.

Self-Help Spirals

When people first become aware of their Victim character, they often fumble through various attempts at change. This is the normal progression of improvement. We go down a path until we realize it's a dead end, and then we improve our methods by taking a different path.

One of the questions on these dead-end paths is, "Why do I still do this?" In reply, the mind thinks, "I must be getting something out of it." The assumption is that there is some advantage to continuing to play the Victim role. In the past, we might have benefited from playing that character role, as explained earlier. However, as adults, we rarely benefit from Victim beliefs and emotional patterns, and in the long term the results are detrimental.

Nevertheless, the Victim beliefs and emotional patterns may continue even though there is no benefit. They may rarely surface, but in times of stress, fearful circumstances, large life changes, or relationship challenges, we are likely to revert to old patterns that reside in our unconscious beliefs. We may not consciously understand that this is happening, but programmed in our unconscious mind, after we have attempted other strategies, is the assumption that if we adopt our Victim archetype role the pain we perceive will stop, and we will get what we want. This isn't reality, but it is the belief bubble the Victim character lives in.

Victim dynamics may also have been reinforced in adult years as a successful emotional strategy to get what we want. For example, if we demonstrate that we feel disappointed or sad, we might unconsciously expect our spouse's behavior to change. If we act upset or show that we feel betrayed, then people might jump into their Hero character to solve the problem we are reacting about.

Within the Victim belief bubble the assumption, "If I am acting/feeling like a victim, I must be getting something out of it," appears true. However, in reality *you might not be getting anything beneficial out of playing the Victim role. And what you do get comes with an emotional price of unhappiness.* Being aware of what you really feel, and what you really want, will allow you to ask for it in other ways.

The problem with looking for an answer to the question, "What am I getting out of this?" is that it assumes there is an advantage. It thereby keeps our mind looking for ways to justify and value the Victim's emotions and actions. Preoccupied with looking for an answer that justifies the Victim behavior, we avoid addressing a better question: "What is this Victim perspective and its accompanying beliefs costing me in terms of happiness?"

The Victim: Summary

Playing the Victim role was not without value in our past and was part of our natural emotional responses to real situations. It was also a learned and conditioned stance that helped us influence other people's behaviors, stop or lessen punishments, or get our way. It wasn't a bad thing in its day, and it is understandable why we learned the behavior and emotional routine, but to continue it as an adult has negative emotional consequences.

Moving Forward with Change

The purpose of spending so much time understanding the detail of these archetypes is not to fill your head with an abundance of intellectual knowledge. That by itself accomplishes nothing. The value in understanding these archetype characters is that you will be better able to spot them in your behavior, in your thinking, and in how you feel. By noticing these characters within your personality you take the step of becoming the observer. The major benefit of being the observer is that you are no longer seeing things from the perspective of these drama-making characters. That is the beginning of change. In this way you have begun to challenge your old beliefs, including basic beliefs about your identity, by shifting out of the perspective that sustained them.

As your perspective changes, so do your interpretations. Once you are outside the belief bubbles of these characters and are established in the observer perspective, questioning and dismantling negative thoughts becomes easier and faster.

Chapter 11

Faith: The Power That Holds Beliefs Together

Like many words, the word *faith* can have different uses. One is in a religious context, referring to a belief in something for which there is no evidence. This is too narrow an understanding for our purposes.

Faith is a form of personal power. It can create a feeling of trust, confidence, knowing, or certainty. When we turn the ignition key on our car we trust that it will start. When we board an airplane we are confident we will take off and land safely. When we mix the ingredients to bake a cake we are sure of what the final product will be before we see it. A person may have faith that their government is running smoothly, or that other people are honest in their interactions. Someone else will be certain that the government is corrupt, wasteful, or that people can't be trusted. A scientist can have faith in his methodology, formulas, and scientific principles. All of these are examples of faith creating a certain state of feeling and knowing that has nothing to do with religion.

We invest faith in some of our beliefs because we can point to evidence that supports them. For other beliefs, we have no evidence but rely on what others have told us or what we read in a book or online. We have faith in our beliefs about the future when our past experience leads our mind to project an assumption about how things are likely to be.

Faith is invisible, something we might rarely notice, yet it is a significant force infused in so much that we do. Whether used consciously or unconsciously, faith is a principal force behind the choices we make, actions we take, the ones we don't, and many of the emotions we feel.

Our beliefs influence our actions and emotions because of the power of our faith that holds those beliefs in place. If we desire to change our behaviors and how we feel, we need to be aware of how we handle this invisible force of personal faith.

The Power of Faith

I use the term *faith* in a general sense. As a form of personal power, faith is a force, a life energy that we command. It is intangible, like an emotion, so it can't be measured, yet we can observe its impact in ourselves and in others.

While we tend to think of confident people as having faith in themselves, the force of faith can be equally strong when it comes to self-doubt and fears: a person with anxiety has a powerful investment of faith in his fear-based beliefs, and a shy person has faith in the idea that she is socially awkward. We can also invest our faith in any of the myriad thoughts that pass through our head during the day, and we often do, even if those thoughts are not true. The cumulative effect of this force of faith has a profound impact on our emotions and behavior.

At times you can perceive how much a person's words are backed by a force of faith. When someone says something with strong conviction, we sense the power behind their words. This is true whether the person speaking is Martin Luther King or Adolf Hitler. Their faith gives power to their voice and words, regardless of whether they are being truthful or lying, whether they are kind or hateful. The power of faith is also evident in your voice in varying amounts when you speak.

—⁓—

***Words and ideas are made powerful by
how much faith people invest in them.***

—⁓—

The Link Between Faith and Beliefs

A belief is a conceptual idea into which we invest faith. When we infuse a conceptual idea with the energy of faith, we give it life and power, and it becomes an active force in our mind. It is too simple to say that words or ideas are powerful. Words and ideas are made powerful by how much faith people invest in them. We can invest faith when we express our own ideas and thoughts, and we can also invest faith in the ideas of others when we accept them as true.

Conceptual Idea + Faith = Belief

The moment you accept an idea as true, the force of faith incorporates that concept into your belief bubble. Faith is like a glue that holds abstract concepts and images in place. The amount of faith you invest determines how powerful the idea becomes and how dominant a place it occupies in your belief bubble.

Not all ideas stick and become part of your belief bubble. For an idea to stick as a belief, you must agree with it. Picture someone coming to your door and offering you a file of papers with ideas to keep and live by; you can choose to accept it or not. People have been offering you ideas via their opinions, books, and movies continually since you were young, but if you don't agree to keep them, it won't become a belief for you.

You forget or ignore many beliefs moments after you accept them as true. They might be added to over time, making them stronger. Sometimes this can go on for years before you are even aware the beliefs are there. They remain stored in the unconscious part of your belief system, often too insignificant to notice, or your attention is on other things in your life. Even though you're not consciously aware of them, these beliefs can affect your emotions, impulses, automatic behaviors, and your thoughts and interpretations of things. You may only become aware of these beliefs when they rise to the surface emotionally or behaviorally, in disruptive ways, or when you go looking for them.

This mechanism of accepting ideas is happening as you read this material. The ideas that make sense to you, the ones you understand, "get," or agree with, are all being digested into your world of beliefs and gaining access to the energy of your faith. As thoughts pass through your mind during the day, and you unconsciously accept them, they are getting little bits of your personal power and growing into beliefs.

When an opinion becomes part of your belief bubble, it becomes part of your paradigm of how the world works. You view the world through that belief bubble and you assume that you are seeing reality. You can lose awareness that it is just a construct of the inner belief bubble you use to describe and interpret outer reality. You are attached to your paradigm and you keep it alive in your mind with your faith. (*Note:* While ideas and beliefs are not technically living in an organic sense, using the model of them being "alive" and having a "life of their own" is useful to understand the dynamics of belief systems.)

Growing ideas in your mind is like planting seeds in a garden. If you water a seed, it sprouts, develops roots, and secures itself in the soil. When you accept an idea as true, you are allowing that seed into the soil of your mind. If you put faith in an idea, it is like giving it the water and nutrients it needs to grow and become a belief. Often, once a belief is rooted in your mind, it can continue to draw on your personal power and grow over years, without your conscious awareness. As the belief grows it can intertwine with other beliefs and create a system.

We saw how this happens with the archetype characters. The beliefs of the Judge need the Victim character to respond and accept the criticism. The Victim then feels unworthy. The Hero and Pleaser beliefs then respond to the Victim's unworthiness with their efforts to prove their worth or get someone to approve of them. The abuse the Victim feels is needed to launch and justify the anger of the Villain.

Later, when you identify a belief and decide that you no longer believe that idea or opinion, you stop investing faith in it. At that point you stop feeding the conceptual idea the necessary nutrients for it to survive. But plants don't necessarily die the day you stop watering them. They may wither slowly over a period of days or weeks. The same is true of your beliefs. Many will continue to be alive for a while after you stop investing any faith in them. Changing beliefs this way is a slow process, but is still effective. If you were to uproot the plant/belief instead, it would shrivel and die much faster. Both approaches are viable and have their place.

Most of our beliefs lie below the conscious level. We have been investing faith in various ideas, self-images, and opinions since we were very young. We don't remember most of what we've invested our faith in, but it can remain alive in our mind for years, operating in our subconscious, sometimes dormant and sometimes active without our awareness. We can call these beliefs part of our unconscious or subconscious mind.

Unconscious beliefs are silent and hidden below what we consciously think and say. The thoughts we have and the words that come automatically out of our mouth can be clues to our unconscious beliefs. By paying attention and reflecting on your thoughts, emotions, and actions, you can gain insights into these hidden beliefs. The purpose of a belief inventory is to bring these subconscious beliefs into your conscious awareness where they can be changed and you can recover the personal power that was stored in them.

Faith Invisibly Drives Our Actions and Emotions

When you walk out to your car in the morning, you trust it will be in your driveway or garage where you left it. Beneath that feeling of trust is the unspoken idea, "My car will be where I left it." You have faith in this assumption, which creates a feeling of trust. No conscious thought is involved in this process—it is just assumed. This is an example of a belief existing without any thoughts or words.

Once you're on the road, oncoming cars may be speeding past only a few feet away, but you feel safe because you have faith in ideas like "Driving is safe," "I'm a good driver," and "Other drivers follow the rules." These are not conscious thoughts either, but rather are operating at a silent assumed level. Because you have years of safe experiences as evidence, you have invested a lot of faith in these beliefs. After a while the paradigm is so ingrained, you trust this idea of safety completely and don't even think otherwise. Or perhaps you just grew up with everyone around you driving safely, so it seemed natural from the beginning that there's nothing to fear on the highway. Your feeling of trust is created and sustained by the faith you've invested in these assumptions over the years. By contrast, people who are afraid of driving have, for whatever reasons, perhaps from having experienced an accident, invested their faith in fear-based beliefs.

If we have years of experience of safe car travel, then our external reality of safe car travel matches up with our internal beliefs about it. We might therefore go our whole life and never notice that we have faith invested in ideas about the safety of car travel.

The same is true of our faith and beliefs about money, relationships, food, our body, love, politics, the environment, scientific theories, our opinions, and our judgments about ourselves and others. We use the power of our faith every day without noticing how we use it. Just about everything we do or don't do depends on the faith we've invested in a belief related to that action.

You can comfortably get on an airplane because you have faith in the belief that it is safe. If you are afraid to fly and don't get on an airplane, it is because you have faith in the belief that it is dangerous. The intensity of emotion is proportional to how much faith is placed in those beliefs. (Feeling completely safe and relaxed may not be an intense emotion but it is still indicative of faith.)

A belief doesn't have to be true in order for us to have faith in it and make it emotionally powerful. A person can believe strongly in the likelihood of a plane crash and therefore feel more comfortable driving, even though flying is statistically far safer than driving a car. Our emotions are often produced based on the belief bubble of the mind rather than the outer, factual reality.

The mind can be a spontaneous generator of thoughts, which tend to be projected like stories. One thought leads to another, to another, and then to another, until the mind builds a whole story, including a conclusion. People without awareness of what they're doing will invest faith in the stories their mind proposes even if those stories are not true. If they invest faith in the conclusion their mind projects, they will create an emotional experience based on something that hasn't happened. For example, if someone assumes that their partner might cheat on them, their mind can weave thoughts about it all day. Their story will include branches about how it will happen and with whom, how they will feel emotionally, and what they will do about it to protect themselves. They build this story with a belief in themselves as a Victim who is hurt, a Villain who will get angry, or a Fixer who will save the relationship. Each character and branch of the story gets an infusion of personal power when it plays in the mind and is accepted as real. The intensity of emotion indicates how much faith we have in the story, not whether the story is true or not.

When we are not conscious that our mind is projecting a story, we fall into these illusions and perceive the projection as "reality." The result is an emotional experience triggered by a projected image or thought. Investing the power of our faith in our mind's imagined scenarios is one of the ways we create emotions.

—◠◠—

Just about everything we do or don't do depends on the faith we've invested in a belief related to that action.

—◠◠—

Faith: A Force in Society

Faith is in common usage throughout our day in all sorts of ways. People use faith when they exchange money. A dollar, euro, or peso has value because people have faith in the idea that it does. People have faith that dollars can be traded for food, gas, clothing, services, and other things of intrinsic value. Without that faith, they would not have trust in the transaction.

When people no longer have faith in a bank, they take their money out and the bank collapses. When enough people lose faith in a currency, there is a run on the bank as they try to convert their money into another currency they have faith in. The result is that the value of the currency and the monetary system in the country collapses. A country's currency or a bank is only as strong as the collective force of faith people put into it. Usually this force of faith isn't noticed until a doubt or fear happens to shake it.

Faith is the power or force behind the price of a stock. The direction of one's faith might shift because of real fact or false perception, but either way, faith is the force behind a person's feeling of confidence in a stock, or their lack of it. When a large group of investors modify the degree of faith they have in a stock, actions of buying and selling ensue and the stock's price changes. We could say that a stock price is a real-world result of a collectively projected belief. The real-world stock price shifts to match people's collective belief bubble price.

It is important to see the conceptual idea, such as a stock's price, as separate from the force of faith that affects it. If you are aware that *faith is the actual force* behind a stock's price, you have a better insight into bubbles. Bubbles in the stock market are a matter of exuberant faith invested into an *idea* of value, and are not a matter of *actual* or intrinsic value. If you accept the price of a stock as its real value, with no awareness of how the force of faith creates value, you might conclude that the stock's price represents something real. If you are aware of how people use and misuse the power of faith, you can see that lots of faith can hold up a stock price, even when there is nothing real to support it. The result is a collective belief bubble that often ends in collapse.

These are just a few of many possible examples that show how often we exercise our power of faith in very tangible and practical ways. In this book we are more interested in how faith affects our emotions, behaviors, and relationships. I just use these examples of stocks, banks, currency, and where you parked your car to heighten awareness of this significant force. Faith is active in our personal and community relationships as well. It is part of the equation of who we trust, how we feel, what stories and thoughts affect us, as well as what expectations we have of other people and of ourselves.

Faith in Yourself

We all have faith in certain abilities we've acquired, such as reading, balancing our checkbook, fixing a leaky faucet, or tying our shoes. With practice and experience, we develop faith in our ability to handle more complex tasks, like doing a skateboard trick, writing a computer program, performing surgery, hitting a golf shot, or playing a musical instrument. Difficult or complex skills are learned with practice. Just as we develop our abilities in steps, over time, our faith in our beliefs about our abilities is built in steps as well.

In the beginning, we don't feel confident about anything we attempt, except maybe a confidence that we can learn something. We assume we will get it with practice. Young kids will spend hours or weeks learning a skateboard trick. They do this because they have faith that they will be able to master it. They also don't have faith in the idea that they won't succeed. If there is some fear and doubt, but it is small, they'll continue taking action to practice and learn, although not as efficiently. They may not be aware that this force of faith is behind their actions, but it is still there.

However, someone who has an illness or an accident and has to *relearn* to walk might struggle with various stories in their mind. A person might be plagued with doubt and fears of never walking again. These doubts and fears are thoughts that have hooked their attention. When strengthened by an investment of faith, these thoughts become part of their belief bubble, if they allow it or are unaware of it.

Cycles of self-fulfilling prophecy are easily set in motion in this way. If we believe we will walk again, or learn a skateboard trick, we practice, and by practicing we get better. If we practice and work at something, we are more likely to get positive results as evidence. That evidence allows us to invest faith in the stories of our successes and feel more confident. This feeling of confidence inspires us to try harder and practice more. It also helps us be skeptical of stories of fear, doubt, and failure. Faith begets action, action begets results, results create evidence, and evidence inspires us to invest more faith and take more action.

If we've experienced failures, we might also invest our personal power in negative stories. Those negative stories project a future of failure. If we believe this projection, we will envision our actions as producing failure and may decide not to take action.

For example, if a student is told he is lousy at math, or just thinks that about himself, he can create that belief. Along with it come implied beliefs such as "Math is a natural talent—a person has it or doesn't, and working at it won't create a different result." He is then less likely to make efforts or practice as much, and as a result he doesn't get better. When he gets a C or D on a test, he accepts it as appropriate and it reinforces his original beliefs. More faith now goes into comparing himself to others and feeling that he is not good enough.

Since he can imagine his future-self character in a belief bubble of failure, he feels as if "he" is failing and will fail. He then decides it's a waste of time and effort to try to study. He stops taking action altogether, so there are no results of success. His lack of real effort results in a failing grade, which "proves" that he's lousy at math. His faith is reinforced in the story and in the failure character identity.

A person doesn't start out being bad at math. It is through faith in the stories they tell themselves that they create the self-fulfilling prophecy of being bad at math. Part of the problem is the associated belief that certain kinds of intelligence or talents are fixed instead of skills that can be improved with practice. Research[2] has shown that people who believed math was a skill that could be learned and improved with hard work did better. Those who believed they were "born that way" tended to stay in that limited fixed identity and performance.

This is one way our belief system shapes the external reality to match it. We can then point to that external reality, whether of failure or success, as evidence proving that our mental model of beliefs and identity was "true."

Whether our experience is of success or of failure, our faith is invested in something for which we have evidence, even if we created the evidence through our own actions or inaction. The direction in which you invest the most faith will spur you towards actions congruent with your belief. Those actions will then validate your faith, and faith will spur you to further action. In this way, faith is part of a cycle where you turn your inner-world beliefs into a self-fulfilling external reality.

—⟡—

Faith begets action, action begets results, results create evidence, and evidence inspires us to invest more faith and take more action.

—⟡—

Congruity and Disparity Between Faith and Experience

Having faith in yourself and your skills is not enough to be good at something. If you are a pilot, you have taken lessons and practiced flying. You have developed your abilities, and over time also invested faith

---

2 Many studies have been done; for an overview, read Miles Kimball and Noah Smith, "The Myth of 'I'm Bad at Math,'" *The Atlantic*, October 28, 2013, http://www.theatlantic.com/education/archive/2013/10/the-myth-of-im-bad-at-math/280914/.

in your ability to fly an airplane. With enough practice and investment your faith is so strong that you feel confident as a pilot. When your faith is steadfast in one area like this, you can act without doubt.

This kind of faith in oneself and one's ability is not a matter of believing in something that has no evidence. Your faith in your ability exists because you created the real-world evidence for it multiple times. This doesn't mean that you are arrogant or cocky. A confident pilot can still be vigilant about weather, fuel, and mechanical problems that might occur. They can also be aware that there are different aspects of flying that they are not comfortable doing. An experienced airline pilot doesn't necessarily have faith in their ability when it comes to doing acrobatics in a stunt plane.

However, our skill and our confidence are not always congruent, because of the different beliefs into which we have invested our faith. A person can develop an ability to an advanced degree and yet lack faith in that ability. We can be capable and accomplished, but not confident. One of my clients, Angela, had enjoyed singing for years. She traveled and sang in groups from an early age, and enjoyed singing for fun well into her forties. Yet, despite singing on stage for decades, always enjoying it and never having a bad experience, Angela would get terrible stage fright before each performance.

If it was a big show, her anxiety would begin a day or two before. Scenarios ran through her mind: forgetting her lines, her voice cracking, tripping on the stage, and so on. The fact that none of these things had ever happened did not prevent her mind from projecting the images, or prevent her from investing faith in those mental pictures. Emotionally, the result was nauseating fear from the perspective of a Future-Victim character convinced of impending failure.

In spite of those feelings, Angela would will herself onto the stage and start singing. It would only take Angela two lines of singing to step out of the Victim perspective. She would move into the present moment and the enjoyment of singing, and her fear of the projected scenarios would dissipate. The belief bubble then remained dormant until the next show.

Angela obviously had lots of faith in her ability, as evidenced by continually taking action to get up on stage. However, even though she had faith in one set of beliefs, backed by solid evidence of experience, she could hold completely opposing beliefs too. By themselves, thirty years of positive experiences hadn't been enough to divest Angela's faith from the negative scenarios that her mind projected. Real-world experience doesn't necessarily equate to changing one's internal beliefs. More specific attention to those beliefs is required, with the intent to recover the faith that's been holding those beliefs together.

You can also have beliefs in the opposite direction, creating confidence disproportionate with your abilities. This kind of arrogance comes from a character that can cause a lot of self-sabotaging damage. It can be somewhat entertaining, like when we're at the karaoke bar and someone believes they have a great voice but then proceeds to spoil a song. However, for the doctor who doesn't refer his patients to a specialist when needed, or the pilot who quickly dismisses the concerns of the copilot, the consequences of arrogance are much more serious. A more common example of a sabotaging belief is when we make an investment in a stock or real estate, completely confident of it being an easy success. After suffering a financial loss, we realize the feeling of confidence was a bubble that we and perhaps others were in.

Faith Empowers Our Archetype Characters

As we have seen in earlier chapters, the actions you take and the emotions you feel begin with the character perspective you adopt. That perspective determines what interpretations you invest your faith in. When you are in a character perspective, the faith you invest goes into its belief bubble. That bubble is the only world you can see, and it appears real from that perspective. To remove your faith from that belief bubble, you have to shift your perspective outside the bubble.

An event does not determine how you feel or what it means to you. Two people can have the same experience of hardship and failure but invest their faith in opposite interpretations about what it means. One person decides they are a failure and that they shouldn't have tried because now they look like a fool. The second interprets that they learned a lot about what didn't work and that they'll have a much better chance for success in their next attempt. Both are using the energy of faith, but they are empowering different beliefs depending on their character perspective.

The insecure and fearful character perspective, with a poorer self-image, will project failure in the future of their world. From this perspective their belief bubble will filter out and ignore possible actions that would result in successful outcomes. As a result, the person will take fewer actions towards achieving changes in their life.

The person who puts their attention on what they learned from the outcome and sees it as a beneficial growth experience leading to future success will build a success mindset. Looking at the world from a character of a "Student of Life's Experiences" focused on growth and learning, they are more likely to perceive possibilities that could work out or that are worth trying. They will put faith in the idea that things are worth trying even if they don't always work out as that person intended. Their feeling of confidence and willingness to take action will result in more attempts and therefore a greater chance of accomplishments. Their focus is on growing and getting better, which is done through trial and error. In contrast, the focus of the Judge and Victim is concerned with measuring oneself according to concepts of failure or success.

Each of these individuals is investing the power of their faith in a different version of their self-image and reinforcing a different character perspective. Each investment of faith produces different beliefs and emotions. One person will generate fear, insecurity, and hopelessness, and the other will become more focused, committed, and confident. Each person's future actions will tend to align with their stronger beliefs and their dominant character perspective. As we saw earlier, their faith and beliefs tend to become a self-fulfilling prophecy for actions and future results.

Misuse of Power: Victim Uses of Faith

Each day, you wake up rested and have a supply of personal power or energy to spend. If you spend your personal power by investing it into fear-based and false beliefs, you won't have much left for being happy.

Growing up, we didn't learn to pay attention to how we use our personal power of faith. As adults, we continue to be unaware of the silent and profound force that we expend every day in our thoughts and imagination. Without awareness, the power of faith seeps into our thoughts, opinions, and judgments, and is wasted like money falling out of our wallet. As a result, we end up feeling weak and powerless, but without knowing why.

Can you imagine the number of judgments and opinions that you have accepted as true? Each bit of faith that you put into a thought about yourself, someone else, or the world is empowering a conceptual idea in your head, often at your own expense.

If your boss makes a critical comment or doesn't acknowledge your work, your mind might associate that with failure and losing, translating it as an indication that you are a poor performer, a failure, or worthless. Your faith goes into these conclusions or beliefs, and the result is that you feel worthless. Or your emotions may arise from faith that was invested in those beliefs years earlier—the boss's comment or lack of acknowledgment may just be a trigger for a belief lying dormant in your mind.

Either way, the comment launches your perspective into a belief bubble where you are viewing the world as a Victim character. Your attention goes to specific interpretations about what your boss did and didn't say or do. Your belief bubble causes you to filter out all previous accomplishments. Your Victim character has control over your attention and fixes it on this one moment out of the day or year and discounts all other successes and accomplishments. The Victim character snaps into a belief bubble world and lines up all sorts of evidence and interpretations to support its perspective.

Sometimes just thinking a thought like "They must not like my work" can be enough to activate a belief bubble and put you in a mindset to feel emotionally worthless. A successful actor who gets passed over for a part can feel the emotional reaction of failure. A beautiful model who gets turned down for a project can feel ugly simply because of what she believes about herself. The external event of getting turned down has no inherent power or emotion. It is our belief system that has associated personal worth to that event. These beliefs then activate other unconscious beliefs and self-images of unworthiness.

Misuse of Power: Judgmental Uses of Faith

Consider the New Year's resolution a person makes to exercise regularly. For a while, they go to the gym every day. Eventually they have the thought not to exercise one day. They accept that thought as a good idea, which infuses it with some amount of faith and creates a belief in their mind. Even if they don't act on it that day, a seed has been planted. Another day, they are running late and have the thought to skip exercising. Again, they accept it as a good idea. That seed grows and builds on their previous small belief that it's okay not to stick with the resolution. In these small ways, they accept the little thoughts that contradict their New Year's resolution, investing more and more of their faith in the belief that it would be okay not to exercise.

Eventually, their "not exercising" belief is stronger than their New Year's resolution. The scales tip and their actions change in the direction of their faith. They still exercise but less often because their faith is split into two opposing beliefs. When they realize how much they're violating their original commitment, their Judge character introduces thoughts that they are a failure, undisciplined, or weak-willed. If they accept these thoughts as true, which is likely if they view the situation from a Victim perspective, then they will use their personal power to build another belief that aligns with the Judge's accusations.

Although the person may believe they are weak, undisciplined, or a failure, they are actually very strong. They have an incredible amount of personal power—however, they are using it to justify not exercising, and then investing more faith in the Judge and Victim criticisms about not exercising. You might say this person is also disciplined. It takes a lot of practice to continually adopt these same points of view and invest in the same kind of imaginary reality until it becomes habitual. While their habit of talking themselves out of exercise or into self-judgments may not be healthy, it is not weak. It is an example of a very powerful belief system that uses a lot of personal power. A weak person could not create such a well-fortified belief system. In this case it is not a question of being powerless, but rather of what their personal power is being used for. As you become skeptical of your thoughts and beliefs, you begin to recover control over your personal power.

Practice: Dig Through Layers of Emotions to Find the Core Beliefs

The process of finding and identifying your beliefs can sometimes be like solving a mystery. This is particularly true of the deeper core beliefs. You begin with a study of your thoughts and the words that come out of your mouth. Then you investigate the meanings of these thoughts and the assumptions that support them. A couple layers of assumptions later you find the core belief. The faith you have invested in the hidden assumptions supporting a thought is often more powerful than the thought or spoken idea itself. It is these hidden beliefs that are usually at the root of our emotional reactions and feelings.

Let's look at an example of finding hidden beliefs. Ed was feeling frustrated and even angry with his adult son Jason. His son was twenty-eight and gainfully employed, but Ed was alarmed at how he spent his money. The cars had to be new. There were ATVs in Jason's garage and he was considering buying a boat. When asked, Ed went on a long rant about his son being irresponsible and foolish. To back up his point, he brought up lots of his own business experience of being careful with money. He felt very righteous and justified in his judgments of Jason. But his thoughts about how to manage money were just the surface layer of the story.

When asked further about what he felt emotionally, Ed eventually got around to a deeper layer: his fear that Jason wouldn't be able to take care of himself, would go bankrupt, and would end up back at home. These fears hadn't previously been conscious or immediately apparent to Ed. They were discovered only when he was asked to share all the different emotions he was feeling.

After exploring his fears for a while, Ed investigated how he would feel emotionally if what he feared actually happened. At that point a third layer, one of self-judgment, came out when Ed realized he judged himself as a failure as a father for raising a son who was so financially careless. Every time Jason spent foolishly, Ed was unconsciously blaming himself for failing as a parent. Ed's attention was on his son's spending, but his deep emotions had to do with his own beliefs of failure. This was part of Ed's core belief of not being good enough. In order to save himself from the guilt, shame, and punishment in his belief system, Ed's

Fixer character was desperately trying to change his son's behavior. This caused great conflict between Ed and Jason.

Ed's thoughts and beliefs about Jason's spending may have been helpful, wise, and congruent with reality. That's not what was causing a problem. The emotional problem that Ed was experiencing resided in his unconscious beliefs about his own self-image and his judgment of himself as a father. As Ed became more skeptical of these self-judgments, his investment of faith began to lessen. The emotional reactions, judgments, and impulses to control his son's behavior had less influence over him.

An effective way to identify the layers of beliefs that give rise to our emotional reactions and sabotaging behavior is to do a *belief inventory*. In a belief inventory we scrutinize all the conceptual ideas in which we have invested faith. By doing this from an observer perspective we can see these beliefs as false and begin to recover our personal power of faith from them. As we reclaim our faith from these beliefs, they lose their power and we recover it, which in turn gives us greater strength with which to make more changes.

Belief Inventory: An Example

As mentioned in earlier chapters, we can have multiple emotions about the same event because we can adopt multiple character perspectives and interpretations and have faith in each one. The following example shows how we can make an inventory of multiple character perspectives and belief bubbles about the same event. By thin-slicing the layers of our false beliefs, we can sort out the truth and illusions in our mind.

Richard's girlfriend recently broke up with him after they'd been together for a year. Now Richard is going through a lot of emotions and there are numerous and conflicting stories running through his head. In one moment he is sad and feels rejected; the next he is angry and wants to hurt her. However, the next day he misses her and thinks of trying to win her back. He quickly dismisses that story with a judgment that she didn't really appreciate him anyway and that he deserves better than her. He fills himself with pride and tells himself he wouldn't take her back if she begged. He convinces himself he is better than her and can find a better partner. Sometimes Richard can go through all these different perspectives and emotions in a few minutes.

Each of Richard's emotions is understandable by itself. But he is being moved from one belief bubble of emotional reaction to another, and they don't make sense when compared side by side. In one moment he feels rejected and wants her back, and in the next he is angry at her and considers her beneath him. If we inventory the archetype characters and their respective belief bubble stories, it will look something like this:

Archetype Perspective	Story/Belief	Associated Emotions
Victim	I'm sad at what I've lost.	Sad.
Victim	I feel rejected because she no longer wants me.	Unworthy.
Victim	I miss her. I am alone. Associated belief: I am lonely. Nobody wants me.	Lonely. Worthless.
Hero/Fixer (with a compensating strategy to shift his emotions)	I want to win her back. That will make me feel better. Multiple thoughts of strategy on what he can do to get her attention. Imagines her wanting him back.	Hopeful: This will change how she feels about him. Feeling accepted, loved, wanted.

Pleaser (alternate compensating strategy to shift emotions)	I'll remake myself into what she would want.	Hopeful but feeling false and inauthentic.
Victim	Why should I remake myself for her? She is the one who dumped me.	Hurt, rejected.
Judge	She hurt me. She is a bad person.	Righteous, authoritative, empowered.
Enforcer/Villain	She deserves to be punished for the way she hurt me.	Angry.
Judge	She is a bad person. By comparison I am a better person than her.	Righteous, proud.
Entitled Princess	I'm much better than her. I deserve to be with someone better than her.	Feeling worthy, positive, better than her.

As a result of all the different perspectives, conflicting stories, and emotions, Richard is confused about what to do and what to believe. All these emotions, driven by the faith he's invested in these characters from long ago, are powerful and drive his attention.

Every time Richard considers an idea from its archetype character perspective it seems to make sense. That's because each belief creates an emotion and the emotion is incorrectly being used to determine what "feels true." The Victim feels rejected and unworthy within its belief bubble of self-rejection. At the same time the Princess feels entitled from within her belief bubble. Each character's story appears true from its own perspective, while the others appear false. And now they're all chiming in with their own stories of what happened, why it happened, and what he should do about it. Only by stepping outside these characters and into an observer perspective will Richard be able to see them side by side and recognize the contradictory and false nature of his belief system.

With the awareness gained from an observer perspective, we can begin to see a more fundamental problem. Richard's mind goes through different cycles of emotions because he doesn't have control over his attention or his perspective. He has also invested faith in the beliefs underlying these characters for many years. The power of his faith is what pulls him into these perspectives and belief bubbles. The problem is not that Richard is weak or powerless. In fact, he is quite powerful. The problem is that he has used his personal power over years in the form of faith to build these belief structures and characters in his mind, even if he hasn't been aware of what he was doing.

Even when Richard has enough awareness to see what his mind is doing, it doesn't mean that he has the personal power and control to immediately stop it. In the beginning it might take all his power just to remain halfway in the observer mode. In the early stages of gaining control of your attention from your belief system, sometimes this is the best you can do that day. While you are feeling all the emotions arising from these beliefs it takes all your personal power not to believe the thoughts and beliefs they arise from. Over time, as you practice being the observer, it gets easier until controlling your attention and perspective isn't a challenge anymore. Like any skill, developing this one will take time and practice. As you practice you will see results, which will help you build faith that you can do it. As you have more faith that you can develop this skill, you will practice more. The other option is to put your faith in a fear-and-doubt story about your chances of success, which will certainly hamper your progress.

Awareness of How and When You Misuse Faith

Having an intellectual understanding of the impact of faith isn't enough to shift one's investment, but it's a start. The way out of all the emotional drama begins with awareness. Becoming aware of how you expend your faith in each small moment gives you the opportunity to refrain from spending it and thereby retain more personal power. When you are aware, you have a chance to refuse to accept sabotaging thoughts as true. You are vigilant and mindful of the passing thoughts and dismiss them as false instead of accepting them as valid. When you are aware, the thoughts that tempt you to react emotionally or to violate a personal commitment have little power over your perspective, attention, faith, and therefore emotional state.

By "aware," I mean that you perceive those thoughts from an observer perspective and can be skeptical of them. You notice them as they arise in your mind and you don't accept them as true. Through this awareness you will be able to conserve your faith. Then you will have it available to invest in what you really want to do. To develop this observer perspective and awareness it will help to write these thoughts out and attribute them to your characters. It is much easier to be skeptical of your thoughts when they are on a page in front of you.

Conflicts of Faith Within Relationships

Often we get into conflicts with others over a difference of ideas. We argue and try to get the other party to change their mind and see it our way. This is what Ed, the father, was doing with his grown son Jason. At a surface level it might seem like an easy thing to move around some concepts in another person's mind. After all, conceptual ideas don't weigh much, so they should move pretty easily—unless, of course, you realize the other person's ideas are anchored with faith.

Getting someone else to change their mind means that they have to withdraw their investment of faith in their beliefs and perhaps even invest it in your proposal. This is a much more involved project than changing clothes or a light bulb. So before challenging someone to change their thoughts, beliefs, or behaviors, consider that you are really attempting to make changes in their investment of faith. Making changes in your own beliefs and behaviors requires a similar calibration in expectations. Once you have spent some time going through the steps of changing your point of view, exiting your own belief bubbles, and suspending faith in them, you will have more respect for someone else undergoing the process.

Chapter 12

Beliefs Are Not What You Think

We can break down and categorize what goes on in the mind in many different ways. There is no "right" or "wrong" way to map this inner world. However, there are methods of understanding that are useful and helpful while others will create confusion. For purposes of this discussion, let's categorize thinking into two different modalities. The first is the conscious, purposeful use of language in our mind, which we call *thinking*. The second is the automatic rambling of thoughts that pass through the mind, often unintended, sometimes with our awareness and sometimes without; we call this the *internal dialog*.

Thinking Versus Internal Dialog

We learned to think at the same time that we learned to use language. We learned to name and explain things, imagine pictures, use or create mental models, and even process complex concepts.

Speech allows us to form symbols of words in a way that they can be understood by the listener. We can also communicate within our own mind as we think through an issue or invent a fictional story plot.

Thinking is typically done with the symbols of words, yet our mind can think in other ways as well. We can communicate with a mathematical system of symbols. Sheet music is written in symbols that our mind converts to sounds, or thoughts of sounds. You are using thinking as you read this page and interpret these symbols to mean something to you. All of these kinds of thinking have their own protocols, learned through conscious repetition. We learned to form words, write, and speak by consciously controlling our attention. What is first learned through conscious use of attention and thinking in a certain way, with repetition becomes automated and unconscious.

Not all thinking is a conscious act. When we're driving a car and the stoplight changes colors, our feet automatically shift position in response. We don't have to tell ourselves to move our foot to the pedal. When we learned to drive we had to consciously think about what to do when the light changed. With repetition this thought process has become automated and is more like an unconscious response. This is an example of unconscious thought happening automatically, in this case without words.

The mind can also have an automated thought process on its own that uses words. When we argue or debate, our thoughts can move so fast we can't keep up with them, and words can come out of our mouth without thinking. They are an automated response. The same can happen in a less heated conversation. The impulse to express something happens and we begin to speak. We might only be consciously thinking a few words ahead of what we are saying, even though the feeling of what we want to say is fully formed. We will begin speaking a sentence without consciously knowing how we will end it. Based on hours of repetition and practice the mind automatically forms the words and phrases in sensible order. When thoughts run through the mind without our conscious guidance, we call it the internal dialog. Sometimes we are aware of our internal dialog, but often we are not.

The internal dialog is what you notice when you sit down to meditate and intend to quiet your mind. It spins in your head late at night during stressful times when you are trying unsuccessfully to sleep. In these two scenarios the internal dialog is most noticeably not under your conscious control the way thinking is. However, the internal dialog is often there throughout our day. Perhaps we are driving, and we pull into our destination and realize that our mind has been wandering in internal conversations for the past twenty minutes. Only when we stop the car do we realize that we didn't consciously think about driving it. In this case we were completely absorbed in the internal dialog, even if we weren't aware at the time or don't remember what it was.

It can be a little disconcerting for people to realize that they are not in control of their thoughts—that thoughts arise from something other than their conscious direction. In truth, as we become adults, our mind takes on a life of its own.

You can check this for yourself by recalling a time in the recent past when you were stressed and your mind was anxiously running stories and projecting conversations. Could you stop it? Could you sustain a quiet mind? Test your theory of control now. Check your watch, or set a stopwatch if you have one. Focus on a blank part of this page with the intent to keep your mind quiet for a period of time. Or just close your eyes and focus on your breath, so that your mind doesn't think. See how much time passes before you begin to hear an internal dialog. How many minutes or seconds can you keep your mind from "thinking" on its own? If you have not practiced skills for quieting your mind this will likely be measured in seconds.

Internal dialog can also take the form of an imaginary conversation with someone we're going to meet, or a replay of an encounter we've already had. The mind even supplies words and thoughts for the other person. The person we're "conversing with" in our imagination is not really the other person but a construct of our mind; their words are filled in by a projection of what our belief system assumes for them. Often, if we have imagined a conversation before the real conversation takes place, we discover that the real one doesn't go at all the way we imagined.

The internal dialog is not the same as conscious thought. It occurs by a means other than our conscious intent, much in the same way a song might be stuck playing in our head. So what projects these thoughts into our mind if we are not consciously doing it? Our belief system does. The internal dialog rises up from our subconscious belief system. There are exceptions, but for the most part the internal dialog becomes quiet and peaceful as we identify and dissolve our personal fear-based beliefs.

Beliefs Are Different from Thoughts

Using spoken or written words, we communicate what these symbols invoke, and perhaps even invoke something similar in the imagination of others. Because so many people use the same language system, we don't perceive the word symbols as abstract and arbitrary—they appear to be inherently meaningful and real. However, when we read or hear a foreign language we are more likely to notice that the word symbols are separate from their meaning. *Sun, sol, taeyang, Sonne, solen, araw,* and *soleil* are a few of the many symbols used by people around the world to convey the same meaning—the star nearest our planet. The symbols made of these letters and sounds are vastly different from that bright heat source moving across the sky. The meaning of a word or phrase resides in the *belief* that people have learned to associate with that symbol.

When we have something to communicate, we start with the meaning, and then our mind converts the message into the symbolism of words. Perhaps we have a certain feeling in our stomach; our mind then translates the meaning of that into words like *hungry*. The same type of translation happens at an unconscious level with our thoughts arising from beliefs.

Earlier we considered the thoughts that come from characters, particularly archetype characters. These characters are structures of beliefs about our identity, and each of them gives rise to its own thoughts. As you become aware you may notice your internal dialog at times is a conversation between various characters. It works the other way too, as it did when we formed our belief system: a thought arises, then turns into a belief when we invest faith in it. That belief, with all its meanings, then produces emotions and more thoughts. If we invest faith in those thoughts, then we are creating a third layer of beliefs, which can produce more thoughts.

This distinction is essential, because when it comes to changing emotions, it is important to put your attention on the beliefs that carry the meaning and faith, and not on the thoughts. It is also helpful not to get distracted by the thoughts or turn them into another layer of beliefs.

Example of an Internal Dialog and Beliefs

A commentary runs in John's mind whenever he spends time doing something fun. He enjoys playing the piano, but after about thirty minutes a feeling of uneasiness arises, along with an internal chatter that says, "I should be doing something productive." After a while, it gets louder and it spurs a feeling that compels him to go back to his office or do a chore, even if it doesn't really need to be done. When he takes a break to play a game of bridge on the computer, the same thoughts chatter in his head. Other thoughts chime in, like "I'm being wasteful" or "I'm lazy."

Initially, we might not think of this internal dialog as a problem. We might even consider it a healthy voice of motivation that gets us moving. But John is sixty-eight years old. He has been retired for several years. The only "work" he really has to do is the part-time management of his investments, and he could ignore those and still be fine. The only deadlines he has are those he sets for himself. Yet the internal dialog of "I should be more productive" continually echoes. It is not a thought that he chooses to consciously think. He has just noticed it as part of his internal dialog. It arises with the feelings of discomfort when he is play-ing piano or bridge, watching a movie, or doing other fun things. The thought continues to arise even when John intellectually knows it isn't true.

John's internal dialog statement is not the sum total of his beliefs. It arises from a set of beliefs that are silently doing a calculation about his character and behavior, and comparing them to imagined alternative choices. The thought that he should do something productive is only the conclusion.

John knows very well where these repetitive thoughts come from. While he was growing up, his father told him many times, "You should be more productive." It happened whenever he was laughing "too much" or having a lot of fun playing. His father might follow it up with, "Go read a book, or do something to better yourself." So now, at sixty-eight years old and financially secure, John still finds himself feeling ill at ease doing anything that's purely for enjoyment.

When John began examining this dynamic, he thought at first that a game of computer bridge would trigger the echoing judgment, which in turn would elicit feelings of guilt and unworthiness. However, after pay-ing closer attention to his emotions, John discovered that it was actually the feeling that came first, before the internal dialog started. The belief system of his archetype characters was unconsciously generating self-judgment and producing emotions of guilt, shame, and unworthiness. Responding to these feelings, the Fixer character would suggest doing a chore to feel better, before John even knew he felt bad. The thought "I should be more productive" would express both a solution and the hidden self-judgment he was feeling. Because John always noticed the thought first, he assumed it came first, but his belief system actually produced the feeling before the conscious thought arose.

Those few simple words, "You should be more productive," carry much more meaning than just a suggestion of alternative actions. His father's statement and tone implied other meanings: "I disapprove, I am disappointed in you, and you do not meet the expectations that I have for you."

By accepting these messages as true, for many years John has maintained faith in a system with numerous beliefs, a false self-image of who he is and who he should be, and expectations of what he should be doing. This "should be" image depicts an idealized standard against which his Judge constantly compares him. When his Judge declares him a failure, his Victim responds by feeling guilty and worthless.

The Tip of the Iceberg

While the words of John's internal dialog were simply "I should be more productive," those symbolic words were associated with many meanings. The associated emotions reveal that the structure of his belief system looks more like this:

- There are criteria I need to meet in order to be perfect/good.
- Productivity is one criterion I should meet and it includes a number of actions.
- Any actions that aren't on the list of productive activities are wasteful and lazy.
- To be accepted and loved, I "should be" this image of perfection/good.
- Since I do things that are not "productive," I am a failure/bad.
- I am a disappointment, unworthy, not accepted, unloved.

These are not thoughts John thinks consciously but are part of his internal dialog in the form of unspoken meaning. They arise from a structure of beliefs residing in his subconscious. His emotions result from these beliefs and are a better indicator of beliefs than is just the thought. The Fixer's thought jumps right over the beliefs and emotions to a compensating strategy of correction. The Judge animates the belief system's images, pointing to the standard of perfection and saying, "That is what you should be." It quickly concludes that John doesn't meet all the criteria for that image, and therefore he is the image of failure. As always, the Victim automatically accepts the condemnation from the Judge.

So John invests faith into this system of beliefs, then feels guilt for failing to be more productive, and shame for being the failure. This entire belief system completely disregards the record of John's productive and successful life and the fact that he is retired. It is still echoing thoughts of the teenager character image to whom these words were first spoken. Inside John's belief bubble those characters still see him as a teenager.

John has been investing faith in this belief structure since he was a boy. Because his faith is still invested in these images and beliefs, he continues to feel guilty and unworthy when he has fun. When he believes the internal dialog thought, "I should be doing something more productive," he reinvests faith in all the associated beliefs and false identity characters connected to this thought. All of this, including the emotional reaction, can happen *even before* the conscious thought about doing something productive forms.

Sometimes, when we notice a thought from the internal dialog, we are only seeing the tip of the iceberg of our belief system. The belief system largely resides below the surface of our awareness. The structure of John's beliefs was made up of three different self-images—the Judge, which resembles his dad; the Victim, which resembles an unproductive teenager; and the Image of Perfection—as well as a catalog of meanings about what was "productive" and what was "unproductive." His thoughts were just internal dialog conclusions arising from this belief system.

John's thought was simply that he should be more productive, but the belief structure beneath this thought was filled with self-rejecting meanings and a failure image of the Victim. It was these beliefs that produced that bad feeling of low worth, not the thought about doing something else. The thoughts were easy to see as they were dressed in the symbols of words. The beliefs were discovered when he looked deeper into his emotions and the meaning those words symbolized.

Often people mistakenly believe that thoughts produce or create emotions. This is clearly not the case. Thoughts are often the tip of the iceberg that we can perceive. The belief structure lies underneath and can be creating emotions before the thought arises. Whether you notice the thought or the emotion first isn't the important thing. What is critical to pay attention to is the structure of beliefs the thoughts and emotions arise from.

Identifying Thoughts, Beliefs, and Core Beliefs

Core beliefs are trunks from which other beliefs branch out. At the core of John's dialog was a Victim belief about being a failure and being unworthy because he wasn't being what his dad wanted. A large branch off that Victim trunk was the belief about needing to be perfect enough for his dad's approval. More specific to that branch was another branch that had to do with productivity. As mentioned in Chapter 11, identifying a core belief is a bit like solving a mystery. It often involves sifting through layers of thoughts and beliefs to find the central belief at the core of our emotional reactions.

Let's use a "fear of public speaking" example to better understand this investigation process. Fear of public speaking isn't a core belief. It is a thought about an emotional reaction. Attributing this emotion to "public speaking" distracts us from the beliefs that are the real source of the fear. A person might explain with, "I'm afraid I will make a fool of myself." But making "a fool of myself" is vague and we can't be sure of the meaning. Making a fool of ourselves could just as easily be a cause for everyone's enjoyment, including our own. Comedians and actors work very hard to be foolish and get people to laugh at them. By itself, the thought of doing something embarrassing does not inspire fear. We have to look for more specific meaning that would create fear.

Fears associated with what other people think of us are very common. This same dynamic can occur when asking for a raise, asking someone out on a date, or asking for what we want. And yet, the thought "I'm afraid of what people think" is not a core belief either. One has to be careful not to jump to conclusions too early. When solving a crime you follow the money. When finding core beliefs, you follow the emotion. Is the fear really created by what someone else thinks? How would thoughts in someone else's head cause us to feel different emotions? What goes on in someone else's head would affect *their* emotions, not ours. If someone else has a fearful thought, *they* become afraid. If someone has a judgmental thought, *they* experience it, not us.

So the question becomes, what belief of ours gets activated when someone else thinks negatively of us? None, actually, because we really don't know what other people are thinking or when they are thinking it. In our mind we are assuming that they are thinking negatively about us. Getting more specific, we might ask: What belief of ours gets activated when *we imagine* other people are thinking negatively of us? It is our own belief about what others think of us that activates our emotion of fear.

If someone pointed at your hair, claimed it was green, and then started to laugh out loud at how silly you looked, would you feel hurt? Probably not, if your hair is not green and you know that. If you know your hair isn't green, you would know this person is being silly, on drugs, or having problems with their vision. You know the issue is with their perception and not with you, so you don't react, except maybe to be amused. It isn't a problem for you; it doesn't activate any of your emotional beliefs. If your hair really was green, as a stylistic choice, you could be indifferent to what others think about it, as long as you like it yourself. Having someone think negatively of you doesn't bother you when you don't think or believe negatively of yourself.

With this understanding, it is obvious that we cannot be hurt emotionally by what others think and say about us. It only hurts if we adopt that belief ourselves, or their actions trigger an existing belief bubble response. It is our own Judge/Victim belief structure that produces painful emotions, and it is those painful emotions that we fear. An activity like public speaking is only the trigger to a belief system. So rather than saying, "I have a fear of public speaking," it would be more accurate to say, "I have a fear that my belief system will create an emotionally painful self-rejection experience when I'm in a public-speaking situation."

Digging Through the Layers of Thought to Find the Beliefs

Jack has a presentation to give. As part of his conscious thought process he wants it to be informative and fun for his audience. He thinks of ways to present the material with examples, funny stories, and anecdotes. Planning the presentation is a useful and essential step.

However, another part of Jack's mind starts to get attached to "getting things just right." Perhaps a good joke to start with. He wants to be funny and relax the room, make a good impression. He thinks of different jokes but wants to be careful not to offend anyone. He then thinks maybe he should make a joke about himself—that way nobody will be offended. Then he thinks that isn't such a good idea because he doesn't want to diminish his image and credibility.

As he works through his presentation, his mind runs more and more scenarios. In his imagination, people ask him questions and challenge his material. At this point, his mind is thinking on its own, based on beliefs he created long ago as well as beliefs about this specific presentation.

One of Jack's thoughts might be, "I need to make this PowerPoint presentation perfect." But if we inquire further, we find other layers of motivation. If we ask Jack *why* he needs to make it perfect, he might answer, "I want it to look good."

Why?

"I don't want to look stupid."

Why?

"I don't want people to think I'm a stupid idiot."

Now we could just simplify this and say that Jack has a fear of public speaking, which might be the case. But since the devil is in the details, it is helpful to break down that fear into some component parts. This more detailed inventory of the fear of public speaking will help in two ways. First, it heightens our awareness of the elements of the mind. Second, when we are aware of these smaller elements we have an opportunity to change them. It is much easier to change a small element, like point of view or single component beliefs, than to drop all of them at once.

The layers of Jack's thoughts and beliefs look something like this. The initial thought, "I need to make this PowerPoint presentation perfect," fits with a reasonable thought process and a genuine desire to do a quality job. The majority of Jack's thoughts and motivation might be part of this desire for quality work and enjoyment of what he does. Only by observing the emotion can we tell what kind of thought and belief we are dealing with. If we continue to let all the thoughts along this line pour out, most of them will be without unpleasant emotions. We might find here and there other meanings and emotions leading to false and fear-based beliefs of the ego.

Suppose there is a belief from the Hero/Fixer character: "I want these people to be impressed and come away with a good image of me." If we look further we find that the desire to impress people is coupled with a fear of failing to impress them. This desire to impress has the same thought, but the emotional motivation comes from a fearful belief. This belief is another layer from the Victim character: "They will see me and think I'm a stupid idiot."

Within Jack's statement, "I don't want people to think I'm a stupid idiot," lies the assumption that people will see him as just that. Why would he believe that's a possibility? Because one of his belief images of himself—likely from the Judge and Victim perspectives—is that of a stupid idiot. It's fundamental to why the thought would arise in his mind. This belief might be one of a hundred beliefs at work, many or most of them very positive. But amongst all those beliefs is one producing fear, and in that one the Victim clings to the image, "I am a stupid idiot."

The story of the Hero/Fixer, "I want to impress these people with a good image of me," is a reactive strategy to compensate for this Victim belief. After undergoing a quick feeling of rejection based in that "idiot" belief, the mind soothes itself by adopting the successful hero image. Notice that in Jack's inquiry process the Fixer version first showed up as a surface-level thought. That's because it was covering the underlying core belief of the Victim. When we asked about the Fixer's motivation to make the presentation so good, we discovered hidden beliefs based in Victim fears.

Had we focused our attention only on Jack's thoughts, we would only notice the agenda of the Hero/Fixer character. This is why the issue of attention was emphasized earlier in this book. To identify these more core beliefs, we must focus our attention not just on the thoughts but on the beliefs and meanings from which those thoughts arise. We have to look behind the thoughts we think and follow the direct emotional connections.

In contrast to these types of stories in our head, consider the type of thoughts one might have when the mind is freed of these ego characters and their self-image beliefs. For that person, the preparation of the presentation doesn't hinge on concerns or thoughts about what "I" will look like or what others will think of "me." Instead, the thought process revolves around delivering the presentation in a way that is best for the audience.

Following a Branch of a Belief

As we have seen, a thought is not the same as a belief. Thoughts can arise with our conscious intention or from our internal dialog, from an existing belief system. Either way, each new thought can become a belief if we invest faith in it by accepting the thought as true. In this way a singular belief can give rise to more layers of thoughts that also become beliefs. This is how a false belief turns into a whole belief system.

In Jack's example, the "fear of public speaking" would not exist unless there was faith in the following as well:

- *Belief:* My assumptions about what others think of me are reliable.
- *Belief:* If someone else believes I am stupid then I am stupid.
- *Corollary Belief:* If someone believes I am smart then I am smart.
- *Extension:* Whatever someone believes about me is what I am.
- *Victim Belief:* What other people think of me can hurt me emotionally.
- *Victim Belief:* I don't have power over my own emotions - others do.

The mind uses these false beliefs to generate fear of emotional pain. We know they aren't true, because thoughts in another person's head don't determine our emotions. What we believe about ourselves determines how we feel. Sometimes what we believe about ourselves is hiding underneath the thought of what someone else believes about us.

153

Someone else's thoughts or opinions—or our imagination about what they *might* be thinking—are just a trigger that exposes the belief bubbles and characters where we have invested our faith.

One branch of Jack's belief system contains the assumption that we can accurately know what other people think about us. When we have a fear of what others think, we are already in a Victim perspective. From the Victim character, the assumption projected on the belief bubble is that someone has a negative opinion of us. If there are thirty people in the room, the Victim assumes that all thirty have the same negative opinion. However, when we become aware that this is a Victim belief bubble, we begin to become skeptical of it. In any given situation, will thirty people all have the exact same opinion? Not likely—it just doesn't pass the commonsense test. Questioning the validity of this assumption makes it difficult to continue investing faith in that imaginary bubble of the Victim. This skepticism helps break the cycle of reinvesting faith in existing beliefs. When we apply awareness we realize what we believe, and we can reclaim our personal power as beliefs fall apart under scrutiny.

Practice: Explore the Source of Thoughts

The next time you meditate, if you do, try going one step further with the following advanced practice. Instead of just observing your thoughts, pay attention to how and where your thoughts are formed. Put your attention on the space and silence that precedes the words. From that silent space an impulse of feeling may arise and from that feeling a thought arises. With practice, you can notice the source belief or feeling that is generating the thoughts.

These underlying beliefs are often silent. You might notice them as a feeling or sensation that precedes the words of a thought. The thoughts of your internal dialog are often birthed from beliefs in your mind. As you recover faith from your false beliefs, you will have fewer of them and your mind will become quieter. This doesn't happen overnight, but rather over time with practice.

This meditation can take you into a deeper state of awareness. As you practice this technique and others, you will develop better control over your attention and perspective. With your conscious attention focused specifically on the silent feeling of beliefs, they modify and change. You don't need to control the thoughts, ideas, and images running through your mind. They are byproducts of the beliefs generating them.

Think of a movie projector. If you watch a movie you see images and a story projected on the screen. These are like the thoughts and images projected in your mind. The projector shoots light through the film and produces what is on the screen. To change what movie is playing you don't go up to the screen and try to move the images around. To change the movie, you go to the projector and adjust the film and the light source. In the same way, the thoughts and images in your mind are projected through your beliefs. To change the thoughts and images you have to go to the beliefs that act as the film and to the energy source of faith projecting them.

—〰—

When we apply awareness we realize what we believe, and we can reclaim our personal power as

—〰—

A Common Self-Help Failure

Often people are not successful at changing their beliefs because they are actually trying to change thoughts. Their attention gets caught up in the thoughts and images on the screen. To find that film and light source of beliefs you need to control your attention and your perspective. With the perspective of an observer or skeptic, you put your attention on the source beliefs. Once you learn to be aware and to control where you place your faith and how to detach it, those thoughts, ideas, and images are no longer projected the same way.

Distraction

One of the ways we are not mindful is that we chase our thoughts. In Jack's story, his mind started to run round and round with thoughts about how to make his presentation perfect. He was following the instructions his thoughts were giving him. Every thought about how to make it better was considered and all the pros and cons evaluated.

Certainly, some of Jack's thoughts were relevant to constructing a better presentation, but many of them were driven by his archetype characters, like the Hero and the Victim. He could look at any idea and talk himself into it as the Hero character or talk himself out of it as the Victim character. These characters run stories that embody their own beliefs. Lacking an observer perspective, Jack didn't have a good way to evaluate ideas, or to perceive that his Hero and Victim were sabotaging his evaluation process with their own beliefs. He couldn't see the line where his good ideas and intentions were being taken too far by his Hero or sabotaged by his Victim.

As you develop more awareness of these archetype characters and their beliefs, you will be able to tell more quickly when it is one of their thoughts that you're hearing in the internal dialog, and not your best discerning assessment. With increasing awareness, the internal dialog has less ability to hook and control your attention, your perspective, or your faith.

Breaking the Rule of Thoughts

The belief system sets up rules within the mind's model of outer reality. If you feel emotionally lousy when you lose (fail) and you feel great when you win (succeed), the belief system sets up the criterion that you *must* win in order to feel good, and creates a pattern of fear about losing. If you feel lonely and miserable when you are alone, and you feel happy when someone is giving you attention, the belief system concludes that you *have to* get attention in order to be happy. It also causes you to generate fear about being alone. These are the rules and "have tos" of your belief system.

Your emotions follow these rules (or beliefs), creating the emotional experience that the beliefs dictated. Because your beliefs dictate it, you will feel better when someone is giving you attention and lonely when you're alone. This emotional result is then used as evidence that the beliefs are true. In fact these beliefs are not true, but they operate to produce these emotions within a belief bubble so they appear and feel true. It's a self-fulfilling prophecy: the belief bubble produces emotional responses and then claims that these emotional responses prove the belief bubble's "reality."

For example, "I believe I am worthless" produces a feeling of being worthless. The mind then interprets this emotion as evidence: "If I feel worthless then it must be because I really am worthless." While this conclusion claims that the emotion "proves" the person is worthless, in reality the feeling of worthlessness is simply evidence of a belief and false character perspective.

John's rule was that he had to be productive in order to feel worthy about himself. If he followed the rules and was productive he didn't have the negative thoughts or self-judgments. If he didn't follow the rules he had the uneasy feelings and self-judgments. The belief in these rules produced emotions that then made these rules feel like they were true. He really couldn't do enjoyable things and always had to work on something in order to feel good about himself.

From that closed-loop reasoning of what determines our emotions, the way to feel better is to obey the negative thoughts. In this way, our false belief system not only defines how our emotions are created but also proposes a solution based on those false beliefs. Look out for these kinds of thoughts that loop you back into following the rules of your beliefs.

A person often comes to a path of pursuing happiness as an *internal* process only after they have achieved some kind of external success and have been surprised to find out that they didn't feel any better. Sometimes they even discovered they felt worse after their success.

The assumption of a direct correlation between our external success or activities, our relationships, and our emotional state fails to take into account the impact of the faith we've invested in our beliefs and interpretations about winning, losing, productivity, success, and failure. It also ignores the influence of archetype characters' perspectives, like those of the Victim and Judge, that determine what we perceive and how we see it.

With awareness, one comes to realize that external events and achievements are often just the triggers to these internal emotional beliefs. With more awareness, one also realizes that it's not necessary to control outside events or other people in order to be happy or avoid emotional reactions.

It's true that many recent studies show a correlation between certain activities and lifestyles and a person's level of happiness. For example, people with strong family ties, healthy social circles, and meaningful work have higher levels of happiness across statistical studies. However, looking only at these external factors is too limited. Statistical averages hide exceptions that would invalidate the conclusions. There are people who don't have these things but are still happy. There are people who have all these things and are unhappy. If there are exceptions where these conditions don't result in happiness, then these aren't definitive rules that govern our emotions.

There is also something different going on within the minds of happy people. What is happening at a more fundamental level has to do with what beliefs they invest their faith in, what they focus their attention on, and the perspective from which they view things. Their core underlying beliefs produce different thoughts and interpretations about external circumstances. These fundamental dynamics affect the different emotions people create and feel but aren't addressed in those studies about happiness.

You may not always have complete control or even influence over the external circumstances of your life. However, there are always dynamics occurring with your attention, perspective, and interpretation that can affect how you feel about your life. Following the trail of your thoughts and emotions to uncover and challenge your belief systems will give you more control over how you *feel* about your circumstances, which is ultimately what determines your experience. Your thoughts and emotions are a clue to the belief paradigms at work in your mind. As with an iceberg, when you notice your thoughts, you are probably seeing less than 10 percent of the belief structure that produced them. Write them out in detail and then begin looking for the meanings and assumptions woven through them.

Chapter 13

Awakening and Acceptance

To take out a splinter you have to put your attention on it. Taking a splinter out will hurt, but only once; then it heals. Not removing the splinter might mean you avoid that pain for now, but you will endure a different pain for a long time. Ignoring it can also cause it to fester and become infected, causing other problems.

When you believe false beliefs (lies), they are like splinters in your mind, causing you pain. Getting rid of a lie can be an unpleasant process, but only once. Leaving it there can cause festering pain the rest of your life.

Steps to Change Beliefs

We've already covered the initial steps to change beliefs. The first step is to be aware. But be aware of what? The component parts:

- Your perspective
- Your attention
- Thoughts
- The beliefs that drive the thoughts
- Your investment of faith
- Your emotions

This might seem like a lot to track. Writing things down can help you achieve clarity and avoid being overwhelmed, distracted, or pulled into them. Using the inventory system of charting the different elements of your belief system can help you stay in the stance of the observer, noticing them all.

The Neutral Observer Perspective

In the beginning, the observer perspective is the most important tool for changing beliefs. Without that neutral perspective, most attempts at change become corrupted. As we have discussed, practical ways to shift into a neutral perspective include:

- Writing in the third person.
- Ascribing beliefs and emotional reactions to archetype characters.
- Breaking those beliefs down into their smaller elements and assumptions.
- Applying scrutiny and skepticism to those smaller embedded, implied, and associated beliefs.

Holding different elements of your beliefs at arm's length can be a great help in shifting your perspective to that of the observer. This ensures not only that you are no longer trapped in the perspectives and reactions of the Judge and Victim, but also that you are free to apply other techniques for dissolving beliefs.

As you begin to be more aware of your own emotions, behaviors, and negative thoughts, another dynamic often happens: you begin to have judgments and emotional reactions to what you discover. Your reactions are likely to knock you out of the neutral observer perspective, since they are coming from various archetype characters. At this point, you have to double down on your observer perspective and apply the same tools of writing inventory to these new thoughts and beliefs. As we will explore in this chapter, actively practicing some form of acceptance will also help you avoid falling into expressions of rejection about what you discover.

Awakening

As you gain awareness, you realize that parts of your mind are automatically making assumptions and interpretations, and drawing conclusions. You notice that the beliefs behind these thoughts are creating emotional reactions. You might come about this realization because you began to do meditation, or something changed in your life like a breakup, a surprise turn of events in your career, or you fell in love. (Yes, falling in love can cause your characters to become loud with fear and sabotaging behaviors.)

Whatever the reason, the result is the potential for a profound realization: *You don't control* the thoughts, beliefs, and resultant emotions your mind produces. Despite years of education, your physical strength, and all your accomplishments, you can't stop a simple negative thought. You might be able to hold it at bay, but not for very long. And, if you have been successful in your life and generally accomplished what you have set out to do, this will be a very uncomfortable fact to accept.

Of course, you don't want to admit your lack of control. Most people resist this fact with various mechanisms of denial. They might point to situations in which they *were* in charge of their mind, moments where they decided to think or believe in something and they did so. Those things may be true, but they aren't relevant to the issue at hand. What these stories amount to is a defensive gesture—gathering evidence to prove that they are in control—or, at a minimum, a distraction from the fact that they don't control their thoughts, emotions, and behaviors. All of this denial and distraction is actually just another layer of reaction by the characters of the belief system.

A helpful step at this point is to notice the part of the mind that resists admitting it's not in control, and name it as another character aspect of the ego. There are aspects of your belief system that don't want to acknowledge this lack of control. Use the same tools of third-person writing, character perspectives, and the inventory to observe these reactions of denial and distraction.

Those characters unwilling to accept the uncomfortable and perplexing fact that they don't control the thoughts arising from their beliefs sometimes try other strategies. They decide they'll overcome their lack of control by adopting quick ways to control their mind, such as hypnosis or positive affirmations, as if this would address the whole problem. Often the result is the creation of a Self-Help Hero belief bubble in which we seem to be in control. It might take the form of repeating an affirmation and making ourselves believe we're in charge of our thoughts and behaviors. This feels much better, but it hasn't necessarily dissolved other belief bubbles, or our habit of adopting various character perspectives when triggered. The underlying beliefs remain intact. These techniques can be temporarily effective, but over time the banished part of the mind generally creeps back in and reclaims old territory. People using these methods may have to implement the technique again, or try something new.

For some people this back-and-forth is enough of a success, and they are willing to do it for the remainder of their life. For others, all these futile attempts at controlling their thoughts and emotions leave them frustrated and confused, possibly even feeling like failures. But the truth is that they are not failures. They have actually done some extraordinary work. In using affirmations they took control over their attention and used it to create a more positive set of beliefs that help control or manage the negative ones. This is a major step forward in controlling their beliefs directly using their attention. However, they didn't do a complete job. The result might be a partial or temporary success. If their expectation was 100 percent success, then the Judge and Victim characters have fuel to justify accusations of failure.

Our scrambling to quickly change our negative thoughts and beliefs often results in a surface-level appearance of success. Not getting to the underlying layers of the problem beliefs might be an unsatisfactory solution. If we go to see a doctor for a problem with our health, we want him to listen to our description of all of our symptoms. If he interrupts us halfway through, makes a quick diagnosis, and prescribes a treatment based on only the half he's seen and heard, he's not likely to do a thorough job. The same is true when we jump too quickly with our approaches to change what our mind is doing. When we try to push a thought away or replace it with a better one, we are acting too quickly and won't be able to notice—and change—the belief it is arising from.

Acceptance

If you want real and lasting change, you are going to have to do something different. A more thorough approach for changing beliefs involves honesty. The ego's fear of losing control causes it to use denial and defense. To maintain control, it scrambles for quick, oversimplified solutions.

Honesty involves acknowledging and accepting the truth. The fact is that we have thoughts we didn't choose and they affect our emotions. The ego part of our mind doesn't like to acknowledge the beliefs we have unintentionally acquired. That's one thing about the ego—it tends to cling to illusions and push away truths.

If distraction, defense, and denial are the path of the ego, then keen observation with your attention, honest assessment, and acceptance of the facts are the path of integrity.

The opportunity to experience a shift in consciousness lies in doing something different from the ego behaviors we've been doing. It might even be completely counterintuitive to the approach our existing belief system would take. But the alternative, doing what your current belief system tells you, will keep you trapped in its bubbles.

A common impulse is to jump in and change thoughts. The counterintuitive step is to refrain from the impulse to control and change your thoughts, beliefs, and emotions. You do this by just observing this desire to change. You will notice it pushing, pulling, or attempting to gain control. That's fine—that desire is just one part of the mind scrambling to control another part of the mind. It's important to step back from this whole game and break the pattern of following the first impulse, or the second, or even the third impulsive reaction of the mind.

This counterintuitive approach is to completely accept that your mind in its current state *is* simply as it *is*. Accept that you do not yet have the skills to change it; after all, you haven't developed them yet. But perhaps you can shift perspective to an observer state and begin to refrain from just following every thought it throws out. The change you are making is to refrain from acting on that one reactive impulse.

This doesn't mean that you give up. It doesn't mean that you have failed or that you are weak, that you can't change or that you won't. It just means that you realize you won't get all these impulsive thoughts and emotions under control in the next five minutes, or even today. It means realizing you are not going to break those reactions by blindly following the new set of impulsive reactions. You are taking a moment to be honest about where you are and recognize the reactions your characters are having to your realizations. You are effectively saying, "I'm tired of banging my head against a wall in a direction that doesn't work. Let me sit back and get a bigger perspective on what is going on here, because there are obviously some pieces that I'm missing in all this."

—ᴡ—

If distraction, defense, and denial are the path of the ego, then keen observation with your attention, honest assessment, and acceptance of the facts are the path of integrity.

—ᴡ—

More Beliefs Were Built Than Dissolved

Most self-help approaches require that you put a lot of faith in their approach. In essence, you are applying a "new technique" to control your thoughts, emotions, and beliefs—but in reality, you often end up adding more beliefs to the structure of your mind.

These layers of beliefs come in the form of assumptions. You assume that the "new" technique will work, that you know all you need to know, that you have all the skills necessary, and that the thoughts, beliefs, and emotions in your mind will respond appropriately to your good intentions for change. You may not notice that you assume all this, or that you put faith in these underlying assumptions, but that's the thing about the mind: most of what goes on in our belief system happens unconsciously until we pay specific attention to become aware of it.

A more effective approach begins with changing our perspective and observing with greater clarity what is going on. We do this by stepping outside some of our belief bubbles. We refrain from putting faith in our first assumptions about what is happening, jumping to conclusions about how to "change it," or rushing in to "fix it." These are the usual patterns that our Self-Help Hero and other archetype characters come up with.

When we first become aware of our negative thoughts and beliefs, our characters start generating an internal commentary about the belief system. If we begin acting on these comments right away, it is because we have put faith in the characters' thoughts and turned them into beliefs. However, if we can remain an observer, we can refrain from investing faith in these thoughts, and that will make it easier to refrain from reacting. This conserves our personal power, not only in the form of faith, but also by not taking unnecessary action.

At first glance the approach of just honestly acknowledging what is going on with your thoughts and emotions doesn't seem like much, but it is a very important part of the change. An important step to eliminating negative beliefs is to refrain from adding more beliefs, or investing faith in our Judge and Victim interpretations about what we discover. Being the observer and practicing acceptance breaks all these patterns.

Do No Harm

"But I don't want to keep having these thoughts, beliefs, and emotional reactions. I want to change them." This is a genuine desire and has a lot of merit. There are things we can change, including the beliefs, but first we have to make sure we aren't making things worse.

Suppose we are driving in our car and we get a flat tire. We park the car safely on the side of the road, get out, look at the flat tire, and make an assessment: the tire is flat. Then we begin to talk to it, saying things like, "You stupid tire. You know better than that. What were you thinking? You know you aren't supposed to be flat. You aren't doing what you're supposed to do. You should be full, inflated, and rolling along nicely. I wish you would stop doing this and do what you're supposed to do. You know all the other tires are doing what they're supposed to. Look around at all the other cars—they all have working tires. You're the only one that's failing. Everyone else has good tires. Just look at them. It's simple, just be like them. Quit being this way and get yourself together."

After a good ten-minute talking-to, we stop the berating, judging, coaxing, and wishing for the tire to be different. Then we get out our lug wrench from the trunk and begin to loosen the lug nuts. Or perhaps we call a friend or repair service and get someone to change the tire.

The ten minutes we spent talking and thinking about the tire and how it should be different produced zero results and wasted our time and energy. The part of our being that accepts the truth that the tire is flat leads us to the next step: taking effective action for change. Once we acknowledge and accept that the tire is flat, the only thing left to do is to take practical action. The longer we stand there telling ourselves how we wish things were, or complaining that things are not as desired, the less productive we are. Our attention is on a belief bubble of an idealized properly inflated tire, instead of the real one in front of us.

The same kind of approach applies to changing our thoughts, beliefs, and emotions. As long as we are involved in the Judge and Victim rants of wishing our mind were different, or thinking how we shouldn't be the way we are, or comparing ourselves to others, we don't change anything. We might as well be talking to a flat tire and expecting it to change. And not only do we not change, but we reinforce the perspectives and habitual expressions of the archetypes.

Some people might say that an image of how things "should" be serves as a good reminder and motivator. The truth is, you don't need reminders like this in the form of beat-downs and rants. You already know what an inflated tire looks like. You already know what it is like to feel good, and you don't need the Judge to remind you by beating up the Victim. It's all energy wasted in the Judge and Victim perspectives, reinforcing negative habits with your attention and faith. It doesn't feel good, and it takes energy away from actions that will bring about change. The assessment part is helpful and only takes a couple seconds, but judgments and rants trip us up and can go on for days.

Acknowledging and accepting a situation doesn't mean giving in or giving up, or that things won't change. It just means that you aren't going to align with the Judge and Victim characters' dialog as a strategy. This by itself is change in the right direction because it takes you out of those limiting points of view. If you don't see it as a step in the right direction, then at least it is a way to avoid a step in the wrong direction. The Judge and Victim approach to change creates loops and spirals of emotional drama. Acknowledgment and acceptance move you out of the loop of yelling at the flat tire and towards grabbing the right tools that will help you change the tire.

Practice: The Great Not-Doing for Change

Detaching from the characters' desire to change emotional reactions and negative beliefs is a step towards changing them. This seems like a paradox, until you look closer and see how the Judge and Victim characters typically corrupt the desire for change by turning it into a rejection of the current situation. It is this expression of rejection that is part of a downward spiral. An inventory can help to separate the authentic desire for change from the expressions of rejection. Below is an inventory of beliefs that you might find when trying to control and change other beliefs and thoughts.

Observing what your mind is doing can be a clean part of the process. You are just observing and noticing. The intention to "fix" or "change" your mind is usually a *reaction* to this awareness. Any faith you put into your intentions to fix things typically reinforces the Judge and Victim beliefs they are based on as well.

Basic Belief Inventory: "I'm going to change my negative thinking."

Perspective	Thought/Belief/Behavior	Emotion/Feeling
	Original issue: "I'm afraid of what other people think of me."	
Observation: Common Sense	I'd be happier if I didn't have this fear affecting my emotions.	Clear assessment.
Fixer	I'm going to stop all that negative thinking and insecurity. Implied belief: Rejection of the situation.	Motivated. Hope and good intentions.

Judge	This is wrong/bad/ unacceptable.	Righteous/correct/know better.
	The fear and insecurity are wrong.	Greater ego.
	My emotions are wrong/bad.	
	My thoughts are wrong.	
	(Associated) I'm wrong.	
	(These beliefs might not be conscious, but they, or beliefs like them, are behind the intent of the Fixer.)	
Victim	What the mind is doing is making me miserable.	Hurt, defeated, feeling powerless over emotional reactions and internal dialog.
	These negative thoughts and beliefs are abusing me.	
	My thoughts/feelings are wrong.	Worthless, less than.
	(Associated) I am wrong for having them.	

The above is a rough inventory and is representative of how things might look in the first pass. As you practice paying attention to the subtleties and gain more skill you will perceive assumptions and beliefs in more detail.

In the following more detailed inventory, we shift the order and place the desire for change arising from the Victim emotions first. In this inventory there are three layers of Victim beliefs and two layers of Judge beliefs. The beliefs around these desires for change can often be more emotionally painful than the initial belief that we set out to change.

Perspective	Thought/Belief/Behavior	Emotion/Feeling
Observer	Observes the feeling of insecurity, uncontrolled activity, negative thoughts, beliefs, and creation of emotional reactions.	Acknowledges the truth of what is going on. Acceptance—it simply is what it is.
Observation: Common Sense	I'd be happier if I didn't have this fear affecting my emotions.	Clear assessment.
	Characters then give their input on what is observed.	
Victim I	Those negative thoughts/ emotional reactions are making me miserable. They are causing me pain. (These thoughts can be somewhat factual, but the tone and point of view add new emotions.)	Abused, hurt, defeated, powerless, self-pity.
Judge I	What that mind is doing is wrong. It's doing a bad thing. It shouldn't have those thoughts of insecurity. It should be different than it is. Implied belief: Expectation of how the mind should be— perfect, quiet, confident.	Righteous/correct/I know better; authority.

Princess	I wish I didn't have these beliefs and insecurities. I wish they would just go away.	Entitled to having her mind change by just wishing it would be different.
Victim II (recipient of the criticism from the Judge)	I am not what the Judge says I should be. I am doing wrong. I am making myself miserable. It is my fault. I am a failure. Victim II accepts the Judge's criticism that it's responsible for the negative thoughts and emotional reactions of insecurity. I should be what the Judge expects me to be, but I am not.	Feeling self-rejection. I'm wrong, bad. Guilt and shame, for what the belief system is doing. Feelings of failure.
Authentic Self	Desire to stop the emotional pain. This is a genuine desire that we have to avoid pain and experience pleasure. This genuine desire is then distorted and redirected by characters.	Genuine desire.

Fixer The first responder to the Judge's critical assessment.	I'm going to stop all that negative thinking. I'll fix this mind and make it better.	Hope, good intentions, confident. Imagines positive outcome.
	Implied beliefs: —I see and understand the complete problem. —I know how to fix/change this. (Perhaps just focus on something positive, etc.) —I know how the mind will react to my actions.	Confident, hopeful.
	Assumption: Expected timeline for success is immediate or assumed to be very quick.	High and unrealistic expectations that become a setup for future disappointment.
	Implied expectation: Things should be different right away.	Positive self-image based in the idea that telling our self to be different will be enough.
	These unrealistic expectations often lead to failed attempts that are followed by self-judgment.	

Observer	Things haven't changed yet. (Nothing has happened to extract faith from any of the existing beliefs or to change perspectives.) However, a stack of expectations did get built and assumptions of the Judge and Victim have been reinforced.	Honest assessment.
Judge II (takes the facts and coverts them into a criticism)	I worked on this yesterday (or last week) and so it should be fixed by now. "You tried to change things but you failed." Implied beliefs: —You understood all the layers of what the beliefs were. —You had complete control over your perspective. —You had all the skills you needed over your attention. —You had complete control over your faith. —You had adequate time to complete the change.	Righteous and confidently knowing "better." Expression of rejection, disappointment, and disgust towards Fixer and Victim.
Victim III	Accepts criticism for the Fixer not getting immediate results. Criticism appears valid because of faith invested in the expectations that change would be quick.	Failure, unworthy, guilty, powerless.

The authentic self's desire to stop the emotional suffering we feel is genuine and real, but it becomes corrupted when it is expressed through the perspectives of archetype characters. Then our efforts are directed through these characters instead of through effective actions like changing our perspective and refraining from investing faith in reactive Judge and Victim stories.

In the beginning we might not perceive the initial expectations, judgment, and victimization that the Fixer agenda is based on. It is common to look past these automatic interpretations as our attention fixates on generating solutions that we assume will make us feel better—even if those "solutions" don't amount to anything more than berating a flat tire.

An important point to note in this inventory is that the judgment and victimization expressions *precede* the "fix it" solution. The whole reason the Fixer goes into action is because the Judge and Victim have proclaimed, and agreed, that the original issue is "wrong" or "bad." Accepting the Fixer's approach means indirectly investing faith in the Judge and Victim assumptions and rejections. These hidden beliefs deplete our personal power of faith and reinforce our alignment with the perspectives of the Victim and Judge paradigms. The original issue was about insecurity and fear of what others think. These are essentially Judge and Victim beliefs forming expressions of self-rejection. For a real change, what is called for is something different from what the Judge and Victim dream up as a solution.

Acceptance: Summary

The process of acceptance has several benefits:

1. You break the automated pattern of judgment and victimization.
2. You practice control over your attention and perspective. If your attention runs off with the Fixer, it's probably because you lost your perspective to the preceding characters of the Judge and Victim. Acceptance is therefore a practical way to return to the neutral observer perspective and regain control

of your attention. Without control over your attention and perspective you aren't going to change anything.

3. You refrain from investing any more faith in the beliefs of the Judge and the Victim, so you have more personal power. The less personal power of faith you invest in reactionary layers of beliefs, the more you will have available for things like directing your own attention and refraining from other reactions.

4. Practicing acceptance is a reminder that *you are not the problem.* Your beliefs might be generating a number of negative thoughts that are causing emotional reactions, but *you* are fine. You, the observer, sitting still in that storm of thoughts and emotions, are fine. Those thoughts and beliefs only become a real problem when you adopt their character perspective, identify with them, and go for an emotional ride.

5. You avoid adding another layer of drama. You may not have changed the first belief or emotion, but at least by practicing acceptance you didn't add more layers of beliefs on top of the original problem.

6. From the neutral perspective of the observer you can then engage in the inventory of and skepticism towards the other beliefs associated with the original thought.

Practicing acceptance is one of the ways to develop your skill and gain control over your attention, perspective, conceptual ideas, and your faith. Once you develop some of this control, changing beliefs like ones that create insecurity and fears about what others think of you becomes easier.

Change Without Judgmental Rejection

We can desire to change something, and actually change it, without judging the existing system as "wrong," "bad," or "unacceptable." We don't need the Judge's and Victim's expressions before we generate the resolve and practical actions that lead to change. Some people profess that you have to get fed up and angry in order to create changes. That isn't true. When people enact changes after getting angry, it isn't because of the anger but because of the resolve and commitment that come along with it. While anger is more noticeable, it is the force of resolve and commitment that really drives change.

Imagine you're a software programmer who wrote a computer program twenty years ago, in your first few years of work. Imagine it's still being used today. Back then you were quite proud of your work; it was a great program. However, because things change, that program has been modified over the years in order to interface with a lot more pieces of hardware and to do extra things today that weren't originally asked of it. Over the years you've added on all sorts of routines and it has turned into a cumbersome program that is cobbled together. It is also written in an outdated programming code that no one would use today.

When you were a young programmer you never envisioned the complex environment that your program would have to operate in today. In a way you are amazed that it has held up and worked so well for this long. At the same time, you would never write a program like that today. You are a much more seasoned programmer and would write more elegant code to accommodate all the complex needs. You would use a different language, omit the archaic routines that slow it down, and add some interface features that would make it more flexible for today's users.

The original program was a beautiful piece of work for its time, but now it is outdated and needs an upgrade. You can see all its limitations and inefficiencies, but you don't judge it as bad or judge yourself for writing it the way you did. At the time it was the best code that you could have written, and you did a great job. While it wouldn't meet the standards of the mature programmer you are today, you have enough sense not to apply today's standards to what was created twenty years ago.

What if you looked at the belief system that you've faithfully stored in your mind, complete with perspectives, emotional patterns, opinions, automated routines, and judgments in a similar way? Those beliefs you formed when you were five, ten, and fifteen years old were the operating code by which you made interpretations of events as best you could at the time. That program of beliefs guided your values, choices, relationships, behavior, and judgment of yourself and others. It worked well enough for years to get you to this point. It's also been working automatically for many years without a conscious rewrite or overhaul. Instead, things have been added to it over the years, making it cumbersome and creating internal conflicts with previously accepted beliefs. There's no need to judge this situation. Since you didn't have the necessary skills to change your belief system, and haven't spent any time upgrading it, it's understandable that this has happened.

While your old system of rules and interpretations might be causing you misery today, it was a work of art back then and served you well for a long time. You created those beliefs with the absolute best intent you could at the time. You did the best you knew how, even if you didn't realize what you were doing—you didn't have the awareness that you were forming beliefs at the time.

With this perspective we can look at our existing belief system and behaviors with acceptance and maybe even some gratitude. They were the best set of beliefs and automated behaviors we could have created at the time. If we had known differently years ago, certainly we would have adopted different beliefs. But we didn't. We didn't know what we were doing at the time we put faith in all those ideas, opinions, and self-images, nor were we aware of the consequences a particular belief would create years later. We couldn't know our life would take a particular direction and that those belief bubbles would have unintended consequences. We just didn't have the awareness at such a young age to know what we were doing.

The result of adopting this perspective and expression of acceptance about your current belief system is a feeling of equanimity. You would write your belief system code differently today, and you can. But you don't need to judge the beliefs you acquired from the past, or judge yourself for still having those beliefs. So yes, you can go about effectively changing your belief system, or anything else, without rejecting what is currently there.

The Art of Acceptance Takes a Lot of Practice

At first glance, it appears that this attitude and expression of acceptance doesn't change things much. To an untrained eye, it seems like accepting the fact that your thoughts, beliefs, and emotions sometimes run out of control means you aren't trying to change them. When you have awareness you realize that the opposite is true. You are changing your expression in the moment and that is much more important. When you refrain from the impulse to fix or change a belief with a Judge or Victim story, you shift your perspective out of the belief bubbles of judgment and victimization. When you refuse to play the Fixer, you refrain from letting the Judge and Victim characters control your attention; you stop acting on their behalf, and you refrain from investing faith in their embedded beliefs. In this way, expressing acceptance allows you to keep more of your personal power.

While this practice of acceptance is somewhat of a "not-doing," it is clearly not without effort. This practice of acceptance goes against years of patterning where we automatically expressed reactions of the characters trying to fix whatever the Judge and Victim concluded was wrong. It will take willpower to resist the temptation to jump into fixing and judgment. You will likely fall down many times. But each time you catch yourself, you'll recover more of the power of your faith and it will become easier to respond with more integrity and kindness the next time.

Adopting the practice of acceptance is a beginning step to adopting a new perspective and gaining control over your attention. As you practice this new perspective from which to express yourself, the belief paradigms of the Judge and Victim will have less and less control over your emotions. At the same time you will be practicing a much more pleasant expression of emotion that is much more enjoyable than what the archetypes come up with.

Putting Things into Action and Behavior

Will you actually put this act of expressing acceptance into practice? For those whose belief system tells them to rely on their unproven strategies, or who don't take their happiness as seriously, it will only be an intellectual idea equivalent to a passing thought. Existing belief bubbles and characters will dismiss this chapter and practice as unimportant or ineffective. What will compel a person to take action is if they invest some faith in the idea that practicing acceptance has value. If you see that it makes sense because it gives you a step towards mastery over all the elements controlling your beliefs, then you will invest some faith that practicing acceptance has merit. If you see that it is worth breaking the cycles of expression the Judge and Victim generate, then you will take the necessary first step.

Until you try it, you won't know for sure whether this approach will help. You will only know after you try it for a while and see by your own experience what happens. So extend a little faith that practicing acceptance of your beliefs will help you gain the skills to change what is going on in your mind. The power of your faith will let you begin to take action, and action will give you a result that you can see for yourself. Seeing the results of your actions will make it easier to invest more faith in this new paradigm and build a new habit.

Two Warnings

The characters and expressions of the Judge and Victim are the principal sources of an emotionally unhappy mind. They create self-rejection, criticism, and abuse. Since they are the ones generating the kind of thinking that is causing our emotional problems, it is unlikely those characters will come up with solutions to stop their own behavior. They are not programmed to form, or even recognize, an effective strategy for changing beliefs and creating happiness. So if your mind spontaneously generates an emotional reaction about another emotional reaction you've had, complete with an agenda for change, consider that this is probably not an effective strategy for change. If you are not sure, do an inventory on the new reaction and the agenda for change, and scrutinize the various beliefs.

In addition, be wary of when your mind decides to adopt the acceptance agenda, but with the motivation that by doing so it will be able to change beliefs, emotional reactions, and negative thoughts. The motivation to "change" can sometimes have underlying tones of judgment, rejection, and victimization. This is the Fixer going at things with a cover story of acceptance while harboring a rejection expression of "wrong" or "bad" underneath. The Fixer is not likely to achieve equanimity about the present-moment situation. As a countermove to this distorted agenda, write out the characters and list each one's agenda underneath this corrupt strategy. This will help you be the observer by focusing your attention on the belief bubble of the Fixer.

Chapter 14

Process for Changing Beliefs

Changing a belief requires more than just wanting it to go away. To change a belief, you need to recognize that it isn't true. For stronger beliefs, it may be necessary to know *why* it isn't true. This entails uncovering the false assumptions supporting that belief.

As we have seen earlier, a belief forms a kind of bubble in the imagination. Even a simple concept can fill your imagination and appear huge. It's then made to seem real by the infusion of your personal power of faith. This investment of faith has the added effect of obscuring your perception, making it difficult to perceive other possibilities. The typical result of creating such a conceptual bubble and investing personal power in it is that you produce your own imaginary reality. Your mind projects its beliefs in various forms: thoughts, rants, stories, or even miniature movies. You then experience an emotional response to your projected beliefs, which reinforces the illusion that they're true.

We have also noted that when you want to change this pattern, the first and most critical step is to shift your perspective and view the belief from outside the bubble. While all elements of the belief will need to be addressed, changing your point of view is often the easiest starting point. Attempts to stop the thought, belief, or emotion won't be very effective unless your viewpoint changes first.

From this neutral observer perspective, the conceptual belief bubble in your mind will begin to change appearance. It will no longer appear as a truthful representation of reality. You will also be able to consider other interpretations, opinions, and facts. To the extent that you still have faith invested in the belief, it is still producing emotions. As you remove your faith from the belief bubble, it begins to dissolve. At a minimum, you refrain from investing more faith in the same belief.

How do you withdraw your faith from a false belief? Often you'll instinctively stop investing your faith in the story and imagery in your mind once you become aware that the story is fictional. It requires little effort to stop believing it when you see that it's false. When this happens, people often experience it as an epiphany. They simply know, and no effort is required for their attachment to the idea to change. Some people assume that it takes a lot of effort to change a belief, but the fact is that it takes more energy, in the form of the power of faith, to keep a belief intact. When you stop investing your faith in false beliefs you end up having a lot more energy available to you. What does require effort during this process is the movement of your perspective to an observer or skeptical point of view.

Sometimes changing your perspective alone is enough to divest your faith from a belief and let it change. Sometimes you have been investing faith into certain beliefs for so long that the whole structure remains intact even when you can clearly see from an observer perspective that they are not true. When dealing with these larger beliefs, you can apply some of the other tools described in this chapter. Some of them will be familiar to you from the many examples you've already read through in this book.

—₥—

**The first and most critical step is to shift your
perspective and view the belief
from outside the bubble.**

Beliefs That Are Difficult to Change

Beliefs that are harder to change usually contain layers of supporting and associated beliefs. They also draw on memories as evidence to strengthen the case that the beliefs are true. As Chapter 12 pointed out, these *core beliefs* are more challenging to change because you must dissolve the supporting beliefs as well. Some examples of core beliefs are "I'm not good enough" or "There's something wrong with me." From that central hub, you may have developed more specific beliefs about not being lovable, smart enough, pretty enough, tall enough, or successful enough.

Overlaying those beliefs is your projection that others see you as "not good enough" in these same ways. You assume that the negative self-image you have in your belief system is what other people have in their mind when they look at you. Since you don't really know what others think, this is only an imagined layer, but your faith in it supports the original core belief. Changing the core belief is more challenging now because you've invested faith in the idea that you saw yourself from their point of view and that it matched the way you see yourself.

A core belief is obscured even further if you build a compensating image as a solution to the negative one in your belief system. Perhaps you project the image of a person you believe others will like and you spend your energy attempting to embody that ideal. You try to say just the right words in just the right way, and dress to elicit positive responses from people. You invest faith and energy in this projected image solution. These behaviors can be evidence of the Hero or Pleaser characters covering the Victim character identity.

Ironically, while it might feel better to get these positive responses when people show evidence of liking and respecting you, you are likely to dismiss them because you believe that people don't see the "real" you. You still assume the "real" you is the false self-image that your belief system has labeled as "not good enough." Even when you have external evidence that people like and respect you, the character within your belief bubble finds reasons to dismiss it. This "not good enough" character and its beliefs are often unnoticed as we are busy trying to impress people with our confident character. These are the two aspects of the ego's self-importance, described in Chapter 8, with one attempting to mask the other.

*A person can have both a negative self-image they try to hide and a
positive self-image that they try to project to the world around them.
Both images exist only within the person's belief bubble.*

The "not good enough" type of core belief is large. It has both supporting layers that tend to keep it intact and compensating strategies
that help you avoid feeling "not good enough" all the time. When dealing with core beliefs, it is sometimes best to manage your expectations
and go one step at a time. Core beliefs are like big trees, not likely to fall
with one blow of an ax, no matter how sharp the ax or how powerfully
you swing.

Addressing a System

A belief is a system. It's composed of the character perspective, faith,
and the conceptual ideas, story, or opinion. Together these parts produce emotions.

Changing a core belief requires changing all the elements of that
system. If you dissolve one element but leave others intact, the system
will rebuild the missing element. It's much like pulling out a weed: you
need to get all the roots or the weed will grow back. If you dismiss a
victim story in your mind, but leave the Victim character intact, it will
re-create another victim story. If you attempt to eliminate the Judge

character but still have faith in its stories, the structure of those stories will influence your perspective towards the character of the Judge again. Just willing away the emotions is the least effective approach because it leaves the character perspective and faith in the belief intact. For lasting results in changing your belief system, all aspects of the system need to be addressed.

Practice: Write Down Emotions You Feel

One of the best ways to identify your fear-based and limiting beliefs is by noticing your emotional reactions. Some emotions can be very subtle so it can take practice just to become aware of them. Emotions like anxiety, worry, or stress may be so common in our experience that they have become part of our normal state of functioning and are therefore hard to discern as being questionable. We may also have beliefs that some of our emotions are "bad" and that we "shouldn't feel this way." These beliefs about emotions often cause us to repress them, or drive our attention elsewhere so we don't notice what we feel. In any case, emotions are a telltale indicator of our beliefs or other issues worth paying attention to.

It takes practice to observe your emotions. As you develop awareness of how your mind reacts to unconscious beliefs, you can actually watch the belief system use other stories to distract your attention from feeling unpleasant emotions. These distractions can take the form of justifications, opinions, and stories about events, or about your reactions to events. Your perspective is pulled out of the observer mode, and attention is pulled away from noticing what you feel. Time spent writing in third person can be useful for conditioning yourself to watch these dynamics.

When working with people to help them identify beliefs, I often ask them to tell me what they were feeling in a given situation. They reply by describing how the circumstance started and who did what wrong, or by justifying their behavior. None of these responses specifies any emotions. When you are trying to identify the emotion connected to a belief, the answer can usually be given in one word: angry, sad, guilty, embarrassed, frustrated, jealous, afraid, and so on. The only time you need more than one word is when you experience multiple emotions. Try to use a single word to describe what you are feeling. If you use more than a phrase to describe your emotions, it is a clue that your mind is distracting your attention from what you are feeling.

The identification and observation of emotions plays an important role in finding these hidden beliefs—so much so that each of the inventory charts used in this book devotes a column to tracking emotions. In the beginning it may be difficult to find words to verbalize the sensations of emotions. If that is the case, start with simple descriptions such as "unpleasant" or "pleasant."

—⁓—

Emotions are a telltale indicator of our beliefs or other issues worth paying attention to.

—⁓—

Changing Beliefs Through Scrutiny and Skepticism

Scrutiny and skepticism are tools that can help you escape a bubble of false beliefs. Scrutiny is a skill of inquiry and examination that we can apply to our thoughts, opinions, and beliefs. Skepticism is the skillful use of doubt. We have used this attitude and approach of skepticism in earlier examples so it may be familiar to you by now.

We begin by assuming that the world within our mind is at times not accurate. Since we can't be sure which of our thoughts are true or accurate, we become mindful and begin to question them. We are most skeptical of our thoughts and images associated with unpleasant emotions, because false and fear-based beliefs commonly produce unpleasant emotional reactions. So we assume that the internal dialog and thoughts surrounding an emotional reaction have some faulty assumptions and beliefs at their core.

In this process of applying doubt, we must be mindful that we are applying doubt to the *thoughts and beliefs* in our mind, and not to *ourselves*. Nor are we applying skepticism to the emotions themselves, which we're sincerely feeling, but rather to the beliefs the emotions arise from. For example, if we have the thought "I'm never going to get this," it means that a doubting thought and a Victim character are trying to attach themselves to us. By applying skepticism, we turn the tables and ask the question: What character is proposing this thought? What emotions come along with this belief? What is this character's expertise on personal development, emotional change, and prophecy of the future that says it can predict results this early? By asking these questions we consciously doubt the character's thoughts and uncertainty about the process.

If you have written out the thoughts you have around an emotional reaction and attributed them to your various characters, this process of questioning them is much more effective. When dismantling a belief system it can be helpful to scrutinize one assumption or supporting belief at a time.

Practice: Ask Questions to Develop Skepticism

To help move the change process along, we can ask questions that not only challenge existing thoughts and beliefs but, more importantly, hold our perspective in the observer stance so we don't reinforce archetype patterns. We can start by asking questions to employ our natural curiosity and engage our mind in the direction of awareness, skepticism, and creativity. Some questions to ask might be:

- What emotion am I feeling?
- What character perspective does this likely indicate?
- What are the thoughts and internal dialog corresponding to this emotion?
- What character is having these thoughts?
- What other characters are making comments about this story or emotion?
- What emotions am I creating when I assume this character's perspective and believe these thoughts?
- What is my attention on?
- What do these characters want to put my attention on?
- What are the factual assessments in these thoughts?
- How are the characters exaggerating or distorting these assessments?

- What are the emotionally charged thoughts from a character that aren't factual?
- What assumptions are being injected into these facts that are distorting a clear understanding?
- What different interpretations can I make about my situation that might also be valid?
- What implied and associated beliefs are blended into these thoughts?
- How might someone else interpret what happened?

If you don't find these questions helpful, come up with a list of your own that work for you.

One of the paradigms of the Victim is a feeling of powerlessness, which often entails not having a choice. Just by asking different questions, we use our attention to look for other choices; in this way, we begin to see that we have other options. As soon as we perceive options, our paradigm of powerlessness lessens, and we shift our perspective away from that of the Victim.

The use of questions to shift our attention can help us step out of the belief bubble of any archetype character. Asking the question "What character am I absorbed into playing right now to produce this emotion?" directs our attention towards observing our current perspective. It doesn't even matter if you answer the questions and identify the particular archetype at the source of a thought. The very fact that you have stepped into this watchful, questioning perspective is making your mind function differently.

Having a Proper Attitude and Perspective

In the process of changing beliefs, it is important that you adopt a new perspective. If this new perspective were a character it would be like Sherlock Holmes, digging into a mystery, looking for clues so he can figure out what is true and what is fiction. You might also think of it as an attorney like Perry Mason, interviewing the belief system in order to find inconsistencies in the story. Or you might see it as a hunter tracking down money or stashes of misplaced faith.

This action of hunting your false beliefs moves your perspective away from archetype characters. Adopting the skeptic's perspective and attitude enables you to ask the right questions. With practice, you develop and strengthen this character in your personality, so that you instinctively ask the necessary questions for a given situation.

I've met many people who consider themselves skeptics. They even have advanced experience, by way of scientific study or from practicing for years as an atheist, to not believe what others think. What these self-proclaimed skeptics come to realize is that they never questioned their own thoughts, beliefs, and system of thinking, to the same degree that they questioned everything else. They learned to implicitly trust their own thought process, interpretations, and conclusions even when those thoughts were from the archetype characters of their belief system. To turn their attention on their own beliefs and scrutinize them is an entirely different level of skepticism.

Practice: Dissecting Hidden, Embedded Beliefs

Some beliefs are hidden and support the larger belief the way spokes hold a wheel on a bicycle. The key is to find and challenge them one by one, and eventually the larger belief falls apart. The way to do this is with an inventory. The inventory examples given in this book are summary outlines of thoughts and beliefs. It may take a person pages of writing all the thoughts of their characters to find the pertinent beliefs they arise from.

The same words can be spoken by different characters, using different tones or attitudes, and mean completely different things. For example, if someone says "You did that really well" in a soft and tender way it means one thing; if they say it with sarcasm or contempt and disdain, those same words mean the exact opposite. If you want to know the true meaning of the message, you have to listen to the tone and attitude of what is said or thought. These kinds of hidden or embedded meanings are within our thoughts as well.

Let's dissect the beliefs behind the comment "I can't do this," a simple phrase that can have many different meanings and produce a variety of emotions. We'll reveal some of the possible supporting beliefs and then see how a process of scrutiny and skepticism can be applied to recover your faith from several "spokes."

Suppose you have tried to make changes in your behavior, perhaps to eliminate a habit or an emotional reaction. You have been working at it for several weeks but, despite your best efforts, you still exhibit the old behavior pattern. After a while you begin to think, "I can't do this." Many different emotions can accompany this one statement. You may feel like a failure, defeated, frustrated, worthless, or even angry. From inside the bubble of the belief "I can't do this," it appears that you really cannot change. You are also unknowingly investing faith in all the hidden beliefs supporting this thought. To deconstruct the belief "I can't do this," it will help to identify and examine each of the beliefs that can be embedded in this one idea.

At first glance the statement "I can't do this" might be simply an observation or assessment without any emotional charge. It's just an acknowledgment of fact if we take it to mean, "Given my present-day skills, understanding of the problem, and attempts so far, I have been unable to make the changes I wanted." Factual observation by itself doesn't elicit much emotional reaction or unhappiness, as it simply reflects reality. However, if the statement carries emotional charge, that's a clue that it also contains other meanings that are false and ego-based.

"I can't do this." → Frustration

When we feel frustrated, it is because we believe in an expectation that a certain outcome should have been achieved by now. Included in that belief are assumptions that we have all the necessary resources, skills, and time required. The fact that we haven't yet achieved our external goal denotes a failure on our part. In our belief system, we "know" we are capable of succeeding, and we are reacting because we haven't done it. But if we become aware that we lack the proper resources, training, or skill level, we won't have the same expectations of success, and therefore we won't feel frustrated.

When accompanied by frustration, the statement "I can't do this" is no longer just an observation. It is a condemnation, based on the expectation that you should have met specified goals by now. If success is expected, then the problem must be you. Included in the statement is the idea that "I have failed to meet expected goals." This embedded belief produces self-rejection and feelings of unworthiness. This negative self-image conflicts with the expected positive one of you being successful. The same thought can produce a number of different emotions because of the different embedded beliefs and meanings that thought arises from.

Character	Thought/Belief/Behavior/ Actions	Emotions
	"I can't do this" (e.g., make changes in my thoughts, behaviors, emotions).	Frustration.
Hero/Fixer	Expectation: I can do this. It should only take me a day or week. Embedded: The behavior issue is small and easily changeable. Embedded: I have all the resources, skills, and personal power necessary to make this change.	Optimistic, hopeful, confident.
Hero	Applies technique (such as affirmation).	
Observer Assessment	The behavior is still going on. The attempt at change was not effective.	Neutral.
Judge	It didn't work. You are still doing it. You failed.	Authoritative condemnation.

Victim	What I did didn't work. I failed.	Unworthiness, failure.
	I can't do this.	
Powerless Victim	Implied: powerless identity.	Powerlessness.
Hopeless Victim	Embedded: I'll never be able to do this. (projected future scenario and character)	Hopelessness.
Hero	I failed where I should have succeeded.	Frustration

Instead of trying to change the belief and its defeating tone directly, we go after the embedded beliefs that support it. The first one is the expectation of immediate success. Questions that Perry Mason or a scrutinizing detective might ask include: Is it reasonable to expect that a behavior which you have spent a lifetime automating will be broken in several days or weeks? How many days or weeks does your Judge say it should take? How long does your Fixer assume it will take? Is this expectation based in any experience or did this character just make it up? How many habits like this have you changed in your past? Have you guided other people through similar changes so that you know what it takes? If a good friend were working through the same emotional change, how long would you expect them to take? How long would you allow them to work on it before you started judging them, criticizing them, or getting frustrated with them?

The second embedded belief is the assumption that you had all the tools, skills, and resources you needed to make this change by now. This assumption supports the preceding expectation of success. Behind it is a positive self-image of success, in which you feel good about yourself and which gives you an optimistic expectation. While these are good feelings and images, where you imagine yourself being successful, they also set you up for unrealistic expectations that lead to disappointment.

The fact that you've been successful in other areas doesn't mean that you are automatically good at changing beliefs. That would be like expecting someone who is good at Ping-Pong to automatically be good at playing piano.

Embedded Beliefs of Powerlessness and Hopelessness

Does past failure predict future failure? As a factual statement, void of emotional charge, "I failed in the past" is true. However, "I will never be able to do this" is a projection of an assumed future. It suggests a kind of powerlessness over the behavior or belief. Once this character bubble is assumed, another layer of debilitating meaning is added. The embedded belief that there is no chance for future success generates a feeling of hopelessness.

There is a projected world of difference between "I haven't succeeded yet" and "I never will." When we use the statement "I can't do this," we might be trying in a shorthand way to express the first meaning of simple history; however, the second version with its projection of future failure can seep through in character identity, meaning, and feeling. When it does, it can foster a debilitating and self-sabotaging belief.

How many times have you tried and failed at something before you got good at it? How many times did you fall down while you were learning to walk? You don't remember all the simple math or spelling mistakes you made in school when you were a kid, but they didn't prevent you from developing the math and reading skills you have today. A good skeptic acknowledges that he doesn't know what a different approach or the next attempt will result in.

Once you see that any of these little embedded beliefs are invalid, you see that the statement "I can't do this" is false in several ways. It is false in its prediction of the future, in its expectation that you have all the skills and training you need, in its dictation of timing that you should have been successful by now, and in its creation of the two opposite self-images of success and failure. If you can perceive that these four words can carry a lot of false meanings, and that all of those meanings can be projected at the same time, it becomes clearer why you would want to scrutinize it and investigate the embedded meanings. All of these embedded meanings are false even though at a surface level the statement appears true about past attempts.

Smaller beliefs feed the larger ones, like roots of a tree feeding the stability of the trunk. When you see the flaw in the assumptions of these embedded beliefs, the larger ones begin to come into question. With the attitude of a detective, you instinctively divest your faith from them. Cut off the flow from the smaller roots, and the larger trunk will begin to dry up for lack of support.

It takes effort to dissect these belief systems. However, it takes much less effort to dismantle them than to support such false mental structures for the rest of your life.

—⟁—

You get to choose how you define yourself
when you direct your own attention and faith.

—⟁—

Implied Beliefs

It's useful to make a distinction between beliefs or meanings that are *embedded* in a statement and meanings that are *implied*. Implied beliefs or meanings are ones that our mind projects on top of what is said or thought.

Consider again the previous example, "I can't do this." These four words might be a statement of fact about your past actions and results. But suppose that you feel like a worthless failure. These emotions are more about an identity as a failure than about a failed attempt at doing something. These feelings clue us in to a separate set of beliefs about identity and self-worth.

In the projected belief bubble, the statement is about what you "can't" accomplish but implies "I am a failure." Although the statement's words were about failed actions, your imagination took it further and implied conclusions about your identity.

Layered beliefs create spiraling emotions of powerlessness and hopelessness. "I can't do this" becomes "I won't be able to do this," which becomes "I am a failure." The feeling of powerlessness engenders hopelessness. From that Victim bubble perspective, the next logical thought is that it is best not to try since it will result in failure anyway. You are tricked into believing that this will be true for future attempts for the rest of your life. Within this character belief bubble there is no chance for change. Now you feel despair and depression about the situation coming from multiple beliefs. From the Victim perspective the future looks bleak.

In fact, this implied identity of powerlessness is made up. However, since a person may have adopted it for many years, it appears valid from within the belief bubble, and possibly so familiar that it feels like "me." Does failing at something mean that *you* are a failure? No. The only thing that defines you as a failure is your own investment of faith in that concept—your own use of your faith to define yourself that way. You get to choose how you define yourself when you direct your own attention and faith.

Where is our power? The irony is that while we might believe we are powerless, we actually have extraordinary power. We use an incredible amount of it in the form of faith to maintain our false beliefs and the false character identity. These conceptual ideas become powerful in our minds because we invest our power in them. Then the beliefs and false identities we created hold us back from action.

No one else can stifle our attempts as effectively as we do with our own beliefs. How do we sabotage our action and our power so effectively? We do it through a stupendous act of power: we hypnotize ourselves with our own belief that we are powerless.

—⁂—

No one else can stifle our attempts as effectively as we do with our own beliefs.

—⁂—

Associated Beliefs: How Our Mind Spirals

Once you lose your attention to a belief, you see things from the perspective of the character within that belief bubble. From that character's perspective more of its beliefs become active and compound the picture. For example, our past memories have nothing to do with our present situation. But when we step into the belief bubble of failure, it can trigger memories of past experiences where we felt and believed we were powerless, and our imagination applies them to the present situation. Even if the memories are from decades ago, they are treated as evidence that we are powerless in our current situation. These associated past memories amplify our emotional state out of proportion with the present circumstances or story. These associated beliefs come from the same character and generate the same or similar emotions, yet they have nothing to do with the present situation.

Associated beliefs sometimes behave differently than embedded or implied beliefs. They distract our attention away from following the particular structure of beliefs, and try to pull our perspective into another character's belief bubble, or into similar beliefs from the same character. The present story of the Victim feeling powerless can start the mind thinking about another time in our life that we felt powerless, which felt just like this time.

Complicating this is the fact that when we are in the perspective of the powerless Victim, we can't perceive anything contradictory to the beliefs it has. It is in a bubble of beliefs in which it is powerless, and anything outside that bubble that would contradict it either can't be perceived or is discounted in some way. Because of this, no amount of evidence to the contrary will shift the belief bubble. We must first shift our perspective away from this character towards a more neutral observer.

When associated beliefs kick in, our emotional reactions are no longer about what is really going on, but rather become exaggerated and out of proportion. One place we commonly see this is if we are having an argument. If we are angry at our partner, we bring up all sorts of things that we were angry about months or years before. The angry Villain merges all the stories about our partner, or even previous partners, and amplifies the emotions. The thoughts of events might jump around but they have the same character perspective and emotions. The result is that we overreact emotionally. Later, if we feel guilty about getting angry, the Victim associates this feeling with other times we've gotten angry and compounds the guilt.

One way to help take the emotional charge out of these past memories is to revisit them from an observer perspective, dismantle the false beliefs behind these past events and characters individually, and reclaim the faith invested in their stories. Divesting faith from interpretations of previous experiences removes the possibility for characters to make these past-present associations.

Practice: Make Use of the Inventory Chart

The inventory earlier in this chapter began with one short sentence: "I can't do this." Behind those four words were numerous beliefs, from different characters, producing several different emotions. You are not likely to discover these layers of beliefs within a single thought by doing this process in your head. The inventory of beliefs is much more effective when you write them down. When a system of belief bubbles is on the page in front of you it is much easier to get outside of it than when it is in your head. The writing of the inventory is emphasized because it incorporates many of the practices into one process. Writing also helps you direct your attention in a systematic, scrutinizing way when other thoughts try to distract you. To reiterate, the inventory examples presented are summaries that outline pertinent beliefs. In the beginning it may take you pages of writing, and rereading your writing, to discover the critical false beliefs. With practice you will be able to hone in on them much faster.

Later, much later, after you've done numerous inventories on different thoughts and emotional reactions, perhaps you will be able to "see" these layers in your mind and not have to write them down. At that point it will be like doing a quick math problem in your head. But in the beginning, in order to train your mind to make these observations, and to be most effective, you will need to write out these inventory mind maps.

Shifting the Dialog

As you become more aware of how powerful concepts become when you invest faith in them, you become much more precise in your language. You speak and even think more clearly. The rough and general statements you used in the past, such as "I can't do this," don't suffice anymore.

Consider this statement: "The person I was in the past, and the way I approached change then, didn't produce the results I intended." That statement is far more precise and leaves out emotionally charged words like *can't, success,* and *failure* that can often carry so many other personalized meanings. It refers to a specific attempt, and doesn't generalize or project into the future. It also leaves out any fixed identities that are negative. It leaves open the possibility of you being different, of trying something new, and of a different outcome in the future.

Shifting your language in this way will help you stay out of many emotional reactions. To do it, you have to be aware of your inner dialog and what's about to come out of your mouth before you say it, so you can express it more accurately. In the midst of an emotional reaction, we don't usually notice our dialog until after we've spoken. Since so much of our thinking and speaking is automated, this part of the change process will take some time and effort.

By using your attention and skillfully controlling your perspective, you can scrutinize your internal dialog and find the implied, embedded, and associated beliefs that are generating many of your emotions. Doing this will enable you to invalidate existing beliefs and recover your faith from them. Then, all the emotional charge connected to those beliefs will dissipate.

Solving a Tree Problem

Sometimes we learn better by story and metaphor. So let me use one to illustrate this whole approach of breaking down beliefs into their smaller embedded, implied, and associated beliefs.

Sometimes, when we decide to change our beliefs, the task can look daunting. We may have been building up all these mental structures for decades. The Victim is likely to chime in periodically with comments like "I can't do this." I suggest you think of that structure of false and fear-based beliefs as a tree that has overgrown in your backyard.

If you have a big tree in your backyard and you want to get rid of it, can you go over to it and push it out? No. You can push and push till you wear yourself out, and after a while you will feel defeated. You will conclude that you're not strong enough, you're a failure, you feel overwhelmed, and that it's a hopeless situation. That tree with all its branches, and many roots, is too big. The comment from the Victim, "I can't do this," would appear true.

But what if you get an ax? Maybe it's a dull ax to begin with because you haven't sharpened it. You hack away at the tree for several hours and it's still standing there. With your ax, you may have cut halfway through the trunk, but it doesn't look like much progress because the tree is still standing upright. You might look at that tree and conclude that you haven't accomplished a thing. When your Judge measures your progress, it puts your attention on the whole tree that's still standing, and not on the part you've cut out. It's a poor method of assessment, but it's a common misinterpretation the Judge makes when evaluating progress.

What if you used a file on your ax? Your ax would be sharper and you could make faster progress. You wouldn't cut the tree down in the first swing, but you might get it done in the first day. For a really big tree, maybe it would take a couple days. Of course, a chain saw would be even faster—perhaps the tree would come down in a few minutes. But with a chain saw you need other items as well: you need a sharp chain, which requires a different kind of file; you also need oil to lubricate the chain and gasoline to run the saw.

While you're sharpening the ax or preparing the chain saw, it might look like you aren't really working on the tree problem directly, but you are. You are working to make your actions more effective, and that will help long-term. It might take a bit more work to get the tools and equipment, but then you can take the tree down faster. The better tools you have and the more skill you have in using them, the more efficient you will be in removing the tree. Similarly, when it comes to dissolving beliefs, getting the right tools and developing your skills won't be recognized by the characters as progress, but it is.

Of course, there is also some fear and resistance in making this change. What if the tree falls in the wrong direction? It might fall on your house, or damage a fence in the yard. How will you take care of the space that opens up when the tree is gone? There's fear in solving a tree problem because there are going to be consequences in other areas of your life.

Now even if you get that chain saw and fell that big tree in your backyard, the job isn't done. It's lying on the ground and it's too big to move.

You have to cut off the branches attached to the trunk, as well as dig up and cut the roots. These are like the embedded, implied, and associated beliefs connected to any core belief. So you take your saw or ax and you start cutting off the limbs. You cut the trunk into short lengths. Then you take your ax and split the large trunk logs into pieces small enough to move. Once each piece is small enough you can pick it up and move it out of your backyard.

That's how you solve a tree problem: you use the appropriate tools to cut it up into a bunch of smaller, manageable pieces and handle them one at a time. If you were to attempt to move the whole tree at once you would conclude, "I can't do this," and you would be correct. However, you can do it if you slice the tree up into manageable pieces that you can carry away.

Dismantling the larger core beliefs of your belief system is done the same way. Sometimes you can't even get close enough to see the main trunk of a belief because of all the branches that are sticking out. So you start with the branch that is in front of you and you work on it until part of it falls off, and then you take on another manageable belief. You may not be able to budge the bigger beliefs when you first find them, but you can inventory the smaller beliefs they are made of and take your faith out of them. This will give you easier access to tackling the bigger ones.

And don't bother wondering if a smaller supportive belief is implied, embedded, or associated. Which category you put them into isn't as important as being aware of them. Just work on being skeptical so that you can see when an idea isn't true.

Example Investigation: Bill's Story

In Chapter 1 we met Bill, a high-achieving cardiologist who, despite his stellar record of outward success and the resultant praise from people around him, had remained depressed his entire life. He'd tried to do all the right things in his efforts to achieve happiness—worked hard throughout school, completed a grueling residency, got married, became the head of a thriving clinic, started his own practice, got divorced, took up yoga, and so on—but happiness continued to elude him. At last he realized that the problem might lie within him and his own beliefs.

When Bill came to me for assistance, I helped him pay attention to what the various voices in his head were saying. He noticed that whenever he received praise or a compliment from someone, a voice within him would silently counter it with "I'm not that good. I'm only average." His inner Judge would chime in to scold him for fooling people with a false image of success. This would give rise to a fear of being found out, a certainty that those who thought so highly of him would eventually realize he was a fraud. Feelings of guilt and shame would ensue, a conviction that he was a terrible person for deceiving others and that he deserved punishment. This was followed by a hope that he would indeed be exposed and punished, and thereby be free of the pressures of maintaining the exhausting charade of success.

These were the stories and emotions that Bill lived in every day. It was emotional hell. And it all rose from a twisted set of beliefs about what constituted success and what was only "average."

From an outsider perspective it's fairly easy to see that this is all happening within the false world of Bill's ingrained belief system. But someone else recognizing this fact from outside doesn't get Bill out of his belief bubble. What's required is that Bill must see his beliefs as false. And to do that, he needs to identify the assumptions behind those beliefs. It's not enough just to know our beliefs are false—sometimes we also have to know *why* they are false.

Scrutiny and Inventory

Let's start with some questions that I asked Bill and see what his answers reveal.

Why, when you get complimented or recognized, do you dismiss it?
Bill: Because I'm not that good.
What are you then?
Bill: I'm average. Maybe even mediocre.
Why do you say you are average? What makes you average?
Bill: I'm not that good. For instance, I procrastinate. I don't manage my time well. I don't exercise or eat like I should. I'm like thirty pounds overweight. That's not healthy, and I'm a doctor and I should know better, and do better, but I don't. I'm like everyone else.

The compliments you receive have to do with your work as a cardiologist, which you have been doing for twenty-five years. It's a very specialized area requiring special skills and talents. You had a case recently where you came up with a diagnosis that others hadn't considered, and it helped the patient tremendously. People commented on how sharp and insightful that was. And you dismissed it because you just think of yourself as average.

Bill: Yes. Others would have come up with the same diagnosis, if not five minutes after me, then later the next day or something.

If you are average, does that mean that there isn't anything special about you?

Bill: Yes. There is nothing special about me.

Is there anything that makes you more skillful or smarter than anyone else?

Bill: No.

I pointed out the way Bill dismisses things. When he gets a compliment for being good at a very specialized skill that he spent decades training for and practicing, he dismisses it based on his conviction that he's only "average," and average means "like everyone else." The fact that he's overweight, doesn't exercise, doesn't eat very healthily, and procrastinates are the reasons his belief system defines him as average. If someone points out what a smart, insightful observation he made in a diagnosis, Bill deflects it by shifting to an unrelated definition of average that has to do with eating habits, exercise, and procrastination. According to his belief criteria, because he is average, he can't be considered "special" or "talented" or "smart" in a specific way because an "average" person can't be special. His locked-in personal definition of "average" pushes away the possibility of being talented or skillful at anything.

Bill worked diligently to develop a skill set of knowledge about cardiology that makes him above average in that area. He has worked very hard in that field and has developed skills that others don't have, but his Average Guy character belief bubble dismisses comments about this based on things like his *exercise habits* being average!

Character	Story/Belief/Behavior	Emotion
"Average Guy"—Authentic Self version	I am just like everyone else. I am average. (simple childhood agreement)	Humble. Humility. I am not more important than others.
"Average Guy"— with a distorted definition of what that means.	Associated agreement: If I am average, then I am not special in any specific way.	
	People compliment me on how smart, capable, or skillful I am.	
Preexisting Belief	It must not be true because I am average and therefore cannot be special.	Dismissive of the compliment.
Average Guy Character (not talented or skilled in any way)	Other people are just as good as me. I really am not as good as people say.	
Judge I	You are not as smart as people say you are. You are only an average guy.	Authoritative condemnation.

Victim As a reaction response to the compliments, Bill creates an identity of being "less than."	I am not as good as people say. People have an image of me that is false.	Not good enough. Undeserving of compliment.
Victim (Future Victim)	One day they will find out that I'm not that smart and not that special.	Fear.
Judge II	You have deceived people into thinking that you are something that you are not. You have done a bad thing. (implied/embedded agreement)	Condemning.
Victim II	I have deceived people into thinking that I am better than I am.	Guilt.
Judge III	You are a bad person. You are evil. Associated belief: Because you have done a bad thing you are therefore a bad person.	Condemning.
Victim III (new identity from this associated belief)	What I did was deceitful. I am a bad person. I am evil.	Shame. Guilt. Worthlessness identity.

| Moral Justice System from Judge | Associated agreement: If I am a bad person and have done a bad thing then I deserve to be punished. | Condemnation, sense of justice.

Need to make amends for his imagined wrongdoing. |
|---|---|---|
| Victim I, II, and III | I don't deserve this success.

I will be found out and punished. | Feeling like a fraud or imposter.

Fear that he will be found out and exposed.

Feeling undeserving of his success. |

Reality Conflicts with Beliefs

In reality, Bill is good at things. Whether it be by hard work, practice, natural affinity, or all of the above, he has areas where he excels. He isn't better than other people because of this. Actually, he is just like other people. Other people excel at some things, are average at other things, and are lousy at others. A carpenter may be brilliant at getting pieces of wood to fit together, but his cooking is average and his violin playing is lousy. So is he brilliant, average, or lousy? None of those. Those words do not describe his identity. They are only adjectives that refer to some of his skills and abilities.

Bill's painful self-judgments hinged on a couple misplaced beliefs that made his other beliefs appear true. His first belief, that he was just like everyone else, no better and no worse, was instilled in him by his parents. By itself it is humble and admirable. However, somewhere it got simplified to a fixed identity as well: "I am average." It's an innocent little belief, not inherently harmful. But viewed through the perspective of the Judge, Victim, and other characters, this concept of average was leveraged to mean different things.

In Bill's mind, *average* implies that all people are the same, and they aren't. They may have the same inherent worth as human beings, but that doesn't mean they are the same in everything. Bill's definition of *average* means that he can't have a skill, talent, or knowledge in any area that was better than anyone else's. When complimented for things other people consider exceptional, Bill's belief system responds with a cascade of reactionary thoughts and emotions.

When his false assumptions were exposed to him, Bill's self-judgments and emotional reactions began to lessen. It was somewhat of a shock in the beginning when this world, as he believed it to be, all of a sudden appeared to be untrue. This included all the statements and beliefs about himself that he'd been so convinced of and emotionally bound by for so many years. The patterns in his mind of how others thought of him and the fears of being found out as a fraud didn't all disappear overnight. His thoughts and emotions weren't gone as soon as he discovered his distorted beliefs about what was "average." But now there is a part of his conscious awareness that doesn't identify with these other characters and doesn't respond the same way with the same intensity.

It has been several months since Bill's discovery, and he is still finding pieces of the old structure to dissect and haul away. However, it is safe to say that he is a different person already.

Self-Help Myths

Sometimes people promote distraction mechanisms as ways to make themselves feel better: "If you are feeling down, then do something that you enjoy, like shopping, walking in nature, or calling a friend." While engaging in these activities may distract you from your emotions by helping you focus on other things, you haven't addressed the belief that caused the emotional reaction. It remains in your belief system and causes you to react in the same way the next time.

Distraction strategies can make you feel better but they keep you from looking at the real issue. For people who don't have the skills to change their perspective, be an observer, and apply techniques of skepticism, distracting themselves is the best they can do to feel better.

Another popular approach to changing a "negative" belief is to develop a "positive" belief to replace it. Although this technique can help at times, it might not be effective for everyone and may even make things worse. Suppose you use a positive affirmation to create an image in your mind that you are good enough and worthy of being loved. You create this image to dispel your old belief that you are not good enough. You draw from many wonderful experiences in your life, create a positive image of yourself, and invest a lot of faith in the belief that this is the real you. By doing this, you create a lot of wonderful feelings and confidence in yourself. This emotion helps you to feel better in the moment.

While this positive image and story are much closer to the truth, they carry some risks. The first is that the positive self-image is used to hide and repress the negative self-image and feelings that you don't like. The beliefs of the negative self-image remain in your unconscious, obscured by the positive ones you laid over them. You haven't reclaimed your faith from your negative self-image. Instead, you are now feeding two opposing self-images. It is quite possible to have faith in a positive and a negative self-image at the same time. The result is that you bounce from one belief bubble to another. In one moment, you might feel unworthy. In the next moment, your perspective and thoughts shift to defending yourself from this belief by holding up the positive image. The opposing beliefs may go back and forth like a debate in your mind. Since you have faith in both beliefs, both appear true. If you are unaware that this is occurring, the conflicting beliefs can be confusing and unsettling.

In the example of "I can't do this" there was also a positive self-image of the Hero. The Hero/Fixer could make the changes in short order. It was capable, smart, and confident. This positive image set up an unfounded expectation of success. When the behavior change didn't happen, the Hero image was used by the Judge to form a comparison and conclude we were a failure. So, while the positive image feels better and is closer to the truth of what we are, it can still be used against us emotionally by the Judge and Victim as an unrealistic standard.

For many people, using affirmations to build positive beliefs is an effective way to start addressing and changing their thoughts. For others, or even for the same person at another point in their journey, it feels like an empty thing to do, just another self-image distracting their attention from a deeper, more authentic self. There is not a simple answer. You find out what works best for you by trying tools and giving them some time to work. Notice the results and make adjustments. Then don't expect that the same tool that works for you will work for your best friend.

Change Your Beliefs About Changing Beliefs

The ability to change our beliefs is a complex skill. It requires manipulating our perspective, directing our attention, maneuvering images in our mind, suspending our investment of faith, refraining from judging what we discover, and oftentimes doing all this while feeling emotionally uncomfortable. This mental balancing act can be challenging in the beginning until we get used to it, but then again so were walking and riding a bike.

At first we are unfamiliar with how some beliefs are layered over core beliefs and how our belief system will distract our attention with reactionary thoughts. In the beginning we haven't yet developed control over our attention; we are more likely to follow a distracting thought than we are to get to the core of the issue with skepticism. If we assume that it will be easy or that we should be able to do it immediately, we are setting ourselves up for failure.

One of the big traps we encounter occurs when at first we don't succeed. The voice of the Judge blames us for failing to change a belief in the expected period of time. The setup to this belief began with expectations about how long it should take, even though we'd never done it before. We didn't take into account the need to develop control over our attention, or the shifting of perspective and faith required. Nor did we know what supporting beliefs were holding the core belief/behavior pattern in place.

It is important to manage expectations. Often the Judge will expect each belief to be successfully changed on the first try. Your awareness that this expectation is unreasonable will make it easier not to believe this judgment. You can adopt alternate interpretations that you did your best, that you haven't developed the needed skills yet, or that the belief has too many supporting agreements, each infused with faith, to fall apart just yet. When working to change beliefs, consider that some of them may take more than a month of consistent awareness. While this might seem way too slow, it might help to keep in mind that we have been investing in and strengthening some of these core beliefs for decades. Also remember that you aren't "doing nothing" during that month. You are spending that time identifying and dismantling the assumptions and the implied and associated beliefs supporting the core belief. Time spent "sharpening your ax" by developing your skills of observation, skepticism, and acceptance is time well spent.

Understand that changing beliefs is not always straightforward and simple. Your effectiveness at changing a belief depends partly on how strongly that belief is held and how many other beliefs support it. Your ability to be comfortable with the emotions that come up, to shift your perspective, and to maintain control over your attention are also critical factors. These skills are so important that it makes sense to develop them before expecting major beliefs to change. It's okay to go through some trial and error as you develop your skills and discover which core beliefs will take more time.

Dancing, flying an airplane, painting, and playing an instrument are skills that we are willing to afford ourselves time to learn. Re-creating your belief system and building a new sense of identity also takes time. If we assume changing beliefs is akin to knowing an answer, we are failing to understand it as a mindfulness skill.

One way to avoid failure in the beginning is to start with smaller beliefs. Expectations about how long the process will take are examples of smaller beliefs. Practicing on smaller ones in the beginning will help you develop skills and gain confidence in the process. Just because it took you only five minutes to read through an example of someone dismantling a belief does not mean that it took them only five minutes to do it, or that you will accomplish the task in the same amount of time.

Chapter 15

Forgiveness

Several years ago I gave a talk that touched on some points related to forgiveness. Afterwards, people gathered around for questions. One woman and her boyfriend remained in the back until everyone else had left. Her name was Theresa. She liked what she'd heard and basically agreed with it, but there was someone whom she felt unable to forgive.

When I asked her about it, she confessed that she couldn't forgive the man who had raped her five years earlier. To forgive this man would condone his action and trivialize the significant effect it had on her life. For her, forgiving him implied some kind of acceptance and, in her view, further implied that his action was okay.

I asked her how she felt about him. Five years after the attack, she still carried anger and hate, along with a deep sadness for herself. She didn't want to forgive him because she felt he didn't deserve it or hadn't suffered enough. These false beliefs about forgiveness kept Theresa in a state of suffering.

Forgiving a person isn't a statement that what they did was okay or to be condoned in any way. We can maintain awareness that an action was wrong, disrespectful, violent, and hurtful, whether we forgive an individual or not. Nor is forgiveness something that you do for the benefit of the person who wronged you, by letting them off the hook. It doesn't mean that there won't be consequences for their action, or that you will be friends or even talk with them after you forgive them. This isn't the kind of forgiveness we learned to do on the playground when we were six years old, where we then went off and played together. The offender may never know you have forgiven them. The benefits of forgiveness are principally for the person doing the forgiving, not for the one being forgiven.

Unable to forgive her assailant, Theresa has been thinking about that event and the man for five years. Most of that thinking has been done by her archetypes. She replays the memory as a nightmare, feeling herself abused again. Although this is taking place only within her mind and not in the physical world, nevertheless the emotional reaction is similar to what it was five years ago. Assuming the perspective of the Judge, her anger and hatred seem legitimate. She continues to relive the event from the same Victim perspective, re-creating the same emotional experience each time. In effect, for the past five years she has been abusing herself from within her imagination. She says she does not want to let her assailant off the hook, but it is Theresa who needs to be let off these hooks.

Theresa's judgments and anger don't punish the rapist; her anger and hatred never reach the original perpetrator. The perpetrator she is dealing with now exists as images in her mind. Anger is a poisonous emotion, but it only gets as far as the imaginary character in her mind that she created. All the judgment, anger, and hatred she feels are received *by her*. One part of her mind, in the form of the Judge and Villain, expresses the emotional poison and another part, the image of her perpetrator, receives that poison. *Who is really receiving the punishment?* It is her mental image, something quite separate from the actual person. One character in her mind generates an emotionally toxic expression, and another character in her mind receives it.

This is essentially self-abuse, and it has been going on for years. That man is long gone, and the pain and anger she feels today are no longer caused by him. What she needs to do now is to step out of this painful cycle of a dream. The perpetrator she should be forgiving isn't the one who attacked her. The person to forgive is the character that she has been carrying around in her own mind. In forgiving herself and her image of a perpetrator, she can be released from the Judge and Victim cycle of narratives. Forgiveness is the letting go of these emotionally abusive stories and beliefs.

In a violent act like assault or rape, there are real physical and emotional responses. There may be fear, hurt, anger, and even rage. These are natural emotional responses from our authentic integrity. The truth is that there was a violent act and an injustice. Those responses and feelings need honoring and respecting. There is also a natural tendency to protect ourself going forward, so we will probably be more vigilant and perhaps fearful. This fearful state can move our perspective towards a Victim perspective where the memory of the past event generates more feelings of powerlessness, injustice, and anger.

At some point we can slip out of the natural emotions and into emotions generated by the repetition of our character-projected belief bubbles. One of the challenges in this process is to develop the clarity to discern and acknowledge truthful interpretation of the event and separate it from the characters' interpretation, even though they might use the same words. This is made more difficult by the fact that strong emotions have a distorting effect on our clarity. Because of these layers of character reactions, it may take visiting such an event in our past more than one time to clean up the false interpretations we have created.

Note: There may be another cause of emotions that we carry years after a painful event. There can be repressed emotions from that event that we never allowed ourselves to feel and release. When emotions are repressed they continue to fester inside and seep out in unexpected moments. We repress emotions with our thoughts and beliefs such as "I shouldn't feel this way," "I should be over this," or "I'm fine, I'll just put this behind me and focus on something else." These judgmental, dismissive, and distracting thoughts don't honor how we really feel, and they keep those emotions under pressure inside us. To heal, we have to address and honor the emotions so they can be released, without believing the thoughts that would cause us to indulge in them further.

—w—

The benefits of forgiveness are principally for the person doing the forgiving, not for the one being forgiven.

—w—

Forgiveness: A Way Forward

Forgiveness is a way to change a nightmarish daydream like the one Theresa keeps alive in her mind. It is a way to take control of the repeated stories of the Judge and Victim and begin to express a different version, one with more peaceful emotions.

Forgiveness is not going to change what happened—the facts of history are facts. But our current point of view, interpretation, meaning, and therefore emotional reactions to it can change. Expressing forgiveness will change *today's emotional experience* of past events.

Theresa assumes that the suffering she experiences is due to an event that took place five years ago. It isn't. If you still suffer emotionally for something that happened in the past, it is not because of the event itself. At a certain point, the emotions arise from the beliefs embedded in the story you tell today. Forgiveness is a way to change your current beliefs so that you no longer suffer emotionally. You do this for yourself because you have the right to be happy and you want to be happy. The Judge will want to continue to be "right" and the Victim will want to continue to blame. To overcome this you need to recognize that these are endless loops of misery and embrace your desire to be happy instead.

Forgiveness allows us to step out from behind false character masks and their beliefs. It breaks the painful dialog between the Judge and Victim with a healing expression. By expressing forgiveness, we shift our perspective out of these roles and refrain from expressing the anger, frustration, disappointment, guilt, and shame they generate. The Judge and Victim characters don't have it in them to express forgiveness, but we do. When we express forgiveness, we push our mind to make a separation between us and the Judge and Victim belief bubbles. At a physical level, this creates new neural pathways for our brain to operate from.

What I invited Theresa to do that day was big. It's a simple thing that looks very small since it happens in the mind rather than externally, but it is not easy. To make that shift she has to leave, even just temporarily, the perspectives of the Judge and Victim that she has been identifying with for years. It might feel like she is abandoning a part of herself, and she is. She is abandoning the identity masks that her Judge and Victim characters have created in her imagination. She is also abandoning their version of what is "right" and "just," which they insist on clinging to even though it makes her miserable. This shift is made more difficult because she has invested faith in their stories and beliefs, and that faith acts like an anchor, fixating her perspective in those character identities.

In any situation that calls for forgiveness, the person we need to "let off the hook" is ourself. If we resist forgiveness, it is because our attention is on the person who harmed us, or it is wrapped up in a concept like justice. To overcome the resistance we must put our attention on our own emotional state, then ask: Have I suffered enough with this resentment, grudge, anger, or victimization? Will I be happier if I let this story and the characters behind it go? Any answer other than yes should be scrutinized, as it is likely coming from one or more characters as resistance.

Around all the expressions of anger, hate, resentment, and judgments are justifications. Justifications are implied and embedded agreements that support and hold fast our expressions of misery. They can play loudly in our mind, telling us why we have every right to be angry, how we were wronged, and why it is another person's fault that we feel the way we do. These justifications are often so intelligent and claim such high moral ground that no reasonable argument can be made against them. We need to realize that these justifications don't include a solution for ending the emotional pain. We must suspend our belief in them if we are going to be happy.

How We Create the Feeling of Being Wronged

Another avenue to forgiveness is to identify the smaller embedded beliefs that limit our perspective. Detaching from these small beliefs makes it easier to step back and become an observer of the large ones.

Suppose someone has done something that you dislike, and as you think about it later, you feel mistreated and abused again, just by imagining it. You are dreaming that memory from a Victim perspective. Your faith is invested in the story that Person A has wronged you. Another common element is the expectation, conscious or unconscious, that Person A "should have" done something else. This alternate version will have a story of what is "fair," "right," "supposed to," and so on. The Judge compares this "should have" scenario to what really happened. Real people or real-life events often appear to be "wrong" when contrasted to an idealized expectation.

In Theresa's case, there is a common use of the word *wrong* that applies to the rape. However, the word is used differently, with different meanings, and creates different emotions when used from a Judge and Victim perspective. It is their embedded beliefs and idealized expectations that generate much of the misery years later. We tend to automatically accept their imagined criteria and comparison judgments as truth, even though we've given no conscious thought to it. Very often, their imagined version will not hold up to scrutiny. Once we bring it into our awareness and dissect it, the belief and subsequent emotional reaction dissolves.

In Theresa's case it is easy to argue that what the rapist did was wrong, and it was. But the idea that he could have behaved differently, that he could have been a different person that day in the past, or that he could have been respectful and polite, is a fiction image. That "could have" scenario doesn't exist except in the world of imagination. That man that day did what he did, acting out of the distorted belief system he had at the time.

As we have discovered, our all-knowing belief system assumes that everyone else should behave according to our notion of what is right, fair, good, and polite. We assume all of this without knowing what really caused the other person's behavior or taking into consideration their life experiences, circumstances, and situation. Our ego assumes that the belief system operating in their head is or should be similar to our own. But if someone got fired from their job or dumped by their girlfriend/boyfriend, would we still expect them to be unerringly kind, patient, and polite? For that matter, if someone was rude or belligerent to us, would *we* still respond with kindness? Sometimes we don't live up to our own expectations, and sometimes others don't either. When we begin to take into account some of the real human factors at work in ourselves and in others, we dissolve the hidden expectations held by our Judge, Victim, and Princess.

Often people pass the equivalent of emotional poison to each other as they react to unfulfilled expectations or ideals. Perhaps our spouse has a difficult day and then vents her criticisms and complaints at us when she gets home. We become frustrated or even angry about her situation; we may also feel upset with her for bringing that home to us. The next day, we go to work and share our upset feelings by yelling at drivers on the road or being short-tempered with our colleagues. If we pay attention and become more aware of how emotional poison spreads through the complaints and criticisms that arise from false expectations, our compassion grows.

As our awareness of the realities of life and how people react emotionally increases, our expectations shift and we become more compassionate. While our imaginary version of human behavior may include high ideals and hopes, these false expectations set us up for more disappointment and judgment, which perpetuates our feelings of being offended.

Honoring our hopes and ideals is important. Through our faith in them, we can facilitate change. However, when the Judge and Victim parts of our minds wield them, the result is criticism and feeling offended. This is a misuse of hopes and ideals against our own emotional well-being. The practice of acceptance mentioned in Chapter 13 is a means of managing expectations. Acceptance involves honestly embracing things just as they are, and this often means detaching from our idealized expectations.

Why was Nelson Mandela able to forgive those who held him in prison for twenty-seven years? Perhaps he understood how his oppressors were trapped within fear-based beliefs, with the resulting oppressive behavior that they could not escape from. He would not expect them to behave any other way. However, he did not let their behavior interfere with his ideals of how he would behave. By being realistic he freed himself from internally generated bitterness, anger, and victimizations that often accompany a person's self-righteous ideals. In this case it is obvious that he, and most of the population of the country, was mistreated and it was an injustice. There was no changing that. However, feeling unjustly treated is a Victim perspective response, and that can be changed. It is possible to use words like *right, wrong,* and *injustice* in a way that has emotional integrity, without getting trapped in the perpetually suffering identity of the Victim.

What Is Forgiveness?

Forgiveness begins with a desire to be emotionally happier. This desire enables us to adopt an observer perspective and view our idealized expectations with skepticism. We begin to practice acceptance of reality. The new story is often akin to "It just was what it was." This is an acknowledgment of the reality of the past, without the addition of alternate versions for comparison. There might still be sadness or remorse, but this is a genuine response, and temporary. It persists only if there is a belief attached or repressed emotions. You might still have thoughts of other possible outcomes, but the thoughts by themselves are not beliefs—they have no power to create emotions because you haven't invested faith in them. Without an investment of faith, over time even the thoughts of an alternate version will fade and the mind will become quiet about this event.

The essence of forgiveness is dissolving your belief that someone "should" have acted any differently than they did. You give up the idealized expectation that they "should" be different than they are. You recover your faith from the imaginary version the Judge and Victim use for comparison. Without that comparison, you accept the facts as they are. Eventually there ceases to be a story to fixate on or to validate a Victim perspective. Without the Victim perspective, there is no longer the repetition of emotional pain or reaction after the experience. Nor are memories viewed from a first-person perspective or compared to an imagined alternative.

The history of the events did not change—the facts remain the same. However, you tell the story from a different point of view, and that makes the story's emotional component different. What has really changed is that there is no longer faith in an idealized version of a different past, so that belief bubble ceases to exist. This is fundamental to forgiveness.

When you come into the state of forgiveness, the most noticeable difference is in how you feel. You can think about the experience or the person without any emotional reaction. There is a quiet calm in the acceptance of life just as it was. The mind doesn't jump to a story of what could have been, nor does it imagine a punishment, payment, or revenge for the past. While we might not be happy about the events we experienced, we are no longer investing our energy in being upset, sad, or angry and the internal dialog becomes quiet.

In order to create peace within herself in the aftermath of the rape, Theresa will have to engage in this process of recovering her faith. She will have to detach from her imagined versions that dictate how it should have been different. Once she recovers her faith, the false images will not seem as real. They will be recognized as imaginations of what could have been instead of emotionally charged beliefs about what *should* have been. This process begins by shifting her perspective away from the character viewpoints of the Judge and Victim in her internal story.

She will also have to detach from any beliefs that the man could or should have been any different than he was. For some people, this is made easier by understanding another person's history, how they were raised or neglected, and/or their emotional experiences in life. When we know someone's history, it becomes easier to understand why they are the way they are, and easier not to believe in the image that our "should" story wishes they were. We don't have to know the personal details of the offender's life experiences that drove him to that behavior. What is important is that we are aware that our imagined idealized version of him is not who he really is.

Tools for Forgiveness

In previous chapters, we examined tools for changing our perspective, increasing our awareness, changing beliefs, and controlling our attention. Many of these tools can be used for forgiveness.

There are additional tools that are especially useful in the process of forgiving another person. One tool is to adopt a stance of *acceptance*. Expressing acceptance of the facts helps shift your perspective away from Victim and Judge expressions of rejection. If you can see some ways that you have grown, become stronger or more aware through the experience, then perhaps you can create a larger perspective of the experience. The larger experience of growth and understanding helps shift the focus on a singular event and will change the emotional expression.

Expressing acceptance of the facts doesn't change the history or facts, just the point of view, emotions, and kind of story you tell about an experience. Expressions of acceptance allow you to transform your present-day experience of past events into something more pleasant. It is the evolution of your consciousness out of the Judge and Victim narrative. This happens only with conscious effort, as our stories and beliefs do not change themselves.

In a case of direct physical abuse such as rape, this kind of acceptance and larger appreciation can be too difficult if the incident was recent. It is easier to start with smaller issues. It is also important to put our attention on how we have grown from the hardship or challenge, not on the hardship itself. Overcoming hardship and challenges develops character, wisdom, humility, and compassion, and it strengthens our will. But it isn't necessarily a quick process—for Nelson Mandela, the growth and benefits that followed from his unjust treatment took decades to realize.

To develop your practice of acceptance and appreciation for growth, begin with small incidents from further in your past. Don't try to see the benefits of growth in a relationship or appreciate an ex-spouse when the divorce is only weeks old. When you have become skillful at shifting your perspective and emotion on smaller issues, then advance to the larger and more recent issues of your past.

A second element helpful in coming to an expression of forgiveness is to understand why the person might have acted the way they did. The challenge here is to shift your perspective to another person's point of view. This is a step beyond just being a neutral observer. You might discover that inside Person A's perspective was a belief system, emotional state, or motivation unlike anything you have known. Seeing from this perspective might dissolve your faith in your expectations of how they should have acted. You might also be surprised at how much you incorrectly imagined about their point of view.

If you have difficulty thinking how it would be to walk in another person's shoes, then engage your mind into that perspective with the tool of writing. Writing and reading engage our imagination in a more rigorous way. If the other person is someone you've known for a while, it may be useful to have a conversation and ask questions about their state of mind.

You don't have to get to know the other person in order to use this tool, and you may not want to. You can make up a completely fictitious version of their perspective congruent with their actions. Your

Victim and Judge versions are fictitious anyway, so why not create a fictitious version that fits more closely with the facts and doesn't cause you emotional pain? True or accurate insight into another person's emotions, challenges, and beliefs is not required in order for you to forgive. Sometimes what is needed is just an alternate version that casts doubts on the idealized expectations and beliefs that your Judge and Victim are using.

One man was regularly upset and frustrated at slow drivers in front of him. His mind would spin judgments and opinions about drivers all day, from his *I* and *me* perspective. But when he began to write fictional pieces about what other drivers were doing in their cars, and why they were doing it, his attitude and emotions changed.

A third tool is awareness of your responsibility for how you feel. When you become aware that you are creating emotions of suffering with your beliefs and character narratives, then you will be motivated to dissolve those beliefs. Taking responsibility for your emotions means that you have power over how you feel—which means you have the power to change it as well. Realizing that your present-day beliefs about the past are creating unhappy emotions will motivate you to change what you believe.

When your attention is on someone else with blame and judgment, your characters have distracted you from noticing the emotions you are creating with your personal power. Blaming others for how we feel is a common narrative in our mind, reinforced in society, so it becomes a habit. Your beliefs don't change when your attention is on someone else or on the past, putting the blame and responsibility for your emotions outside yourself. Your beliefs change only when you look inward and put your attention on them.

—⟪⟫—

Taking responsibility for your emotions means that you have power over how you feel—which means you have the power to change it as well.

—⟪⟫—

Overcoming Resistance to Forgiveness

Forgiveness sounds like a simple and elegant solution to release unhappy thoughts and beliefs. And when we were five or six years old, it was. But as we have gotten older, our minds have developed more complex structures like characters and ideals that resist the process of forgiving. To actually accomplish forgiveness as an adult requires that we push through these resistant layers. Breaking down these layers into smaller pieces and working through them step by step makes the process easier and manageable.

Resistance One: Attachment to Ideals

To truly forgive someone for not meeting our expectations, we must recognize and relinquish those expectations. In the forgiveness process, some people resist letting go of their idealized versions of themselves and others. They make the case that these idealized versions are goals that give them something to strive or hope for.

When ideals are used in a genuine way they inspire us to acts of kindness, compassion, and achievement. When these same ideals are used by the archetype characters they produce misery. The Judge uses ideals for comparison and generates criticism, disappointment, anger, and disgust, while at the same time having a feeling of righteous authority. The Victim creates a story using the same conceptual ideals and produces betrayal, guilt, shame, and other painful feelings. Having ideals is not a problem. However, problems are created when those ideals are used against us emotionally by our archetype characters.

Often our beliefs associate certain ideals with being happy. We believe that living in that perfect world with those perfect people who are all operating according to our idealized expectations would keep us safe from being hurt emotionally. In the ideal scenario none of the Victim belief bubbles get triggered so we don't feel offended. In that perfect world, we are the idealized people our Judge says we should be, so the Judge no longer criticizes us and we aren't victimized anymore. This feeling of being safe and happy is conditional on living within a narrow corner of the belief system where no other feelings get triggered. It is very appealing even if it is only created by an image in our minds.

Detaching from the concepts that make up our idealized expectations also means detaching from the emotions associated with those ideals. It feels like we are letting go of the possibility of emotional safety, the thing that will make us happy, and venturing into something scary if we detach from these ideals. If we are convinced that having the "perfect" life will make us happy, then we might also be afraid of having anything else.

However, those blissful emotional states could only be achieved if the real world and real people fit our imagined version of them. Everyone and everything would have to act in accordance with our expectations in order for us to love, be happy, or even feel safe. The problem with our imaginary, idealistic world of emotional safety is that it is only imaginary, and clinging to it will only lead to disappointment and other emotional reactions as reality bursts our bubbles. To get off this cycle of hope and disappointment we have to dissolve our attachments to these false beliefs.

What does this look like? Roger is angry and hateful towards his ex-wife Diane, who is now making a new life with another man. Roger has an idealized version of his ex-wife that his Judge and Victim use in their stories in his head. The Victim feels betrayed because the real Diane left him. Idealized Diane would never leave Roger—she adores him and only wants to be with him. Roger's Victim feels betrayed and rejected by the real Diane. Roger's Judge condemns and is angry at the real Diane for not measuring up to Idealized Diane's fictional behavior.

Roger also has an idealized version of himself. Idealized Roger never would have treated Diane the way the real Roger did. When Roger's Judge compares Roger's actual behavior to that of Idealized Roger, he is condemned and hated. The Victim receives these criticisms from the Judge and feels unworthy, ashamed, and angry at itself. Idealized Roger is obviously so much better than the Victim and so, in the Victim identity, Roger feels unworthy and ashamed.

In this system of beliefs, happiness is dependent on Idealized Roger being together with Idealized Diane. This keeps Roger's Fixer busy trying to get back together with Diane, or to make her behave like Idealized Diane by punishing her with anger when she doesn't fit the image. From this bubble, asking Roger to let go of these ideals is also asking him to give up his chance for this scripted version of happiness. Because of that false association to happiness Roger resists letting go of the ideals the Judge and Victim are using against him emotionally.

It is possible to keep our high expectations and goals and use them for self-motivation while we dismantle the Judge and Victim aspects that cause unhappiness, but it's a very difficult way to go about it. Dissolving beliefs in your mind is hard enough in the beginning. Leaving some of the idealized structures intact and having to work around them makes it even more challenging. It might be helpful for Roger to hold in his mind the possibility that Diane would forgive him in the future, but to have the expectation that she should have already done so is harmful. Holding on to ideals in this way raises the risk of confusing the hope of a future possibility with the expectation that it should happen today, which makes it harder to get free of the Judge and Victim narratives. Sometimes the easier and faster approach is to dissolve the goals and expectations altogether. Later, if you want, once the Judge and Victim no longer dominate the narrative in your mind, you can consciously rebuild your goals with a practical timeline for their future attainment.

By detaching our faith from the false beliefs such as these conceptual ideals, we clear away illusions, giving us more clarity to perceive and accept life and people as they actually are. The result may not be a story of such idealized hope, but it is a *real* story, and one that has a real chance for peace and happiness. The fictional one with false beliefs and illusions has no chance. A life based in truth can lead us towards happiness, humility, acceptance, understanding, respect, and compassion. These may sound like empty concepts to someone steeped in self-judgment, but with practice and work they become a tangible way to live our life.

Resistance Two: The Victim Identity

Oddly, as much as the Victim character cries out for change and seems to run from any possible unhappiness, it seems to resist healing even more. The Victim part of our mind resists forgiveness and clings to its expressions of misery. Not surprisingly, almost all expressions of the Victim are accompanied by unpleasant emotions. Avoiding forgiveness is a matter of survival for this part of the ego-mind. If the Victim allowed forgiveness, then it would have no story to tell, no emotional reactions to create, nothing to do. Its drama stories would cease, and the Victim character would essentially die—and it is the nature of living things, ego included, to resist death in every way possible.

The critical step in overcoming this layer of resistance is to distinguish yourself from the identity of the Victim character. Use awareness and attention to notice the different parts of your mind and name them as archetype characters; in this way, you can separate your perspective from that of the Victim. This gap allows you to perceive that the Victim's resistance and fear of its death is not yours. Its resistance story then becomes less believable, and its fear of change will have less power over your choices. With awareness, you will observe that what seemed to be "your" resistance is really the Victim's resistance. You will realize that the Victim is suffering not only because of a belief against forgiveness, but also at the prospect of losing its life if that belief is dissolved. Awareness of the irrational nature of this part of the mind will help motivate you to fearlessly let it die.

Resistance Three: Unwillingness to See from the Other Person's Perspective

Our belief system may resist seeing the situation from another person's perspective. The ego system of characters wants the other person to understand *our* perspective and adopt our story and beliefs. The ego-mind is invested in being right and seeing others as wrong. It shuns differing beliefs and points of view and thereby impedes our growth. When we consider expanding our perception to other points of view, the ego digs in its heels. If you find yourself trying to convince another person that they should change or that they were wrong, it is likely that you are trying to get them to adopt your belief bubble.

Seeing from another's perspective makes our imagination stretch and become more flexible. We might have to put forth some effort to accomplish this mental and emotional stretch. A practical way to help is to write out what might be going on in the other person's mind. Writing encourages us to sustain the shift for a longer period of time. Writing also engages our mind to use language more precisely. This makes writing a more rigorous and effective use of our attention and perspective than just thinking.

—⟋⟍—

No one is harder on us than the inner critic of our own Judge, because it has more expectations of us than of any other person.

—⟋⟍—

Self-Forgiveness: Releasing Yourself from the Injustice System

It is often more challenging to forgive oneself than to forgive someone else. No one is harder on us than the inner critic of our own Judge, because it has more expectations of us than of any other person.

In the past, we looked outside ourselves for forgiveness: a parent, teacher, or priest apportioned punishment and absolution. While we were growing up only others had this power, so we never developed the habit of forgiving ourselves. As adults, no internal character voice says, "I've suffered enough with this story! It's time to forgive myself." It's not that we lack the ability—it's just that we never acquired the habit, nor is it in the nature of the Judge and Victim to offer forgiveness. Therefore we mustn't leave it up to our existing belief system. A new part of ourself has to stand strong and engage in this new authentic expression of self-acceptance.

False beliefs and our authentic nature compete in the quest to forgive ourselves. Since childhood, many of us have been taught that forgiveness of others is virtuous. Our belief system labels it as altruistic and noble, reinforcing our emotional motivation to forgive other people. It is also healing because we can let go of the grudge or resentment we felt towards them.

Forgiving ourselves presents a different situation. In the view of our belief system, forgiving ourselves doesn't make us a noble, compassionate, altruistic, or good person. Rather, we are seen as "letting ourselves off the hook." Our characters use the calls of idealism, responsibility, and justice to keep us on the hook. They don't stand up for us and say,

"We have been berated and emotionally punished enough. Now it is time for compassion and healing." While we might recognize that someone else has been chastised a number of times and withhold further reprimand, our belief system doesn't care how many times we've criticized ourselves for the same error. The Judge and Victim have a lousy memory. They don't keep track—they just keep going, compelled to point out and repeatedly punish our failings, possibly for years. To end the criticism, berating, and self-judgment that go on in your internal dialog, it is up to you to say for yourself, "Enough!" If you haven't had that voice within you before, you have to create it.

In self-forgiveness, we divest our faith from expectations of what we "should" or "shouldn't" have done and how we "should" be, just as we do when forgiving another. As long as we hold those expectations, the Judge believes that we've done something wrong, warranting criticism. The Victim receives this pronouncement and believes that we deserve emotional punishment for our failure. This seems to be a sensible conclusion if the original expectations are accepted as valid. Agreeing with the conclusion that we deserve to be punished fixes our perception in the Victim character, which also holds the implied belief "I don't deserve to be forgiven," or "I don't deserve to be happy." This makes it difficult to even consider forgiving ourselves.

Our faith in this Victim belief, and in any embedded beliefs hidden behind its statements, is a barrier to practicing presence and accepting ourselves just as we are. It's impossible to solve the problem from within the Victim's bubble of beliefs. The Victim always believes negative things about itself and will make no expression of acceptance or forgiveness. Getting out of the belief bubble perspective of this character is the first step. To begin dismantling this structure of false beliefs, we can adopt the stance of the observer and do an inventory of the embedded and implied agreements.

Another way to challenge this belief is to imagine punishing someone else to the degree that we punish and berate ourselves. You could even say out loud, as if you were talking to someone else, all the harsh things the Judge and Victim say about you. Would you treat anyone else the way these characters treat you? This is a kind of commonsense test for these self-punishing thoughts. If you wouldn't repeatedly send those thoughts to anyone else, then perhaps you don't deserve to be treated that way either. When you really challenge these self-judgments and victimizations you become aware that this part of your belief system really behaves as an *injustice system.*

Theresa, the woman mentioned earlier, can forgive herself also. Many rape stories contain an element of self-judgment that lies below the surface of the anger directed towards the rapist. Within our Victim stories there is usually anger directed at ourselves. Theresa's inner Judge concocts stories of how the rape wouldn't have happened if she had done X, Y, and Z differently. The Judge may assert that she shouldn't have opened the door, gone to that party, trusted the man, had that drink, or ignored her instincts. It can invent numerous fictional versions and outcomes based on something she did or didn't do. With faith invested in these alternate versions, the Judge and belief system conclude it was at least partly her fault.

There are two false assumptions hidden here. The first is that she should have known all of this before it happened. We've already acknowledged that "could have" and "should have" scenarios are purely fictitious. However, Theresa may fail to notice this false assumption because the voice of the Judge is treated as an all-knowing authority, so she doesn't scrutinize the embedded and implied beliefs behind its statements. Instead, she adopts the Victim perspective and accepts the condemnations of the Judge as right.

The second false assumption is that any of those alternate paths would have led to a different outcome; there is no proof they would have, only speculation. It is up to us to be skeptical on our own behalf and challenge the false assumptions made by our Judge and Victim characters, removing the blocks to self-forgiveness.

Forgiving the Judge and Victim

You are your own harshest critic. There is no sterner judge than the one in your own mind. That is why self-forgiveness is necessary if you are to create peace and happiness for yourself.

The most challenging aspect of forgiving yourself is to forgive your internal characters of Judge and Victim. As you become more aware of them and the emotional havoc they cause, you will likely begin to wish they would go away. You might even react by hating them at times. The mind begins to imagine an alternate reality where there is no Judge or Victim. Wanting to rid yourself of the Judge and Victim can look like a worthy goal. This is fine, until the imagined Judge- and Victim-free version becomes the standard for the Judge to use in comparisons and criticisms. It finds your current state of mind unsatisfactory. The result is more judgments, victimizations, and corresponding emotions based on the newly created fictional ideal. The Judge and Victim characters use your new ideal to create more thoughts about what is wrong with you! Some sample thoughts that signal this trap are "I know I should forgive him for this, but I can't"; "What is wrong with me that I can't get over this?"; "I should have just forgiven myself and I would be over this by now."

This pattern of judgment continues until you adopt a different perspective and expressions. It begins with being an observer and then extends to acceptance, which is the opposite of rejection or judgment. Neither the Judge nor the Victim can subscribe to or even survive in this perspective. The Judge's habit is to express rejection and the Victim's habit is to receive it. Stepping out of the perspective of Judge and Victim and expressing acceptance of the way things are breaks the old habits of expression and creates new ones.

Once you have developed some skill in being the observer and controlling your attention, you can speed up the transformation process. To move towards self-forgiveness faster, express forgiveness to your Judge, Victim, and other characters. Forgive the Judge for its actions, expressions, expectations, condemnations, criticisms, and rejections. Forgive the Victim for its role in believing the stories and receiving the abuse from the Judge and from others. Both characters are doing the best they can. Not knowing any better, and being trapped in a very old and outdated program of beliefs, they've made the best possible understandings and interpretations of your experiences in life as they could. As was said by a great teacher, "Forgive them, for they know not what they do." By the same token, forgive yourself for not knowing any differently than you did at the time.

Release the Judge and Victim in your mind from any expectation that they should be different than they are today. This means detaching from that idealized version. With time and practice the automated expressions in your mind will change, but today they are where they are. Forgive yourself for any beliefs that you should be different than you are. As much as you would like the Judge and Victim to vanish forever, that expectation only creates a basis for more comparison and judgment. Much like yelling at a flat tire, your rejection of these characters is just another Judge and Victim bubble. If you really wish for the Judge and Victim, as well as their stories, to be gone, then forgive them. The expression of forgiveness is what will make the difference, not wishing. The real noticeable change happens in our emotional state as we express differently. By practicing a different expression, you eventually become different—not the other way around.

This action of forgiving your Judge and Victim is not a starting point. To anticipate that you'll be effective at this technique upon reading this book is a dangerous expectation. The fact that something makes logical sense doesn't mean that you have the personal willpower over your attention and perspective yet to make it happen. Attempting to do this advanced level of forgiveness without first developing skill in controlling your attention and perspective can lead to more self-judgment because of unrealistic expectations. Maybe you've gotten some good ideas from this discussion of forgiveness, but that doesn't mean you are skillful in applying them yet, or in preventing the Judge and Victim from using these concepts against you emotionally. Only awareness and practice can prevent that.

In spite of your lack of skills, you have to begin somewhere. By practicing and engaging in expressions of forgiveness you become better at it. The practice is the important part. You will have to suspend belief in these judgmental thoughts many times until it becomes the dominant habit. You will have to practice expressions of acceptance and forgiveness until it becomes a bigger habit than the expressions you are replacing.

Practice: Forgiveness In Action

The practice of forgiveness is the same as changing other beliefs. In the case of forgiveness we focus attention on specific beliefs of the Judge and Victim. The first step in this process is to separate your perspective from the Judge, Victim, and other characters using the practices previously mentioned.

Put your attention on your expectations, images of perfection, and assumptions about how you are "supposed to be." Then break them down into details, looking for the underlying embedded and implied beliefs. The more aware you are of these expectations, the more you will perceive them as illusions, dreams, belief bubbles, and abstract constructs in your mind. They are just conceptual ideas, very different from the reality of who and what you are. The more clearly you see how your implied and embedded beliefs are disconnected from reality, the more your expectations will begin to appear unreasonable and, at a certain point, ridiculous.

The recognition that your expectations are ridiculous becomes possible when you use the observer perspective and are skeptical of your beliefs. The glue holding these artificially constructed stories together is your faith. When your beliefs no longer pass the test of common sense, you naturally reclaim your faith from them and your personal power grows.

Chapter 16

Emotions: Why Do I Feel This Way?

Up to this point we have developed the understanding that emotions arise from beliefs. While this is the most common source of unpleasant emotional reactions, and the first cause we should consider, it isn't the only source of emotions. People who change their beliefs and quiet their mind may feel confused when they still experience certain emotions. They find themselves feeling sadness, anger, gratitude, joy, and love without any accompanying thoughts or beliefs. This is because there are sources of emotions unrelated to our thoughts and beliefs.

When we notice a particular emotion we ask ourselves, "Why do I feel this way?" Sometimes we draw a blank, because we simply don't know. If this not knowing results in a sense of confusion, our inner Victim may extrapolate that to feeling like a failure. We have the assumption that we should know why, but we don't know the answer.

To avoid these feelings of confusion and failure, the mind quickly proposes and accepts a justification for our emotions. Any answer we believe is right will make us feel better than not knowing. It's usually a simplistic, one-sentence answer to the question. We are quick to blame traffic, someone at work, or point to someone we are close to. The justification ignores the impact of our belief system and other sources such as those described later in this chapter.

Emotions arise from a number of sources. The impact of each source varies from person to person, depending on our past experiences as well as how much control we have over our attention and over what we believe.

But before we explore those sources, let's discuss our emotional system.

Your Emotional Body and Its Functions

Imagine that, just as you have a physical body, you have an emotional body as well, which can perceive the entire spectrum of emotions. You can't see it, but imagine that your emotional body surrounds your physical body like the skin and also has depth, permeating and connecting all your cells. This explains how we can perceive emotions at different places inside our physical body. Our nervous system is able to sense these emotions in areas of our body the same way it can sense physical sensations.

In the same way that understanding the functions of our physical body helps us care for it wisely and use it skillfully to express ourselves, understanding how our emotional body works will help us in gaining mastery over our emotions.

The Emotional Body as a Feedback Mechanism

One of the functions of the physical body is that it gives us important feedback in the form of signals of pleasure and pain. If you touch a hot stove, you feel pain, which is accurate feedback and causes you to pull your hand back and prevent further damage. Stretching, affection, and movement can feel good and create a pleasant experience that encourages healthier activities. These sensations are appropriate feelings resulting from what we are doing.

A painful sensation is a useful signal because it is telling us to change something. The pain in our hand when we touch a hot stove is alerting us to a dangerous situation. The problem is not the feeling of pain. This is the sensory feedback you are supposed to get from a hot stove. The problem is that we have our hand on a hot stove.

Our emotions work in a similar way. Emotions are not the problem, even if they are unpleasant and painful. They are just the feedback that informs us of something that needs to be changed. Change the cause of the emotions and the emotion will change. A person with a lot of angry outbursts may want to get rid of their anger, but that wouldn't be effective. The anger emotion is being created as a result of something else. They would do better to put their attention on the causes of their anger—and that doesn't mean the immediate triggers, like traffic, the other driver, or people around them, that their Victim character or denial system points to as justification.

Emotions give us the appropriate pleasant or unpleasant feedback for what we are doing and help us make decisions. If we watch a horror movie and find it to be a miserable experience, we've gotten some very useful feedback about the kind of movie we no longer want to see. Or perhaps we go to a classical music performance and have a beautiful emotional experience. This provides great feedback to tell us what brings more happiness and enjoyment into our life. When your friend calls and invites you out for dinner or drinks, you picture the scenario, get a feeling as a result of thinking about the imagined evening, and then decide whether to go, depending on how it feels.

This is when the emotional body works well: generating the right emotions for the situation or imagined scenario, in the right proportion. Emotions are an important component in guiding us to make decisions. But the emotional body doesn't always work in such a straightforward way. When we have multiple conflicting beliefs it is more difficult to sort out an answer about what we should or want to do.

The Emotional Body Responds to Things Real and Imagined

The emotional system responds to just about everything we perceive, whether real or imagined. Our emotional body can't tell the difference. It even responds to a sleeping dream as if it were real, because it appears real while we're in the middle of it. When we're awake and operating within a belief bubble (essentially a daydream), in an archetype character perspective, that belief bubble appears as reality and the emotional body responds accordingly. The more faith we've invested in these belief-based dreams, the greater intensity of emotions we'll feel, just because there is more personal power behind them.

Our emotions are generated in response to our inner world of beliefs in the same way that they're generated in response to reality. This is how emotions are supposed to work. While emotions may feel unpleasant and painful, the emotions aren't the problem. Emotions are just the sensations you get as a response to painful beliefs, judgmental rejections, and false belief bubbles.

Emotions Conflict

Our imagination is well able to generate multiple scenarios, and our emotional body responds to all of them at one time. This can be confusing; if we can't sort out the conflicting signals, we may be unsure what to do. Our emotional body is doing its job, trying to help us make a decision. The problem is that our conflicting beliefs and imagined scenarios generate conflicting emotions. It is up to us to develop our awareness so we can discern between reality, helpful projections of our imagination, and distorted character projections.

Suppose two people are engaged and their wedding date is getting near. If one of them is experiencing uneasiness but is uncomfortable talking about emotions, they may simply say they're "getting cold feet." If they are more comfortable and honest about their emotions they will describe their feelings of fear and doubt, which seem to conflict with their feelings of genuine love and adoration for their partner. There may also be a gut feeling that something isn't right. That feeling might be authentic, but it might also be a Victim character afraid of experiencing unconditional love. It could also be the expression, emotionally, of an unconscious belief like "all married people are unhappy." Then there is the layer of emotion about how awful it would be to call off the wedding because people have already spent money on airfare and catering, and there's a fear of disappointing them. Exploration and scrutiny are the only way to find out where the uneasiness is coming from.

Several different emotions in a scenario can be a lot to observe and monitor consciously at one time. When we're considering a big decision we may be harboring numerous beliefs with strong emotions plus emotions from other sources. If we don't have a great deal of awareness to discern the several different emotions we're feeling, we tend to just lump them into one vague pile and say we feel confused or upset. In these situations, you can use the tool of the belief system inventory to sort out how much of each emotion you feel, and the different beliefs behind each one.

All of this is to say that our emotional body is an amazing feedback system for what we are perceiving, both real and imagined. It is giving us emotional responses even to ideas and beliefs that we may not be aware we have.

—⚡—

**When you change your false beliefs,
your emotions will also change.**

—⚡—

Changing Your Emotions

The important thing to understand about changing emotions is that *you don't have to change them.* They are authentic responses to your real-life circumstances, imagined scenarios, conscious and unconscious beliefs. If you don't like the emotions you are feeling you will have better results by addressing their causes. If you simply try to repress or deny your emotions, it will be more difficult to discern their cause. Typically, when your emotions are unpleasant and painful, the real cause is false beliefs. When you change your false beliefs, your emotions will also change.

While sorting out these emotions and their causes it's important to refrain from expressing them inappropriately. If you are angry, it can be wise and helpful to refrain from venting that anger at another person. Dumping your toxic emotions on someone may make it seem like you're getting rid of them because you feel better, but it's not a real solution. For one thing, that anger might just come back to you from that person later.

Refraining from expressing toxic emotions to others is different from repressing them. When we repress emotions we push them down in an attempt not to feel them anymore. Burying emotions deep inside and making ourselves believe they are not there, or not important, doesn't make them go away. It just makes them come out later, usually in unhealthy ways. (We'll look more closely at repressed emotions later in this chapter.) Refraining is different. Refraining means allowing ourselves to feel emotions without acting on them or venting them to other people. By feeling emotions we are allowing them to dissipate and be released from our emotional body. While allowing our emotions to be released, it is important not to believe the thoughts that justify these emotions as this will bring us into a character loop and generate more.

There may still be actions to take. Real-life situations have to be addressed with real-life solutions. For example, you may need to set boundaries with a person who is criticizing or expressing anger at you, perhaps by removing yourself from the situation or confronting them. However, even when there is a real-life situation to address, there are usually also thoughts and negative beliefs that run in your mind about that person, yourself, or the situation, which add other emotions to your experience. These beliefs and thoughts can be dissolved as well.

Perhaps a friend is going through a tough stretch and you let them stay with you for a while, but what you thought would be a few days turns into a few weeks. In the meantime the person is behaving like a slob in your home and isn't contributing anything towards your household expenses. You're cleaning up after them and incurring extra expense. You have a real-life situation where you intended to be generous but are now being taken advantage of and victimized in a real way. At the same time, you have Victim thoughts and beliefs running in your mind. Emotions you feel from the real situation exactly match those generated by the stories in your head, and now you need to really focus your attention to find the line between the two. You will need to do a belief inventory process on your stories to address the belief-generated emotions. You will also need to address the real-life issue with your friend, establish boundaries, and agree on expectations.

—⁓—

Refraining means allowing ourselves to feel emotions
without acting on them or venting them to other people.

—⁓—

Major Sources of Emotions

While most of the unpleasant emotions that make us feel miserable originate from our beliefs or are magnified by them, there are actually numerous sources of emotions. Some are internal, others are external. Some emotions are generated by humans, and some are naturally occurring. In short, we are immersed in energy fields of emotions all the time.

Source One: Natural Emotions

Natural emotions are emotions that arise as a direct response to the perception of something real in our environment. A beautiful sunset or sunrise stimulates feelings of awe, love, and appreciation. A beautiful piece of music lifts our spirits. The sight of a young child running into the street evokes a response of alarm. Loss of a loved one can create grief. These are natural expressions of our emotional body that don't come from conditioned beliefs.

A baby's emotions are natural, occurring without prior conditioning. Their emotional response to the world around them is predominantly love and joy. An infant will cry out when in physical pain, hungry, or because of an uncomfortable wet diaper. These are natural emotional responses aligned with and appropriate to real experience.

Young children's emotional expressions are also predominantly of love. A young child's mind, before it is engulfed by conditioned beliefs, is different from that of an adult. It is imaginative, creative, curious, and most often happy. It easily and naturally expresses unconditional love, lacking the criticism, self-judgment, fears, pride, jealousy, envy, and other emotions of the ego-mind that come later with social conditioning. A child looks at things it doesn't know or understand and responds with wonder and curiosity.

Children are taught to make interpretations that create a fear of cars, high falls, animals that could injure them, and they learn to fear what others might think of them. Children eventually learn that they should know things and to feel uncomfortable when they don't know. As that process takes place, it becomes impossible to know how much of their fear is natural and how much of it is added on by their mind's interpretations, associations, and conditioning. Throughout our lives, some of our emotions are natural responses arising from a natural mind and emotional body. By the time we are adults, our mind's natural functioning might be layered over with internal dialog and false beliefs, but it is still there. Perhaps it finds its way out when we are playing with our children or doing an activity we love, like painting or playing music, where we connect with those expressive elements of play, creativity, and love.

In any case, it is possible for our mind to imagine and dream in the ways that it did when we were younger, ways that are completely different from the internal dialog chatter and stress that arise from fear-based beliefs. By detaching from our false beliefs it is possible to become more aligned with this happy, curious, and loving state, and still operate responsibly in the world.

Source Two: Emotions from Beliefs

Through repetition and conditioning, children learn to associate certain emotions with specific experiences and then with words. This expands to phrases and larger concepts. *No, yes, bad,* and *good* are examples of words that adults ascribe to children and their behavior. When a child does something they shouldn't, their parents will use the words *no* and *bad*. The message will come with a certain tone of voice, facial expression, gesture, and possibly even a spanking. The child learns to feel a certain emotion about the words as well as about a specific behavior. The words and actions, along with the child's emotional response to them, form a congruent message and become a way to modify the child's behavior. Over time, the message can be condensed into a smile, for example, which can evoke an immediate response of feeling like a good child who is loved.

This is social conditioning through punishment and reward. The punishments and rewards can be verbal, have an emotional component, or be physical. Through repetition of punishments and rewards we build a library of associations in our mind that includes beliefs about our behavior and ourselves. When we do a certain behavior, or think of doing it, our mind flashes the associations and we feel guilt and shame even if no one else is around. We learn to believe that this world of associations and beliefs, complete with emotions, is reality.

One of the confusing things about emotions that come from beliefs is that they very often match natural-response emotions. Grief is a natural-response emotion to the loss of a loved one. However, that grief can be exaggerated and prolonged with our character stories and beliefs about loss. From our stories about our loss we can generate more feelings of grief long after the natural emotions would have dissipated. The process for change is to respect the emotions we feel, allow ourselves to feel and release them, and not believe the thoughts in our mind that would generate more emotions via stories.

Source Three: Emotions in One's Personal Emotional Field

One characteristic of emotions is that they can linger. If you have an emotional reaction of fear or anger, and the cause is removed, that emotion doesn't immediately end. It can hang around you like a cloud and dissipate over time. The time can be very short or sustained for days, depending on the strength of the feeling. This is one way that feelings make up your *personal emotional field.* While some emotions in your field come from beliefs or from current experiences, past emotions are still hanging around there as well.

Sometimes we say that a person is surrounded by a "dark cloud," meaning that they are carrying a lot of negative emotions. Someone who is generally happy and joyous has a cloud too—it's just that their emotional field is pleasant and enjoyable. There's no question that we all have a kind of cloud or field of emotions around us. The important question is, what is the quality of that field, and do you want to change it?

If you meditate in the morning on gratitude, you can consciously create and experience the feeling of gratitude. As you go about your day, that feeling can stay with you for a while. You get to continue feeling the emotion that you created earlier in the day. If you practice this regularly the emotion of gratitude becomes stronger and is present for longer periods.

Similarly, if you have an outburst of anger, you might remain angry for a few more minutes, hours, or the rest of the day. Even if you talk yourself out of whatever interpretation caused the anger and no longer align with the belief you had, the emotion doesn't necessarily leave you right away. The emotions you expressed into your emotional field are still there until they dissipate. Even though you aren't adding any more faith to the belief or generating any more anger, the emotion you created takes time to dissipate.

Emotions from Unconscious Beliefs

While some of the emotions in our cloud might seem obvious, others are more layered and long running. Some of the emotions that make up our emotional field are continually being reinforced by unconscious beliefs. A thought or image might arise from an unconscious belief and our emotional body responds. For example, the fear of what others think of us can be triggered many times during a day as we are around people. The emotion we unconsciously created is now part of our emotional field. We can have many beliefs stirring many thoughts and we can unconsciously generate emotions all day long. As we become more aware of our thoughts and beliefs, the emotions we are adding to our emotional field become more obvious.

Even if we are able to be the observer and not believe our thoughts about something, our faith might still be stored in the underlying beliefs and in associated beliefs from the past. While we may recognize intellectually that the thought or belief isn't true, it still has the power to create emotion. Our perspective has shifted, but it may take a while for our emotions to reflect that change.

We might think of our many beliefs that contribute to our emotional field as clothes we wear. Once we put them on, we don't notice them much throughout the day, yet our skin senses the material texture and pressure of the cloth on every inch of our body all day long. While we are busy with other things and aren't paying attention to these sensations, our physical body is still experiencing them. Each belief we acquired during our life is like a thread or patch of clothing. Some are very beautiful and smell like flowers, and some beliefs stink with fear, anger, and disappointment. By the time we are adults we have been collecting beliefs for years and have lost track of how many layers of beliefs we are wearing. There might be dozens or even hundreds of layers of beliefs, like different pieces of cloth. Each of these beliefs produces an emotion and contributes to the emotional field around us, even if we are unaware that we are dragging those beliefs around.

Since so many of our emotions arise from unconscious beliefs, we could call our emotional field an *emotional-belief field*. An emotional-belief field is the sum of all our belief bubbles plus the emotions they produce.

Studies have shown that people who experience external life-changing events that strongly affect their emotions often return to their previous level of happiness or unhappiness within a year or two. This is the case whether someone goes through divorce, has a child, loses a leg, or wins the lottery. The resultant theory is that people have an emotional set point and that is what they return to. This return to a baseline emotion makes sense in terms of a person's emotional-belief field determining their overall emotional state. They may temporarily have positive or negative emotional responses to things, but they return to feeling the emotions normally produced and maintained by their composite emotional-belief bubble. The exception to this is when a person makes a strong commitment to become aware of and change their beliefs. Internal changes in your beliefs produce lasting and sustainable emotional changes.

The overall effect of the emotional-belief field is that it creates default emotional states for a person's personality. A long-term strategy for eliminating unhappiness and misery would be to shed the layers of fear-based beliefs. Then you have more room in your emotional field for emotions based in love. This strategy has a higher probability of working than does winning the lottery, and will have longer-lasting results.

Source Four: Other People's Emotions

The impact of the emotions of others is usually small compared to that of our own natural reactions, beliefs, and emotional field. Additionally, our emotional-belief field creates a barrier that is difficult for other people's emotions to penetrate, and for us to perceive beyond. In spite of this, other people's emotions do affect our experience.

Feeling the emotions of others generally happens in one of two ways. The first is when we focus our attention on another being, in effect extending our consciousness as a feeler from our emotional body. This is easier to do when we are quiet and intently paying attention. Sometimes a person walks into the room in an intense emotional state, and what we perceive is more than just body language and facial expressions. We sense a feeling, like the cloud around them. We might not be aware of this sense consciously, but it is within the range of our ability to perceive. If we are busy with thoughts and filled with our own beliefs, we are more likely to imagine what someone else is feeling and project our assumed emotions onto them rather than perceive what they're actually feeling.

The second way we can feel another person's emotion is when someone expresses their emotions to us, such as anger, guilt, or sadness, and we perceive it with our emotional body. Our clarity in recognizing their emotion can quickly get muddy as we have our own emotional reaction to their expression. For example, if they express anger, we are more likely to feel our own fearful fight-or-flight reaction than their anger. Some of our fear could be from a natural response if we sense danger, and some fear can arise from the interpretation made by our belief system. In either case, we have moved beyond noticing their anger and are mostly experiencing our emotional response.

If we project ideas of what might happen to us because of their anger, we no longer feel natural fears. Now we have shifted to belief-generated fears as we react to our imagined scenarios. The emotion is the same, but the source is no longer our natural response to a real stimulus—it's a response to our beliefs generating imagined scenarios about the stimulus. An emotion from an imagined scenario on top of a natural response can amplify its power to an irrational level.

Empathy and Distortion

If we are consoling a friend whose heart has just been broken in a relationship, we are likely to perceive the emotions of another. By intently listening, our attention opens a channel and we can sense their emotional pain. This is empathy.

However, sensing other people's emotions like this often turns into creating our own similar emotions. When we just perceive the emotions of another there is no story or interpretation in our mind, but this is not usually what happens. As we listen to their story we identify with the perspective it is being told from, which is typical when we hear any story. The ideas create a bubble in our mind with us in the center, viewing it the same way the brokenhearted person is experiencing it. The result is that we make a copy of their experience. The distortion happens when we include ourselves in the character perspective they are in. Then our emotional body produces the same emotions they are generating instead of perceiving theirs.

The same thing happens when we watch an emotional scene in a movie. We imagine ourselves in the situation of the actor on screen and feel the emotions accordingly. At this point it is our own emotions we are creating and feeling and not the actor's.

We may also become judgmental and angry at the person who dumped our friend. When we do this we are no longer simply perceiving our friend's emotions. Our sadness and anger about their pain is not compassion but an unhappiness and suffering we create with our belief about their situation. Our judgment about their ex comes from our belief system, from copying our friend's bubble instead of perceiving our friend in their own bubble. We have now fallen into the same kind of emotional reactions we hoped they would be free of. If we are not aware of our perspective, attention, and beliefs, we can get caught in emotional reactions generated by our own mind from someone else's story.

Sometimes people feel exhausted when they spend a lot of time with someone who is full of grief, brokenhearted, or in other intense emotional states. This is common for social workers, therapists, teachers of special-needs students, and others working in service fields. They feel that the other person is draining them. This is a misinterpretation of what is happening. It is not exhausting to perceive a person's emotional state and be compassionate with them. What drains our energy is creating a similar internal world and investing our personal power in the thoughts and interpretations we generate there.

Accepting someone and witnessing them in their experience does not take a lot of effort. If your emotions become very strong and match those of the person you are listening to, consider that you may have created your own belief bubble. It may be one matching theirs or in reaction to theirs that creates emotions such as sorrow, worry, or anger. At this point you are no longer perceiving their emotions—you are generating your own. If you do this often, you will be expending a lot of personal power on emotions and it will be exhausting.

Source Five: The Collective Field of Emotions

Just as you have an emotional field surrounding you, everyone else has an emotional field surrounding them as well. They might not express it outwardly, but they are generating those emotions and filling the space around them. Imagine walking into a room full of people who are all generating the same emotions. You would probably feel their collective emotional field.

There are billions of emotional fields throughout the earth, generated by all the human beings on the planet. A group of people generating similar emotions create a collective field of that emotion. For example, if your country's soccer team is competing for the World Cup and is winning, excitement and joy resound throughout the country. Those emotions will be more concentrated and intense in the stadium where so many fans are gathered. But even if you are at home by yourself, simply putting your attention on the game can connect you to that larger field of emotions. If your team loses, a collective vapor of disappointment fills the air. Together, all the individual fields of emotions make up the larger collective field of emotion surrounding groups of people.

Specific fields of emotion also connect people in their personal relationships. When two people are in love, they have a connecting channel of love that links them. There is an external, shared emotional field between them. Each person connects to others in their relationships through these channels of emotions, extending their emotions and therefore their personal emotional field to others they are in relationship with. We contribute to the collective field of emotions through what we express, and we feel the impact of these external sources of emotions through these channels as well.

Getting Caught Up in an Emotional Field

When two or more people express similar emotions and share similar beliefs, their investment of faith in those beliefs produces more emotion in their individual and shared field. Their feelings can be contagious, such as feelings of excitement or fear. Because there are many people in the same state of excitement, the collective field is stronger and more seductive.

This is what happens when a friend talks to us about a stock or real estate investment in an excited way. We feel their excitement and are more likely to see the situation the way they see it. Although we are talking with one person, the ideas they are sharing connect us to the collective field of all those who share the same emotion and beliefs. We hear about other people making money, which confirms our thought that we can make money as well. We might also get caught up in a collective fear of missing out on the opportunity. In the obscuring fog of the collective field, commonsense analysis of earnings, price, and value are too easily discarded. We don't have to be on the floor of the stock exchange to have these emotions come over us. We can connect to these collective fields when we're by ourselves, looking at the computer screen, watching the news, or thinking about it later in the day.

When we are swayed by a strong collective emotional bubble, we may describe what happens to us as simply being "swept away." That simple dismissal blinds us from understanding the mechanics of our own behavior and changing it. Failing to understand the specifics of how a wave of emotions affects our imagination, perspective, faith, and beliefs leaves us at the mercy, or tyranny, of these forces of emotions and beliefs in the future.

Strong collective emotional fields can produce herd mentality or mob-type behavior. Whether people are pouring money into overpriced real estate, rioting in the stands at a soccer game, or fearfully or angrily calling for war, the mechanics in the mind are the same. Like swimmers unaware of the deeper currents in the water they're swimming in, people can be carried by the tides and undertows to painful and costly experiences. Sometimes these influential fields are spontaneously and unconsciously generated. At other times marketers intentionally work to generate a frenzy about their product, cause, or political candidate. They might also try to create a fearful field about their opponent or competitor's product. Marketers know such mass emotional appeal is powerful. If you develop your awareness, you will have control of your personal power so that you are immune to the influence of such emotional marketing.

Collective emotional fields can also exist where there are no people present. If you enter a church, temple, or memorial site, the feeling of the place can be palpable. Many people describe having powerful emotional experiences at the Vietnam Memorial or the Holocaust Museum, even though they have no personal connection to those past events. These residual emotional fields exist because people have been there before them and expressed strong emotions which have not dissipated.

The collective emotion in a location lingers the same way an emotion lingers in our personal emotional field. When emotions are expressed by people intensely, or for a long period of time, those emotions can be felt days, months, or even years later. As people pass through those emotional fields, they perceive them and often adopt a congruent perspective, thereby generating more of the same emotions. In this way a continuous flow of visitors who produce the same emotions keeps these places charged for many years.

As we work through inventorying and dissolving our beliefs, our personal emotional-belief field begins to clarify and we are better able to perceive external fields of emotions. Sometimes these larger external emotional fields are bigger than our personal fields. However, having recovered a lot of our personal power from our own false beliefs, we have more control over our attention and can detach ourselves from these collective fields. We may notice that some of the thoughts we hear in our internal dialog, or the emotions we feel, are not arising from our own belief system or from our own real experience.

Collective emotional fields do not just affect us—we create and affect them, too. When you change your beliefs and move towards love and acceptance, you change the field of emotions that you create around you. As more people engage in this conscious action, we change the larger fields of emotion that everyone is moving in. This means that by changing your false beliefs and being happier, you can have an impact on the collective happiness and consciousness of humanity.

Source Six: Emotions from Nature

Nature also contributes to the emotional field. Go into a place of natural beauty, undisturbed by the emotional fields of human beings, and it is possible to perceive how a place feels. If nothing else, there is an absence of humanly created collective fields with their thoughts, beliefs, and drama stories, so the environment will have a different feel just for that reason. You are more likely to notice a sense of contentment and calm in natural settings. The living landscape of trees, rivers, sun, earth, and sky all have an emotional component that we can perceive. Peacefulness and calm might be subtle and even hard to discern as we are not used to putting our attention on things that are silent.

The expressions of emotions from nature fall almost entirely within the pleasant spectrum of emotions we could call love.

We often don't notice the field of air that surrounds us and that we breathe into our lungs thousands of times a day. It is so continuous that it doesn't stand out and we take it for granted. In the same way, we are living in a sea of emotions made up of different connecting channels and fields that we move through all the time. We have the capacity to perceive these different fields with our emotional body, provided we put our attention on them, much in the same way we can perceive any area of our skin as we shift our focus to it. But even if we don't place our attention on all these emotions, we are still perceiving and experiencing them at levels we are not aware of.

Source Seven: Repressed Emotions

The physical body has the ability to store energy in the form of emotions. Memories are a similar kind of informational energy that we can store for years.

Imagine that little Johnny is three or four years old. It's time to go to bed and he is told to put away his toys. Johnny is having such fun and loves what he is playing so much that he ignores the direction. After a few failed attempts at getting him to comply, Mom or Dad takes Johnny's toys out of his hands. Johnny has an emotional response of sadness at the loss, or perhaps hurt at losing the feeling of joy he was having with his toys. Some of these emotions can be genuine, some generated by attachments through belief systems.

As a defense mechanism against these unpleasant emotions, Johnny becomes angry. Anger is a natural response that we use to protect ourselves from danger. Johnny isn't in any physical danger, but his automated system responds the same way to pain and, in this case, to emotional discomfort. Anger may also arise from a belief system of Victim/Villain because of his attachment to his toys. Regardless of whether his anger has one or more sources, Johnny expresses it to his parents.

But this doesn't go over well with Mom and Dad. Disrespect and angry behavior are not going to be allowed, so they respond by raising their voices, scolding, physically lifting him off the floor, or even expressing anger back at him. Mom and Dad's response scares Johnny. After a few experiences like this, Johnny finds that when he gets angry he starts to feel afraid. Johnny learns to be afraid of Mom and Dad's response and associates this to feeling angry. Johnny becomes afraid of his emotion, and even more afraid of expressing his anger.

The next time Johnny gets told to stop playing, he still feels the hurt and has the emotional reaction of anger. That part of the emotional response hasn't changed yet. However, as the anger starts to build, so does the fear, and he instinctively pushes down the energy of anger back into his body so it doesn't get expressed. He holds it in and doesn't let anyone know that he has anger inside. After doing this awhile, Johnny becomes so good at it, and he does it so quickly, that he has no conscious awareness of the responses of anger going on inside him. Later in life, he feels afraid of letting his anger out because of what might happen or what he might do. The fear of feeling anger is bigger than the anger itself, as it is a layer of energy and emotion holding the anger in.

In later years a person's repressed anger may not be so easily controlled. The anger being held in the cells of the physical body has built up too much pressure and needs to be released. The emotion may come out at traffic, employees, oneself, or one's spouse for the smallest of reasons. When a repressed emotion bursts out, it's often completely out of proportion with the cause or trigger. This is confusing, and the mind scrambles to come up with a reason for it. When we have enough awareness to recognize that the justification we give is bogus, our Judge and Victim characters pile on with their stories and condemn us for our outburst and inadequate excuse. The characters use what we did to make us wrong again, which encourages us to return to repressing our feelings. We then add guilt and shame, as well as fear of angry outbursts, to our emotional layers. We might also express some anger and hate at ourselves for being so angry, thus increasing our level of hurt and ensuring further repression. In a vicious cycle, this kind of expression from our characters adds more emotion to our emotional field and makes it more likely that we will have an outburst again.

Commonly repressed emotions are anger, sadness, guilt, shame, and grief. We are most fearful of these emotions because of how we will behave, what others will think, or how much we will judge ourselves for feeling them. These fears and judgments about our emotions interfere with releasing them. When these emotions are not released in a healthy way, they can take a toll on our physical body, often manifesting as a physical pain. Or they end up getting released by venting to other people in inappropriate ways, taking a toll on our relationships.

A solution out of these fears and judgments is to make an inventory of the thoughts, beliefs, and judgments your characters have about the emotions you feel. A better understanding about why we feel what we feel, and a compassionate acknowledgment of those feelings, will help remove the forces of fear and judgment that keep these emotions repressed.

While some of these repressed emotions are belief-based and have an accompanying story or belief, some do not. We may have repressed natural-response emotions as well. For many of the natural emotions there are often no stories, thoughts, or beliefs to dismantle. When they are released there can be a great deal of emotion with no connecting thought or memory. For example, when we lose someone we love there is often grief. It is a natural response that even animals have, despite having no belief systems. There are no words, thoughts, or beliefs that accompany these natural-response emotions. As humans, we also have a mind that will project thoughts, beliefs, and images to form stories. Both these belief-based emotions and the emotions that have no story have to be allowed and released.

At first the healing and change process is just a matter of letting the suppressed feelings empty out. The emotional body, much like our physical body, has its own guidance and healing system and release mechanisms. It will have bouts of crying or rage for no apparent reason. As best you can, allow the process and let the emotions be vented off without inflicting them on others. What will take the most work, particularly in the case of anger, will be to refrain from expressing that anger at anyone. The mind will try to justify and explain in some simple way why we feel what we feel. In these intense emotions it is looking for an answer. In reality, you don't need one. The work that needs to be done is to let the emotions move through you in a healthy way without sending them to anyone or believing the accompanying thoughts. It will be helpful to suspend belief in any of the justifications for these emotions. Investing faith in justifications just adds more emotion-producing beliefs to your system.

—〤〤—

The work that needs to be done is to let the emotions move through you in a healthy way without sending them to anyone or believing the accompanying thoughts.

—〤〤—

The Repression of Love

Surprisingly, one of the biggest emotions that we repress is love. As very young children we were free to dance and express excitement and joy through our body. While growing up, we were told not to be so silly, that laughing is inappropriate, and that we should be more serious. We learned that how we appeared to others was more important than expressing our joy. As we learned to be more responsible, we also tried to act more serious. All of these little moments add layers of energy that hold back our natural expressions of joy, wonderment, humor, creativity, curiosity, and love.

As we sort out career choices we may put aside interests we love, like art and music, dismissing them in favor of more "practical" fields of work. Our worries about making money and financially providing for ourselves and our family take precedence, and the expressions of love that come with those other, cherished activities are repressed. We try not to think about what we gave up because it hurts too much not to express that love for things we are passionate about.

If we fall in love and then have our heart broken, we can make an internal agreement that love hurts, or that we have to be careful, which really means to be afraid of love. We become hesitant to love again, un-aware that it wasn't the love that hurt but rather the pain of not lov-ing when it ended. We create false interpretations and beliefs about our emotions and future actions. We hold back our feelings of love as if love itself were painful. Like the child who stopped feeling joy when his toy was taken away, we also repress our painful reactions at the loss of love by covering it with layers of denial about feeling anything. "I'm fine" is a convenient statement to repress the hurt, and to repress the love we want to express underneath.

As we remove these layers of denial and notice what we feel with honest acceptance, we first find fear and judgments of our emotions. Beneath that are repressed layers of sadness, grief, and anger. But below those layers are the repressed layers of love, passions, and an abundance of joy in great reserves. Some of those emotions based in love have been held back for years and may at times rush out in overwhelming waves. Once that repressed love is no longer under pressure, it returns to a normal authentic flow in a balanced and sustainable way. However, there isn't one specific way this looks for everyone; each person's experience of this process will be unique to them.

—⁓—

**We become hesitant to love again,
unaware that it wasn't the love that hurt
but rather the pain of not loving when it ended.**

—⁓—

Source Eight: The Conscious Will to Create

As we have seen, many of our emotions are created in reaction to what our belief system imagines. In effect, our belief system controls our attention, makes its interpretations of what we perceive, and then our emotional body responds with emotions. However, we don't have to create emotions only as a response. If we take the belief system out of the loop, we are free to decide where and how we focus our attention, and therefore what emotions we create.

It is possible to create emotions deliberately by directing our attention, without the use of thoughts or beliefs, and expressing whatever emotion we choose. This requires two things: (1) conscious control over our attention, and (2) enough willpower to generate that emotion.

When we master the art of expressing emotions, we can generate love, gratitude, and respect without any identifiable reason. Instead we do it simply because we want to, or it feels good. At first it will be easier to use ideas, memories, or affirmations to focus attention and generate certain emotions. We might use a guided meditation, listen to inspiring music, or call to mind someone we love. If we want to consciously create gratitude, we can focus our attention on the blessings in our life. We can use our attention to direct our story, and then respond emotionally to the story or imagery we created. At a higher level of mastery over our attention, we can create those feelings without using the intermediate steps of imagery, stories, reasons, and justifications.

A simple practice might take the form of a meditation on serenity. Sit still, focus your attention within, and deliberately express calmness, contentment, and peace. Sitting there in your room alone, you are choosing to express a certain emotion, not as a response to reality or a belief, but just because you consciously decide to do it. It's like voluntarily exercising a muscle, but in this case it's an emotional muscle, and in a way that feels good. With practice, your personal willpower and your emotional muscles become stronger. When you gain enough mastery over your attention and emotions, you can express emotions of love and acceptance even when people or circumstances are acting against you. This is much easier to achieve once you have identified and dissolved your ego-based beliefs so they no longer distract you.

This way of creating emotions runs counter to our usual experience of emotionally reacting to other people and to our own beliefs. Can you imagine being at peace at work when someone wrongfully blames you for something or even fires you? Or maintaining your serenity when your relationship partner is doing emotional drama or being unkind to you? Can you imagine not losing your attention to stories of injustice about political, financial, or environmental issues? It isn't a common experience, but that doesn't mean it's not possible. If we only hold ourselves to the habits and practices of what people commonly do, then we only feel the range of emotions people commonly feel. If we do something different we will experience something different.

A trap to avoid falling into with this practice is using this conscious expression of emotion to repress other reactions. If you are angry with someone, the attempt in that moment to consciously will yourself to a state of gratitude might be an attempt to override and repress the anger or other emotions. While this may help you feel better in the short term, it becomes an exhausting way of keeping emotions repressed and leaving false beliefs intact as the source of emotions.

It is possible to be aware of all these issues of drama and deal with them while maintaining a state of equanimity. However, deliberately generating love and gratitude in these circumstances can be much harder than when you are just sitting in your room with no distractions. When dramatic emotions are triggered in us we defend them as being passionate, caring, or justified, even if they are creating suffering for ourselves and adding it to the collective field for others.

The archetype characters of drama will resist the deliberate creation of love and gratitude. The most common reactions I hear when I describe this practice of choosing love and gratitude are, "Are you suggesting that I just be an automaton?" and "I like my emotions, all of them—they are what make me human."

No, I am not proposing that we be unfeeling automatons. I am suggesting that we be more aware of our emotions and that we recognize that we can consciously create emotions as well. At the same time, I am suggesting that we *stop* being automatons that just react in the automated ways our conditioned belief systems would have us behave. I am proposing that people be aware enough to consider a full range of choices, even choices regarding their emotions. When you have emotional mastery, you will have more choices in every moment. You can express more than just what your conditioned belief system or the collective field of emotions is offering. Exercising your personal power to consciously express love, compassion, and respect is being human too.

Some of the most dangerous emotions are those that seem justified. We achieve the biggest impact when we dispense with the typical emotions that people expect. If we are angry with someone, we probably feel justified and don't believe they deserve to be forgiven. But if we can take our faith out of our reaction story and invest it in acceptance of things as they are, we can forgive them and love them—not because they deserve it, but in spite of the story that says they don't. You can do the same for yourself. Consider giving love and acceptance to yourself, not because you've done something to deserve it, but for no reason, or just because it feels good. This is approaching a completely unreasonable kind of love: a love that is unconditional.

When you achieve emotional mastery, you don't have to go through the reaction process of first taking offense, then forgiving, and finally finding peace with it. You can skip the step of "being offended," and therefore not have to bother with the forgiveness work. You can just remain in peace about things to begin with. It's actually a lot easier. It's just that it takes some work to learn how to live that effortlessly.

The challenge of emotional mastery involves more than mastery of your expression when everything is going well, or when you are sitting alone in your favorite meditation spot. The real test is whether you can express love, acceptance, and respect when things in life go against you. That's why we consider people like Nelson Mandela and Mahatma Gandhi heroes. Part of their journey was invisible. They were heroic in that they conquered the inner temptation to believe in interpretations that would result in hatred, victimization, or anger. In the beginning, emotional mastery is about consciously willing an expression of love and respect when you can. As you strengthen your will and control over your attention, emotional mastery is about expressing love and respect when the thoughts in your mind are tempting you to believe that you can't.

Achieving this kind of mastery isn't easy and should not be considered a beginner's practice. However, it is good to be aware of the possibility. If others have done it with time and practice, then perhaps you can do it too. Maybe you won't get it "perfect" in the beginning or even before you die. That doesn't matter. The important thing is that you will be happier every moment of your life that you become better at it.

—⁓—

Emotional mastery is about expressing love and respect when the thoughts in your mind are tempting you to believe that you can't.

—⁓—

Obstacles to Emotional Mastery

In the beginning, it can be challenging to consciously create emotions that we choose, such as love, gratitude, and acceptance, because we don't have complete control over our perspective and attention. Even when we have some control, much of our personal power is still stored in beliefs we created in our past and still carry around. These beliefs act on our personal emotional field and make it difficult to access elevated emotions and other points of view.

If we are even a little bit aware during an emotional reaction, it might occur to us that we could respond differently; we might even try to compel ourselves to feel differently. But if the story of the Judge or Victim is strong and a lot of faith is invested in old beliefs, we won't be able to make the change yet. We might have enough awareness to realize we are caught up in a reaction to our beliefs, but not enough to become the observer. We don't yet have enough personal power to adopt another perspective or express a different emotion. The effect is just enough awareness to know that there are other possibilities, but not enough awareness and personal power to change our situation yet.

At this stage of the process, practicing *acceptance* for where we are and what we are doing is one of the best steps we can take. We didn't stand up and walk the first time we tried, but we didn't give up either. Expressing acceptance slips us out of the Judge and Victim loop, and we can begin to recover control over our perspective. Also, honestly acknowledging the other sources of emotion can help keep our expectations in check. It's easier to focus our attention and create emotions we choose when we aren't in the midst of an emotional reaction.

One of the keys to staying out of self-judgment about our progress is to manage our expectations—in other words, our beliefs about how well we "should" be doing. A common hidden assumption is that, because we were able to accomplish something yesterday with our attention and willpower, we should be able to do it every day. That assumption would make sense if shifting our attention and creating emotions were knowledge-based. Once you know that the capital of France is Paris, you should be able to get that question right every day. This is how knowledge and memory works.

But controlling your attention and exercising the will to express an emotion are skills, like public speaking, hitting a golf ball, or playing piano. Because you played a song through with no mistakes or hit a golf shot one day doesn't mean you will do as well the next day. Those activities require skillful practice, and even then, some days can be more challenging than others. Understanding that the process of emotional mastery is a skill to be practiced and developed will help you avoid the self-judgment that the Judge attempts to trick you into.

Source Nine: The Force of Life

Lastly, there is the transcendent emotional experience that defies definition. Spiritual traditions give it names like *nirvana, samadhi,* or *Christ consciousness.* However, it doesn't have to have a religious or spiritual connotation. In her book *My Stroke of Insight,* Jill Bolte Taylor, a scientist studying the brain, describes her experience of expanding consciousness, love, and beauty during and after a stroke. In that experience her consciousness perceived a reality beyond her previous experience and all her social conditioning and beliefs. Whenever an experience exceeds the normal realm of emotions, it is typically described as a beautiful, intense feeling of love that extends far beyond the physical self.

Some have experienced it during near-death situations, as their body lay on an operating table and they floated above it. Some sit in meditation for years, seeking to achieve such an emotionally expansive experience, not knowing if it will ever happen. For others, it can happen spontaneously. One woman I spoke with experienced an emotional and conscious awakening of love as she walked across her college campus one morning. She said it was like being struck by light and then seeing that the physical world was actually made of light. The emotional quality of that light was love, and it overwhelmed her. I call that experience seeing Life as it is.

A friend, Charlotte, described an experience she had while parachuting. Her parachute didn't open—there was a problem with the release, and lines got tangled. Her reserve chute became tangled as well. After a brief moment of fearful panic, Charlotte was struck with a sense of calm and peace and she completely accepted the situation. She accepted her mortality, that life is fleeting, and that everything in her life was in perfect order, even this surprise moment where she was face-to-face with death. Often, such a direct encounter with death directs our attention to look past all the illusions of our belief bubbles and perceive and experience Life directly in a very real and loving way.

With complete peace, Charlotte did all that was necessary. She tried to untangle the lines that were collapsing her chute. The canopy would open in a lopsided way and slow her fall. Then it would start spinning, lose air, and she would drop like a rock again. The speed of descent would cause the canopy to catch air again and billow out, and then it would spin some more in freefall. This cycle continued until she hit the ground. Fortunately, the landing happened in a moment when the chute was open, and Charlotte survived without any broken bones. Throughout the ordeal, Charlotte was in a state of peace. Her body was in physical pain for weeks, but emotionally she felt great. Better than great—better than she had ever felt before.

This emotional experience, so new and different from anything Charlotte had known in the past, caused issues for her as she went back to her regular life. In previous years she'd been miserable and depressed. Having such an expansive experience of love and peace contradicted every thought and belief in her mind. The contrast between the experience of love and the familiar bubble world of her belief system forced her to challenge everything she believed. Years later, that expansive field of love is something she regularly perceives and enjoys.

Experiences of expanded consciousness and awareness are always accompanied by a boundless experience of love. This is because the innate emotional quality of the force of Life is love. There is no physical evidence for this, as there is no quantifiable measurement of love, or of consciousness. These experiences are personal and subjective, but when they happen time and time again they show a pattern. Some people who haven't had this experience will say that it's purely imaginary, that such a limitless, loving consciousness doesn't exist. That's understandable because in their realm of experience, and therefore within their belief bubble, it *doesn't* exist. However, for others, these expansions of consciousness and love are very real.

These experiences are also usually accompanied by a quiet mind, which indicates that the nature of this force of Life is silent. It operates without language and precedes language. While it can use language, it is not limited to the construct of knowledge encapsulated by words and is often more easily perceived in the absence of language. Thinking and mind chatter are often a distraction from this force of Life. This is also why many mindfulness and spiritual practices involve quieting the mind.

Each person who experiences these expanded feelings of love and consciousness finds it difficult to express in words what they have perceived. It's similar to the problem a person would have if they tried to explain what a symphony sounded like to a deaf person, or describe a rainbow's colors to a blind person. Without the experience as reference, the words are empty. The expansive feeling of love beyond the personal self presents the same challenges in communication. The words are just empty symbols until you have an experience that gives them meaning.

There are many traditions that offer paths to this conscious and emotionally expansive experience. They range from contemplative prayer, meditation, shamanic journeys, and Kundalini yoga to mindfulness and awareness practices. My intent is not to present a study of those paths but simply to point out the realm of emotions those paths can lead to. This chapter would be incomplete without mentioning these emotional experiences of love and a connection to a force of Life that transcends all traditions and practices.

Reading Your Emotions

One of the biggest misinterpretations we make is about what our emotions mean. We assume that if we feel something, then it must be real and legitimate. This is partially true. If we take our hand and physically touch something, we can say it is real and explain where the sensation came from. However, we're mistaken if we make the same interpretations about our emotions. If we feel anger, our mind will quickly make an interpretation about what caused that anger. Our simplified justification could be something like, "I'm angry at that driver for cutting me off." The emotion of anger is real—it exists, and we feel it. However, the assumed reason or cause of that anger is not necessarily true or real.

Anger could be coming from our belief system, associated beliefs unrelated to traffic, anger triggered by other aspects of our life that week, or repressed emotions from years ago. We might also be feeling emotions from the collective field around us. Sometimes the emotions you feel aren't even yours. Just because you feel emotions doesn't mean they are about what your mind says they're about. Actually, what the belief system proposes as the cause of emotions is usually wrong. This is why an inventory and skepticism are so valuable.

Someone else got cut off by a driver that morning in traffic, maybe even the same driver, but they didn't respond with the same emotion of anger. They might not have felt any unpleasant emotions at all, or perhaps they felt gratitude that they didn't get in an accident. Since most of the emotions we feel come from our own belief system, we feel the emotions that we ourselves create. The emotions are real, but the meaning and cause that our mind assigns to them are up for questioning.

After you have emptied your mind of false and fear-based beliefs, you will find that there are other emotions available to you. Those other emotions are mostly aspects of love, both coming from inside you and present in the world around you. Through your growth, the very world of emotions you learned to fear and repress through social conditioning becomes an incredible world of experiences to enjoy and love.

Chapter 17

Journey to Authenticity: Authentic Living in a New Belief System

We are on a journey towards what we could call "the authentic self," a perspective in which emotional expressions no longer arise from the conditioned belief system but are genuine. Emotions arise naturally, rather than from the projection of a belief bubble, or from the distorted interpretations conceived by our ego "characters." Embracing a new sense of identity, we feel, speak, act, and react to others in ways we hadn't considered before. Our emotional palette and choices expand as we are free to step back from the archetype characters we previously identified with. In this chapter, I hope to convey a general sense of what this new world looks like.

We change in unexpected ways, and a person's own set of beliefs guides and sometimes impedes the process; there isn't one "timetable" that works for everyone. As you change belief bubbles, your perspective and the way your mind interprets events will change. From an old belief bubble, the first interpretation might be offered by the Victim character. Without awareness, you'll believe and act on those Victim thoughts. From an observer perspective, you can refrain from believing that thought and consider others. Choices appear where before there were none. It becomes possible to offer compassion where previously judgment and fear were the only automated routines available.

This is somewhat like learning a language, except it is an emotional language. You might still be speaking in the words of your native tongue, but the emotional tone and meaning are different. An old thought like

"That was a wrong turn" might have carried a tone of accusation and ridicule, suggesting that if you do something wrong, then you are stupid; and if you are stupid, then you are a loser and unworthy of love. So the thought and the words were accompanied by implied beliefs and feelings of unworthiness.

These same words will have a different feeling once you shed the perspectives of the Judge and Victim. You might miss a turn while driving and still think, "That was a wrong turn," but now in a lighthearted way, and you can laugh at yourself and your folly. You can even say it with a sense of love and acceptance, as you have the clarity to know that this act was of little importance in the scheme of your life, and certainly is not the one moment that you or anyone else will use to measure your worth.

In any case, it takes more than a week and a half to learn a new way to express yourself, so be patient and accept where you are. You are attempting to master an entirely new language of emotion and meaning, and to make it more challenging, it uses many of the same words as your old language.

In the meantime, here are a few markers to help identify how things change along the way. They will help guide you towards kinder, more respectful and loving expressions and relationships. These markers are also here to help you dismiss the resistance that the characters protest with as you dismantle their beliefs. Those protests show up as fear and doubts hidden inside comments like "This is too hard"; "Where is this all going?"; "Sounds like I won't have any personality left after I do this"; or "I'll just be an emotionless automaton."

Authenticity

As our perspective changes, conditioned beliefs that created fear and emotional drama will fall away. As our beliefs change, the false identities of the Judge, Victim, Fixer, Pleaser, and other characters will also fall away, along with their habitual interpretations.

What, then, is an alternative perspective that we can adopt, as opposed to these ego identities? The neutral observer or witness perspective is a start, but it is not the end point of the journey. Becoming an observer of our mind leads to skepticism about our conditioned beliefs and the recovery of personal power. This is useful in dismantling the beliefs, but is too detached to engage in and enjoy life in a connected way. We need an entirely new point of view to move forward and create a new life.

Expanding to an Authentic Perspective

Our ego tends to perceive every situation from the perspective of *I* or *me*. Because of this, we are blinded to the possibility of any other point of view. It is difficult to understand the perceptions of others when we are stuck in such a rigid framework, especially when there is a lot of emotion to anchor it.

However, if we can imagine someone else's life through *their* eyes, our point of view shifts and we have a new understanding. To take it further, what if we looked at *ourselves* through the eyes of our loved ones, or even our enemies? This is an incredibly effective exercise for fast change. It takes us out of our belief bubble, and now there is room for something fresh and new. This is an advanced exercise, requiring significant skill over one's attention, so it's often not very effective for a beginner. Ultimately, it is a much more conscious way to live in the world.

Whether you shift perspective in order to change beliefs, or your perspective becomes more flexible because you *have* changed beliefs, the result is the same. The following story is an example of such a shift.

Jeffrey struggled with his father throughout his adolescence. They were always at odds. Jeffrey's father was continually pressuring him to excel in school and restricting his choice of friends. If Jeffrey violated his dad's rules, a big confrontation would ensue and Jeffrey would be grounded, with even more restrictions. Desperate to escape, Jeffrey joined the merchant marines when he was just seventeen, and rarely came home for a visit.

Decades later, Jeffrey attended a meditation retreat, where he explored the repressed emotions of anger he had towards his father. Eventually he allowed his perspective to shift. For the first time, he saw their relationship through his father's eyes. Below the controlling anger was extraordinary fear. His father worried that Jeffrey would fail, become destitute, and have a hard life. Below the fear was a strong desire for Jeffrey to succeed and be happy. All the pressure and strict rules really came from caring. He expressed it through exerting control, but it originated from his caring.

Once Jeffrey realized this, he was able to perceive something unexpected: love. His father had the best intentions, all originating from a feeling of love. He wanted Jeffrey to be successful and happy. But his fears that his son would fail were so great that this desire was expressed through restrictive rules, judgment, and anger. As a child Jeffrey recoiled from the fear and control aspect of his father's personality; it blinded him to the layers of love and caring underneath.

Jeffrey's father was trapped by the emotions and beliefs that were driving his behavior. He had no self-awareness and so could not perceive other choices.

Once Jeffrey was able to see things from his father's perspective, all his hostility and rebellion drained away. His father was not the demon he had imagined. The victimization and rebellious righteousness that Jeffrey had felt all his life ceased to exist when he expanded his perspective beyond the confines of his own personal belief system. His anger dissolved, along with all the beliefs that were driving it. His sense of being "right" about his father also dissolved, as well as the sense that his father had "wronged" him. He no longer needed to judge, nor did he feel like his father's victim.

As these false identities fell away, Jeffrey became more compassionate, authentic, and humble. This happened not because he tried to be authentic, but simply because he dropped all the false beliefs he was carrying. It followed naturally from looking at the situation from another perspective.

This is a very fast way to dissolve false beliefs, but it is not necessarily easy. Our own beliefs tend to fixate our perspective in existing bubbles. So begin with something with which you can have success. Become skillful at adopting an observer perspective and build skepticism from there. The methods in this book and in the online Self Mastery course will help you to break down these belief structures in a step-by-step approach. If by chance you have transformative experiences like Jeffrey's, ones that allow you to see things from other people's viewpoints and to let go of decades of struggle in relationship in one day, be thankful. If it doesn't happen this fast, then keep taking steps so at least it dissolves slowly.

After this experience Jeffrey no longer described the situation in terms of who was right and who was wrong. For Jeffery, these labels were part of the problem, fixating both men's identity in the Judge and Victim characters. Each of them felt he was right and the other wrong in a relationship where both suffered. In authentic relationships of respect and acceptance we refrain from these oversimplified Judge and Victim perspectives and statements.

Humility

So what is our identity once we shed these archetypes of ego? Our authentic nature cannot be distilled down into a finite number of descriptive phrases. It is much easier to identify what it is not and strip those pieces away. What is left is the truth of what we are.

At its basic level, the authentic self is happy and at peace with the world. Many different words could describe it: genuine, peaceful, or self-realized. It is not the label that's important, but rather the state of emotion, perspective, and calmness of the mind. When you strip away the false identities that constitute your self-important ego characters, an attribute that grows is humility, a kind of non-self-image.

Characters have a big agenda to define us with words. Your mind will wonder what the "right" or "authentic self" point of view is or is supposed to be. This is the Hero wondering what he should make himself into so that he gets the conditional approval, acceptance, and praise. Don't fall for it. Our authentic self doesn't have a need to define and label itself.

As you journey into your more authentic self, your understanding of humility deepens as well. You live with a central emotional integrity that is made up of natural emotions and which stabilizes your attention. Your attention is no longer hooked by images or concepts that your mind projects, nor is your sense of love, respect, and acceptance for yourself or others swayed as easily by the opinions of others. Simply put, your mind is a great deal quieter, and you experience a lot fewer emotional reactions because your self-important characters aren't there to tug at your attention. *Humility* is a good word to describe this state of perspective.

—ɱ—

Humility isn't something you gain or achieve.
It is what remains after you strip away the layers of the ego,
false identities, and false beliefs.

—ɱ—

Humility and Personal Power

Humility isn't something you gain or achieve. It is what remains after you strip away the layers of the ego, false identities, and false beliefs. Humility is like snow: indescribable until you have experienced it. Once you have seen and felt snow, descriptive words make sense—*cold, wet, white*, even *beautiful*. But until that happens, the words only serve as a construct in the mind; a close approximation, perhaps, but not the truth. Direct experience is the only way to have a true understanding. Until then words are empty of meaning.

Humility is often associated with timidity, shyness, or submissiveness, qualities we sometimes view as negative. But true humility is not any of these things. A humble person is more likely to be quiet and listen to others, but that doesn't indicate the magnitude of their personal power or strength. When we have invested a lot of our personal power of faith in ego characters and false beliefs we can generate a lot of emotional drama, negative thoughts, opinions, stress, anger, frustration, and judgment. That's a lot of energy. Imagine having all that power and consciously directing it towards a heartfelt agenda.

When the ego characters are no longer controlling our attention, we have the power to be a better and more patient listener. Our energy and attention aren't being used by false characters, and we don't feel compelled to project our opinions and ideas. The humble person doesn't consider themselves better than anyone else, nor do they consider themselves less than others. They don't spend energy comparing themselves to other people at all, or comparing other people against each other. All these attitudes and behaviors are absent in the state of humility. Perhaps humility is difficult to describe because, in a way, it is an absence of things. It is really the absence of ego characters, their beliefs, and their corrupted expressions.

Mahatma Gandhi was a humble man. Because so little of his faith was invested in false self-images, judgments, or personal comparisons, he had an astonishing amount of personal power to devote to his actions. A humble person has extraordinary personal power at his or her disposal because the ego isn't wasting it. Because a humble person doesn't expend their personal power getting others to pay attention to their *I* and *me*, they are better able to accomplish what they set out to do and to serve others.

Nelson Mandela is a more contemporary example of the power possessed by a person of humility. His demeanor demonstrated that one doesn't need to think of himself as great in order to do great things. To accomplish things, you must have faith in your actions rather than in a self-image. The more power of faith a person invests in creating or maintaining their self-image, including their concerns of what others think of them, the less faith and attention they will focus on their actions. When you are no longer spending energy concerned with being right or appearing wrong, you will have much more personal power to do the right thing.

In the best-selling book *Good to Great*, author Jim Collins describes the accelerated growth of several extraordinary companies. He found that the common denominator was a powerful leader. What was surprising, though, is that these leaders were not the charismatic types we have come to expect; rather, they were quiet and soft-spoken, people who asked questions and listened more than they talked. You wouldn't know the names of these CEOs, yet they are historically some of the best. They surrounded themselves with talented people, drew out their best ideas, and stayed true to a level of personal integrity. They held a personal strength and unbending intent, even in times of challenge. This can only be done by a person with a high degree of self-awareness. Jim Collins described these individuals as Level 5 leaders.

While he did encounter the charismatic, visionary personas that we often stereotype as "leaders," he categorized them as Level 4 because their success was not as substantial or sustained. Often, the company would falter after reaching a certain level of success, as the CEO began to think his ideas were infallible. Or he became enamored with the spoils of success and neglected the company. This is the path where the ego directs a person's attention, and the illusions of their belief bubbles interfere with effective running of the company and accurately perceiving the marketplace.

—ɷ—

When you are no longer spending energy concerned with being right or appearing wrong, you will have much more personal power to do the right thing.

—ɷ—

The Near Enemy of Humility

One of the obstacles we will face as we shed our ego is our attempt to be humble. This is somewhat of a catch-22. We may have a concept of what it means to be humble, but when we try to live up to it we become inauthentic. We are not being what we genuinely are. Humility is expressed in action; it is not a state to be attained. This isn't to say we shouldn't make an effort, but it is helpful to be aware that our ego will attempt to use this goal for its own agenda.

Often our mind creates an image of what a humble person *should* be like. Our Hero attempts to project that image and take the actions necessary to achieve it. The Judge character then uses that image as a basis for comparison and looks for any instances where we are failing. Our Victim accepts the Judge's criticism of our failure to be humble enough. Conversely, the Judge might point out what we are doing well and tell us how great we are—"Oh, look how humble I'm being"—which then triggers the backlash judgment of how arrogant we are for thinking we were sufficiently humble. Our mental image of our humble self can trick us into thinking that we should have already transformed, but just having that image of humility doesn't make all our thoughts, emotions, and behaviors immediately shift.

When it comes to humility, you can't "fake it till you make it." However, you can practice and try your best. Simply notice where you are in the process. Look at your beliefs and the characters behind them and just acknowledge them. You will be best served by ruthless honesty, a clear-sighted assessment of what is really there. As you struggle back and forth with your ego characters, being kindly honest about your progress and setbacks is being authentic.

Authenticity isn't a fixed state. At each stage along the way, you can express authentic honesty. Authenticity changes as you dissolve false beliefs and your consciousness grows. As you recognize that this collection of beliefs isn't really you at all, you'll take another step towards love, self-acceptance, and humility. This awareness will grow with time and practice. With each step of change the genuine self develops and grows stronger.

Backing Up into Humility

In truth, we don't have to learn how to be humble. We only have to become aware of the various ways in which we are false and stop doing them.

Children are generally humble by nature. They are apt to be kind, respectful, and love a lot. They also ask a lot of questions as their curiosity is strong, and they actively explore what they don't know. They haven't yet developed a fear of revealing how much they don't know. However, they are also naïve and innocent. They are not aware that believing what they are told has consequences, or that not all the thoughts that pass through their heads are true. Nor are they aware of a belief system, the power of their faith, how their mind dreams and imagines its own reality, or the power they have to create their own emotions. Without intending to, as they grow, they learn how to think of themselves as a winner or a loser, right or wrong. They learn over years to compare themselves to others and to assess themselves as better than or less than someone else.

We do all of this as we mature, without any awareness of what we are doing. In the process, we learn to believe in false self-images, stories of victimization, and judgments. We invest our faith into these opinions for years, until we become masters of creating beliefs and emotionally reacting to them, even when they are not true. Later, if we choose to be happy by dissolving our fear-based and limiting beliefs, we have to unlearn these automated roles.

When we begin to recognize the characters that are at work in our mind, we become self-aware and practice becoming happy again. As adults, we are no longer naïve like children; we understand the power of our imagination and faith. We know that even false ideas may appear to be true, if we put enough faith into them. Once we become more vigilant and recover our faith, we become powerful, humble, happy, and wise.

With this recovery of faith, we have the power to love and accept, even when stories of judgment and victimization tempt us to do otherwise. We can love with the unconditional acceptance of a child, but without that degree of innocence. We are aware that stories in the mind will attempt to shift our perspective and grab our attention. A child often lives in a protected bubble of safety under his parents' care. As an adult, we are no longer that naïve. We can see that the world is full of chaos, emotional drama, injustice, and physical danger. However, once we have developed awareness, we don't have to succumb to the opinions and oversimplified explanations that the Judge and Victim offer about the world. Like Jeffrey did with his father, we can see past these layers of emotional fog and perceive the love and caring underneath.

To free your mind from false identities and gain control over your attention is not easy. Self-talk comments like "I should be over this by now" or "I'm better than this" are lines of internal dialog that point to a belief used by the Judge and Victim to interrupt your happiness. When the expectation of a positive self-image is not met, it can only lead to a story that you "failed." By dismantling the beliefs that you are either "less than" or "greater than" some imagined ideal or other people, you will be dismantling your ego, and in the process humility will happen of its own accord.

Another common reaction is, "This is too hard. I'll never make it." The Victim identity is central to these interpretations, along with some kind of Fortune-Teller personality that claims to be all-knowing about the future and what is possible. The Victim is totally pessimistic, yet absolutely confident that the future can be known! This is an incongruity where you can apply a wedge of skepticism.

At the same time, we can acknowledge that changing beliefs is hard, just like learning to walk was hard. Each time we stood up we were going against the flow of gravity. However, continuing to get around by crawling is much harder than learning to walk. Similarly, although we are going against the flow of our own thoughts and emotions when we challenge our beliefs, it is far more difficult to continue to live in the flow of Judge and Victim emotions.

The Emotions of Humility

The Judge could be characterized by an emotional attitude of righteousness, indignation, or moral superiority. The Victim embodies feelings of fear, unworthiness, powerlessness, and inferiority.

In contrast, if we had to pick one emotion or attitude that most characterizes humility, it would be *gratitude*. There are certainly others, like respect, compassion, and peacefulness, but gratitude is the central emotion. Gratitude is about developing an appreciation for what you actually have, as opposed to feeling entitled, the desire for more, the fear of not having enough, or a sense of authority and dominion over others. These are conflicting feelings that swing us from one emotional drama to its opposite. The Princess feels a sense of entitlement, while the Victim holds the opposite belief: "I don't deserve what I have." Neither viewpoint is accurate. From the stance of the authentic self, we simply appreciate what is present right now.

Gratitude is an emotion we easily generate when we notice the reality of what we have, not in comparison to what anyone else has, but with the perspective that it is amazing we have anything. We come into this world naked, with nothing, and we will leave with nothing. Everything in between could be considered a bonus. The galaxy is largely cold, dark, and largely devoid of biological life, yet on this little speck of a planet where you sit reading this book, you can be comfortably warm. When you consider how many cells and organs in your body must work together just to take one breath, it is extraordinary that the body does this at all. If you try to fathom the intelligence of just the human body as it breathes in and out, you face an incomprehensible miracle with every breath.

You can either look at something like breath as a miracle that happens in every moment or you can just take it for granted. The first leads you to a sense of awe and gratitude for whatever level of health is maintained in your body, and for your capacity to perceive. The second leads you to expect it just to be there and to ignore it as long as it's working properly. That expectation sets up a sense of entitlement about the health and functioning of your being. If at some point real life doesn't match your expectations, you are likely to feel betrayed or victimized by your lack of health. The feelings you end up with depend on the perspective and expectations you start with.

With a perspective of humility, we don't take the health or functioning of any part of our body for granted. We are aware that complex systems don't have to work as seamlessly as they do. This perspective lets us maintain a kind of childlike wonder and awe, even if we have a PhD in biology.

A sense of entitlement usually goes hand in hand with a Victim reaction when the reality doesn't meet expectations. On the other hand, when we don't take things for granted, or we have very few expectations, a feeling of gratitude can be evoked from something as simple as breathing, drinking a cup of tea, or eating an orange. This is what happens when we shed the self-images of ego expectations.

—⚍—

The feelings you end up with depend on the perspective and expectations you start with.

—⚍—

Perspectives of Authenticity

Authenticity doesn't entail adopting a single perspective. A singular fixed perspective labeled "me" is a construct of the ego. When we are authentic, we have the flexibility to adopt multiple perspectives: our own and, like Jeffrey did, the perspectives of other people. Our awareness expands beyond the limitations of any singular belief system. This is the process of becoming aware and wise.

Naturally, the reasoning part of our mind will be confused by this. Multiple perspectives create multiple interpretations. Which one to choose? Each perspective appears right within its own belief bubble. While it can be quite confusing initially, at least now we are free. We can choose or reject the interpretations the mind offers, instead of reflexively using the ones we learned over the years from others or through socialization.

The self-important ego will tend to resist the flexible approach. It will protest with statements such as, "But I feel like I don't know who I am anymore," or "That seems so wishy-washy." The ego is looking for a fixed version of self that it can define with words or an image and lock us into. Once the identity is defined, the ego's agenda grows with fears of change and the need to be projected and defended. It clings to its definition in spite of the fact that the meaning of words can change, and the imagination itself is not a very solid place. If we are honest, we recognize that we are not the person we were in our youth, or even the person we were last year. Since we are constantly in a process of change, being authentic and truthful to ourselves doesn't necessarily mean being static.

As we have seen, a step towards authenticity is to adopt the perspectives of others, if only to practice flexibility in our point of view and develop a greater consciousness. This doesn't mean we need to invest faith in the other person's beliefs; but we gain greater understanding from a view into their experiences, and this can only enhance our process of change. It expands our perspective, our consciousness, and our understanding of the world. If we find someone else's perspective and beliefs beneficial, we can adopt them—at least for a while, until we find better versions.

It is immensely freeing when you discover that your personal belief system is very arbitrary and largely not true. You may also realize that personal beliefs tend to divide human against human and are at the core of conflicts in humanity. The belief systems conflict and drag human beings along. This happened to Jeffrey and his father and the other people whose examples are described in this book. The same happens on a collective scale between political parties, religions, cultures, and nations in larger, more destructive ways. As you dissolve your belief system and gain the ability to perceive from multiple viewpoints, your conflicts with other people will dissolve. You still might not agree with them, but you will have the wisdom to refrain from disrespecting their beliefs or fighting with them. Part of being aware and wise is to acknowledge that you didn't consciously choose the beliefs you grew up with, and neither did they.

Authentic Beliefs and the Truth of Life

So, when you are authentic, what do you believe in? The answer is simple: not very much—at least, not much in terms of concepts and ideas. The mind makes a mental model of the world with its concepts. Mental models are helpful to understand and communicate, but they aren't the real world. When you are aware that concepts in the mind are not the real world, you don't invest much faith in them.

The characters of the ego believe in illusions. The Judge and other characters would say they believe in the truth, but their "truth" is only true within a character's belief bubble. Those "truths" are often nothing but very tightly held opinions. A hundred years from now, much of our so-called scientific knowledge will have seen many revisions. The genuine truth of life is vaster in the macrocosm, in the subatomic world, and through time than we can fathom.

The characters of our belief systems are very concerned with believing in something. They need concepts to invest faith into so they can continue to live in their belief bubbles. Without our ego characters we don't feel such a need. We are more concerned with enjoying life and feeling alive. We seek out enlivening experiences and the enjoyment of emotions like love, gratitude, compassion, and respect.

The fullness of feeling alive and being present in the moment can't be captured in words and spelled out on a page. Language, thoughts, and words are symbolic and largely empty. Try to describe to a blind person how sunlight scatters in the sky to produce a rainbow, or explain to a deaf person the way a symphony builds individual notes into an emotional experience. The mind can't accurately put into words the feelings you feel in those moments when you perceive beauty and love directly.

Words and concepts are convenient tools for communicating about real life and understanding one another. However, as ideologies and life philosophies they have less value. Investing faith in concepts just makes those concepts powerful. Without our awareness, those concepts, opinions, and beliefs, such as "right" and "wrong," have had power over us and ruled our emotions. When we are aware and wise, we regain dominion over our concepts and the faith we invested in them.

An authentic person doesn't have to believe in concepts or ideas, but will use them to communicate. Ideas that are true won't need anyone's faith in order to stand. That leaves the authentic person free to invest faith in themselves instead of in thoughts, opinions, judgments, or ideologies. When you aren't expending your personal power of faith on concepts, opinions, and judgments, you have a great deal more power to love, be kind and compassionate, and to create your life as you choose. This unhindered expression of love for yourself, for others, and for the world helps create a life of happiness and feeling alive.

About the Author

Gary van Warmerdam is the creator of PathwayToHappiness.com, an interactive website with lessons for changing beliefs that drive negative thoughts, emotions, and behaviors. In 1994, due to his own unhappiness with work and emotional drama in his relationships, Gary became motivated to learn about how his beliefs affected his emotions and decision making. He studied extensively with Dr. Miguel Ruiz, author of *The Four Agreements* (a favorite of Oprah Winfrey) and other best-selling books. Gary realized that with a proper approach he could gain greater control over his mind and emotions. With practice he developed the power and the freedom to choose the peace and happiness he was seeking.

Educated and experienced as an engineer, Gary brings a common sense approach to changing beliefs, emotions, mindfulness, and living in greater happiness. Since 2001 Gary has been lecturing, leading retreats and coaching individual clients so they can live happier lives. His methods are not limited to a particular philosophy or approach, but are based in careful observation and getting practical results. When not helping others to be happy, you might find Gary with his wife Lisa enjoying the beaches or hiking the hills in Santa Barbara, California. You can explore more of Gary's work at his website www.PathwayToHappiness. com which has extensive free material and online courses for changing beliefs, emotions, and creating better relationships.